Use and Abuse
of
America's Natural Resources

Use and Abuse
of
America's Natural Resources

Advisory Editor

STUART BRUCHEY
Allan Nevins Professor of American
Economic History, Columbia University

Associate Editor

ELEANOR BRUCHEY

SOIL EROSION
AND ITS CONTROL

BY

QUINCY CLAUDE AYRES, C.E.

ARNO PRESS
A NEW YORK TIMES COMPANY
New York • 1972

Reprint Edition 1972 by Arno Press Inc.

Reprinted from a copy in The Newark Public Library

Use and Abuse of America's Natural Resources
ISBN for complete set: 0-405-04500-X
See last pages of this volume for titles.

Manufactured in the United States of America

Library of Congress Cataloging in Publication Data

Ayres, Quincy Claude, 1891-
    Soil erosion and its control.

    (Use and abuse of America's natural resources)
    Reprint of the 1936 ed., issued in series: McGraw-
Hill publications in agricultural engineering.
    Bibliography: p.
    1. Soil erosion. I. Title. II. Series.
S623.A96 1972   631.4'5   72-2832
ISBN 0-405-04501-8

McGRAW-HILL PUBLICATIONS IN
AGRICULTURAL ENGINEERING
DANIELS SCOATES, A.E., Consulting Editor

SOIL EROSION AND ITS CONTROL

SOIL EROSION
AND ITS CONTROL

BY

QUINCY CLAUDE AYRES, C.E.

*Associate Professor, In Charge of Drainage and Conservation Engineering,
Agricultural Engineering Department, Iowa State College; Member American Society of Civil Engineers; American Society
of Agricultural Engineers; Society for Promotion
of Engineering Education; Iowa Engineering
Society*

FIRST EDITION
THIRD IMPRESSION

McGRAW-HILL BOOK COMPANY, INC.
NEW YORK AND LONDON
1936

THE MAPLE PRESS COMPANY, YORK, PA.

To that tireless little band of erosion technicians who have labored through the years, unmindful of aught save the good of the cause, this book is respectfully dedicated

PREFACE

This book is offered to meet the need for a general treatise on erosion control for the use of students in colleges and vocational agriculture departments, county agents, engineers, farmers, public officials, bankers, investors, and others who may be interested in the subject. A reversal of attitude and action in American agriculture, whereby soil wastage is eliminated and fertility accretion equals or exceeds extraction, should be a matter of grave national concern to every citizen regardless of occupation.

For the first time, it is believed, an attempt is here made to bring together under one cover a general introduction to and correlation of all phases of this rather complex problem with the quantitative application of such data as are at present known. In spite of the rapid strides in research of the past few years and the mass attention devoted to the subject many questions regarding the relative value of various control measures cannot as yet be answered with scientific exactitude. This, however, does not lessen the need for better understanding of fundamental principles and of the research position as it at present exists.

If it should appear that disproportionate emphasis is accorded to engineering phases of control, the fault is not due altogether to the author's training and experience in that field but also is partly attributable to the fact that more information of a practical and time-tested nature seems to be available. By means of numerous conferences and interchange of ideas and printed matter in recent years a very good mutual comprehension of the scope of each other's contributions to the assault on erosion has come to agronomists, foresters, soil specialists, botanists, economists, engineers, animal husbandmen, and sociologists alike. General principles may be grasped by all, but important applications in practice is, and should remain, the job of specialists in the various fields.

One of the functions of technical authorship, it is believed, is to canvass available data, sift out that which is unsupported by facts, and report the remainder in an accurate, impersonal manner. Where insufficient facts exist, and competent opinion differs as to the value of various processes or methods, the author considers it his duty to report all versions of important practices as impartially as possible.

Necessarily, in a book of this kind, numerous sources of information are drawn upon. These are accorded recognition in the body of the text, in footnotes, and in the bibliography found in the appendix. In spite of the most scrupulous attention to this detail, however, it is probable that occasional credit omissions will occur. For these, and for typographical and other errors characteristic of first editions, the author asks indulgence.

Special acknowledgment is due to three mimeographed booklets which are extensively quoted and have been most helpful. These are: (1) An instruction manual prepared in 1935 by the technical staff of the Bethany, Mo., region of the Soil Conservation Service, U. S. Department of Agriculture, (2) a similar manual prepared in 1934 by C. L. Hamilton and associates in Region 9 of the U. S. Forest Service, and (3) a manual called "Brief Instructions on Methods of Gully Control" prepared in 1933 by C. E. Ramser, U. S. Bureau of Agricultural Engineering. The material on gully control found in Chapters X, XI, and XII is based very largely upon *Bulletin* 121, which was prepared by the author and published in 1935 by the Iowa Engineering Experiment Station.

Sincere thanks are extended to Dr. P. E. Brown, Head of the Department of Agronomy at Iowa State College, who read the manuscript and offered valuable suggestions for improvement.

A certain amount of repetition is intentionally included. This is believed to be justified, not only for the sake of emphasis, but also to round out the pattern structure of the several chapters.

Admittedly the text is quite elementary in character, but differs little in that respect from other pioneer works.

QUINCY C. AYRES.

AMES, IOWA,
August, 1936.

CONTENTS

PAGE

PREFACE. vii

CHAPTER I

INTRODUCTION 1
Significance of Erosion—Old-world Object Lessons—Extent in the
United States—Erosion Inventory—Annual Expenditure for
Control—Water Erosion—Sheet—Gully—Stream—Wind Erosion
—Combating Agencies.

CHAPTER II

FACTORS AFFECTING RATE OF EROSION 20
Effect of Rainfall on Runoff—Of Land Slope on Runoff—Of Soil
Variables on Runoff—Soil Tests—Soil Qualities Affecting Erodibil-
ity—Effect of Vegetation on Runoff—Of Cultivation on Runoff—
Of Overgrazing on Runoff—Of Frost Action on Runoff—Of Mis-
cellaneous Factors on Runoff and Erosion.

CHAPTER III

METHODS OF CONTROL. 39
Absorption Range of Soils—Use of Vegetation—Results of Experiments—Interpretation of Plot Data—Contour Farming—Mechanical Aids—Explosives—Strip Cropping—Strip Cropping with Terraces—Permanent Pastures—Contour Ridging—Forests and Wood
Lots—Use of Terraces—Correlation of Methods.

CHAPTER IV

RAINFALL AND RUNOFF 83
Source of Runoff—Annual Precipitation—Rainfall Characteristics
—Factors Affecting Runoff—Quantitative Determination of Runoff—Runoff Formula—Runoff Coefficient—Rainfall Intensities—
Time of Concentration—Rainfall Durations—Frequency of Recurrence—Application of Data—Runoff in Terrace Channels—Economics of Terrace Sizes.

CHAPTER V

TERRACE DESIGN. 100
Terrace Types—Design Principles—Spacing—Grades—Level Ter-
races—Graded Terraces—Special Gradient Tables—Length of
Terraces—Terrace Cross Sections—Capacity Formula—Shape of
Channel—Depth of Flow—Dimensions of Cross Section.

CHAPTER VI

TERRACE LOCATION—PRINCIPLES AND PRACTICE 120
Planning the Layout—Illustrations of Various Layouts—Surveying
Procedure—Farm Levels—Turret Type—Peg Test for Adjustment
—Dumpy Type—Utility of Farm Levels—Use of Level—Applica-
tion to Terrace Layout.

CHAPTER VII

TERRACE CONSTRUCTION METHODS AND MACHINERY 135
When to Terrace—Making Pilot Cut—Direction Earth Should
Be Moved—Preliminary Preparation—Construction Details—
Construction Equipment—Plows—V-drags—Light Terracing
Graders—Four-wheel Graders—Special Two-wheel Graders—
Heavy Elevating Graders—Light Elevating Grader—Multiple-
disk Plow—Whirlwind Rotary Terracer—Completion and Check-
ing of Terrace Grades—Illustrative Example.

CHAPTER VIII

TERRACE CONSTRUCTION COSTS AND MAINTENANCE. 165
Factors Governing Costs—Effect of Variation in Implements and
Power—Extra Work Required to Complete Terrace—Extra Work
on Outlets—Cost Data—Whirlwind Terracer—Light Elevating
Grader Terracer—Two-wheel Blade Graders—Heavy Equipment
—Miscellaneous Equipment—Form for Cost Data—Terrace Culti-
vation and Maintenance—Plowing Terraced Land—Row Crops
and Terraces—Contour Farming.

CHAPTER IX

TERRACE OUTLETS 187
Need For—Location—Natural Outlets—Constructed Outlets—
Channel Design—Vegetative Control—Vegetative Species—Estab-
lishing Vegetation—Outlet Structures.

CHAPTER X

CONTROL OF GULLIES 202
Order of Priority—Gully Terminology—Treatment of Small
Gullies—Principles Governing the Use of Check Dams—Notch
Capacity Required—Height of Check Dams—Spacing of Check
Dams—Overfall Protection—Use of Brush—Flumes—Watertight
Structures—Diversion Ditches.

CHAPTER XI

TEMPORARY AND SEMIPERMANENT CHECK DAMS 217
Distinguished from Soil-saving Dams—Brush Dams—Single-post
Row—Double-post Row—Pole Type—Woven-wire Dams—V
Type—Suspended-net Type—Fixed-basket Type—Cost Com-
parison—Loose-rock Dams—Log Dams—Plank Check Dams.

CHAPTER XII

PERMANENT OR SOIL-SAVING DAMS 235
Economics of Comparison—Rubble Masonry Dams—Concrete Dams—Earth Dams—Side Spillway—Drop Inlet—Low Head Designs—High Head Designs—California Type—Pondage Fill—Storage Dams—Drop Inlets on Existing Culverts.

CHAPTER XIII

SPECIAL USES OF VEGETATION 273
Gully Control—Trees in Gully Control—Advisability of Tree Planting—Check Dams for Gully Planting—Sloping Gully Banks —Planting Trees—Tree Species—Shrubs in Gully Control—Vines in Gully Control—Grasses in Gully Control—Sodding—Stream Bank Protection—Forms of Bank Cutting—Remedies—Inclined Tree Planting—Use of Retards—Woods System—Large River Bank Protection—Eroded Material in Lower Mississippi River—Bank Revetment—Articulated Concrete Mat.

CHAPTER XIV

SOIL CONSERVATION AND LAND USE. 303
Self-perpetuating Basis for Agriculture—Fact-finding Experiments and Methods—Federal Experimental Farms—List of Experiments in Progress—Map of Bethany Farm—Measuring Equipment—Air Photo of Clarinda Farm—Data Collected—Demonstration Projects—Plan for Conservation Farming—Data Required—Soil Map—Cropping Plan—Herbaceous Cover and Conservation—Coordination of Physical Factors—Classification of Lands According to Best Use to Promote Conservation—Human and Economic Handicaps to Adoption of Erosion Control Practices—Adverse Influences—Helpful Influences—Eventual Outcome.

APPENDIX

SIMPLE METHODS OF CALCULATING LAND AREAS 331
PARTIAL LIST OF SOIL CONSERVING AND DEPLETING CROPS. 335
PARTIAL LIST OF PLANTS FAVORABLE TO SOIL CONSERVATION AND WILD LIFE. 337
TWO-THIRDS POWERS OF NUMBERS 338
SQUARE ROOTS OF DECIMAL NUMBERS. 339

BIBLIOGRAPHY 341

INDEX. 353

SOIL EROSION AND ITS CONTROL

CHAPTER I

INTRODUCTION

SIGNIFICANCE OF EROSION

Nothing in Nature is absolutely static. Fortunately, eternal *change* is a fundamental law, for, were this not true, it is doubtful if man could have survived. Natural processes, including erosion, have brought about the formation of soil from the parent rocks; and the distribution and assortment of the soil by wind, water, and ice have been immensely encouraging, if not indispensable, to all forms of life.

A basic distinction should be made, however, between the *rate* of change as it occurs in nature, whereby soil-building forces are substantially in balance with those of destruction, and the rate of change precipitated by man in the conquest of his environment. The one is inherently natural, and the other must be considered artificial. What takes Nature hundreds or even thousands of years to manufacture, man can and often does destroy almost overnight by haphazard land use and improvident husbandry.

How else are we to interpret the wholesale cutting and ravaging of our forests, the widespread removal of native grasses on hillsides to make way for cultivated crops, the senseless overgrazing of range and pasture lands, indiscriminate drainage operations sometimes resulting in needless exposure to drought damage and dust storms, and the inadequate safeguarding of vast tracts of forest and cut-over lands from denuding fires? All of these offenses and more are chargeable to man in his pursuit of temporary advantage at the expense of lasting economy in the use and conservation of natural resources.

1

Old-world Object Lessons.—A permanent consciousness must be developed on a nationwide scale, with a firm resolve to do everything possible to restore, or at least approach, a natural rate of change or balance between fertility production and consumption. We in the United States have object lessons to behold in the history of older civilizations. The ruins of once flourishing cities standing amid barren wastes long since stripped of fertile topsoil are found in the Orient, Central America, and other parts of the world. They bear eloquent testimony to the significance of uncontrolled erosion and its power to destroy.

While the note of hopelessness and finality in examples such as these is impressive, to say the least, there is a temptation to consider them merely as remote relics of the unenlightened past, not comparable in any real sense with the things we do today. For those who fall into this error there is ample evidence to the contrary. In fact we do not need to go beyond the limits of our own country to find a situation ominous in the extreme.

Erosion devastation has now become so apparent in the older cropping regions of the United States that there is no longer any doubt about the gravity of the menace. Good farm land, topsoil gone and gutted with gullies, has had to be abandoned over extended areas during the past few decades. Desultory attempts to reduce hillside wash on cotton and tobacco fields by means of contour plowing and miniature terraces have been tried in the southeastern states for 150 years but have not been generally effective. Indeed, small terraces of the narrow ridge type may easily do more harm than good by funnelling the water from ordinary rains at points of washouts in the ridges. The evolution of terrace design has paralleled somewhat that of Mississippi flood control levees as the need for more adequate protection became apparent.

Extent in the United States.—A graphic portrayal of the extent and some indication of the severity of erosion in the United States is presented in Fig. 1. This map was prepared by the Soil Conservation Service of the U. S. Department of Agriculture and shows the situation as it existed late in 1934. The distribution of the shaded areas can partially be explained by a consideration of rainfall and watershed characteristics, length of time that the land has been in cultivation, type of farming practiced, and the degree of economic compulsion to

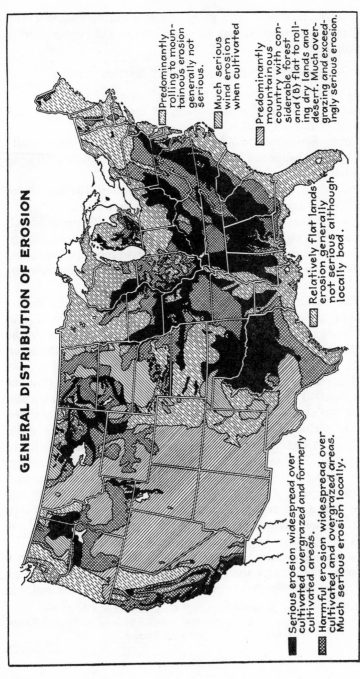

GENERAL DISTRIBUTION OF EROSION

Predominantly rolling to mountainous erosion generally not serious.

Much serious wind erosion when cultivated

Predominantly mountainous country with considerable forest and (B) flat to rolling dry lands and desert. Much overgrazing and exceedingly serious erosion.

Relatively flat lands erosion generally not serious although locally bad.

Serious erosion widespread over cultivated overgrazed and formerly cultivated areas.

Harmful erosion widespread over cultivated and overgrazed areas. Much serious erosion locally.

FIG. 1.—Map showing location, extent and severity of erosion in the United States.   (*U. S. Dept. Agr. Soil conservation service data.*)

grow cash crops year after year. In later chapters these factors and their interrelation and effect on erosion will be discussed in detail.

EROSION INVENTORY IN THE UNITED STATES

According to estimates of the U. S. Bureau of Chemistry and Soils[1] and other authentic sources, an erosion inventory in the United States is as follows:

Thirty-five million to 50,000,000 acres of cultivated land totally ruined and abandoned in 1935 as compared with 10,000,000 acres in 1910.

Partial to complete stripping of topsoil on 100,000,000 to 125,000,000 acres of remaining cultivated land.

Five hundred and thirteen million tons of suspended silt annually transported to river mouths, in addition to vast quantities of soil and sand from uplands that never reach the open seas but spread out and lodge on rich bottom lands and choke culverts, public streams, and reservoirs.

Two hundred and seventy million tons of dissolved matter containing 63,000,000 tons of plant food material removed from the fields and pastures of the United States and delivered to the oceans every year. This represents a rate of fertility exhaustion 21 times greater than that required to produce a crop of corn.

Overgrazing on 165,000,000 acres of the public domain that has lost from 40 to 50 per cent of its productivity in consequence. That 640 acres is too small a unit for stock grazing is attested by the virtual destruction of all grass on the sparsely covered range; and 15,000,000 acres of abandoned homesteads testify to the futility of attempts to cultivate land suited only for grazing.

In Iowa,[2] a survey conducted by the author in 1934 exposed 200,000 acres of abandoned farm land eroded beyond redemption, 4,000,000 acres seriously infested with gullies, and 8,000,000 to 12,000,000 acres more suffering loss of topsoil at a rate of one inch in four years to one inch in twenty years by sheet wash.

In Missouri, recent studies of the Soil Conservation Service revealed that "more than three-fourths of the soils of the state have lost one-fourth of their original fertile surface soil. If

[1] "Soil Erosion a National Menace," U. S. Dept. Agr. Cir. 33.

[2] For a more complete account of the situation in Iowa see Special Report No. 2 of the Iowa Agricultural Experiment Station.

lands not subject to erosion are excluded, the survey shows that approximately two-thirds of the rolling hilly upland soils have lost one-half or more of their original fertile surface soil.

"The survey further shows that 20,850,000,000 tons of soil have left Missouri farms since they have been cultivated. This means that Missouri's agriculture has lost 26,090,000 tons of nitrogen, 13,030,000 tons of phosphorus, and 300,240,000 tons of potassium."[1]

Six inches or more of top soil washed off of many cultivated fields in a generation of farm life is a common experience in the southeastern states, according to the U. S. Bureau of Agricultural Engineering.

In one old South Carolina piedmont county 90,000 acres of formerly good land has been ruined by gullies. And 46,000 acres of bottom land, once the richest soil in the state, have been so covered and otherwise damaged by deposits from the upland farms that they are now mainly useless. A Georgia piedmont county has suffered in much the same way; 100,000 acres of former crop land in the upland region has been so badly washed that it is now about worthless for anything except trees; erosion is still cutting steadily into every cultivated sloping field.

And so the story goes. Six million acres terraced in Texas alone is some indication of the severity of the problem in that state and also of the enterprise of Texans in meeting it. One of the first systematically conducted erosion surveys in the country took place in Oklahoma in 1929, where enormous losses were revealed; the vulnerability of southern California farm land has long been recognized (see Fig. 2); and probably some of the most disheartening examples of ultimate erosion to be found anywhere are located in the red clay hills of Mississippi and Alabama. Georgia's contribution to the ghastly toll is illustrated in Fig. 3. Erosion is truly as widespread as man's efforts to exploit sloping lands; and, in the attempt to describe the havoc wrought and the portent for the future, superlatives are not only warranted but necessary. To combat the menace on a scale commensurate with the need is indeed a staggering challenge.

[1] Manual prepared by the technical staff of the Soil Conservation Ser., Bethany, Mo., 1935.

Fig. 2.—Extreme erosion in California. Typical of much of the areas shaded black in Fig. 1. (*Photograph by U. S. Forest Service.*)

Fig. 3.—Present condition of formerly good farm land in Georgia. This gully is reported to have started under the eaves of a barn less than 75 years ago. It now extends across two counties and has consumed and disgorged enormous quantities of soil. (*Courtesy Caterpillar Tractor Company.*)

From the above it is seen that erosion produces losses in three distinct categories; (1) valuable plant food in solution, (2) fine silt and humus in suspension, and (3) removal by scour of the soil itself. Potentially an area exceeding one-third of the entire cultivated acreage of the United States is either totally ruined, or soon will be, unless the erosion menace is subjected to vigorous, concerted, and unremitting attack on a nationwide front. Seventy-five per cent of all our farm land is affected in some degree.

Benefits of Erosion Control.—Erosion control measures result in great benefit both to the private owner and to the public; to the landowner in the form of soil and moisture conservation, and to the public in the form of reduced flood heights, clearer streams, and lower maintenance charges for bridges and culverts, drainage ditches, and navigable waterways. Furthermore, adjoining owners of level lands are insured against overwash by barren soil from already denuded slopes, and there is a vital community interest in maintaining the ability of all citizens to pay their pro rata share of the tax burden.

Justifiable Annual Expenditure.—Estimates by a distinguished committee of the National Resources Board[1] place the tangible money loss suffered by citizens of the United States on account of erosion at $400,000,000 annually. In the judgment of the committee this justifies a federal expenditure of $20,000,000 a year for erosion control and prevention.

Diagrammatic Representation.—A diagrammatic representation of soil erosion and its effects, as conceived by L. D. Baver, Assistant Professor of Soils at the University of Missouri, is shown in Fig. 4. This chart might be considered a thumbnail summary of the foregoing discussion.

TYPES OF EROSION

The three most active eroding forces are water, wind, and ice. Wind is directly responsible for sand and dust storms and is indirectly responsible for wave erosion along the shorelines of oceans and lakes.

[1] Report of the Mississippi Valley Committee of the Public Works Administration, Oct. 1, 1934, now known as Water Planning Committee of the National Resources Board.

WATER EROSION

Water erosion is generally considered to manifest itself in two forms: (1) sheet washing, and (2) gullying. Usually these two forms represent different stages in the same process; and gullies, as a rule, do not appear until sheet erosion has been under way for a considerable time. Gullies, however, sometimes occur

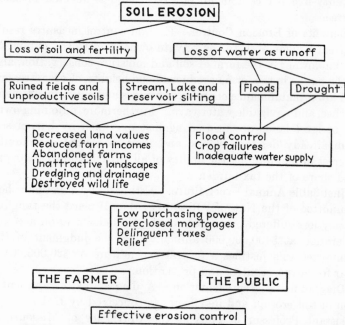

Fig. 4.—Chart showing how soil erosion affects the general public as well as the farmer. (*From Missouri Agr. Exp. Sta. Bull.* 349.)

without being preceded by sheet erosion; and conversely, sheet erosion has been known to continue indefinitely without the formation of gullies. Nevertheless, the normal sequence, when virgin sod is plowed up and replaced by cultivated crops on sloping land, is about as follows:

Sheet Erosion.—To make a good seedbed the soil must be worked and smoothed into a loose pulverized condition. The season of planting is also the season of frequent and abundant rainfall. When intense rains fall on ground in this condition the first tendency is to pack the soil, but in so doing many of the soil grains are pounded loose and left free to float away. Soon after the rain begins, excess water starts flowing down the slope carrying soil and humus with it. Since water is falling simultaneously on all parts of the field, the mixture of soil and excess water progressively increases in thickness as it moves in a thin sheet from top to bottom at accelerating speed, until, if the slope is long enough, a "terminal" velocity has been attained.

Fig. 5.—Silt detritus removed from moderately sloping corn field by sheet erosion.

The result is a rather uniform skimming off of the cream of the topsoil with every hard rain by an insidious process known as sheet erosion. The process is insidious because it may or may not leave any visible trace of damage and may continue for years under the eyes of an owner who does not realize his loss and cannot understand why the productivity of his land is rapidly decreasing (see Fig. 5). In the spring or fall when fields are prepared for planting, any "educated eye" can detect on almost any hillside in humid regions the telltale lightness of color that bespeaks a near approach to subsoil and complete exhaustion.

Figure 6 is a striking example of the damage that can be wrought in a comparatively short time by sheet erosion. It is a photographic record of two fields of similar characteristics, the only difference being that one has remained under its native cover of sod and the other has been injudiciously cultivated.

Incipient or Finger Gullying.—In a great many cases fields are not absolutely smooth laterally nor is the soil of perfectly uniform texture; water will tend to concentrate into small rivulets soon after it leaves the hillcrest, and the rivulets in turn converge into stem channels. If the slope is long enough the stem channels

Fig. 6.—Comparison of two fields in Missouri with same soil type, showing amount of topsoil lost by sheet erosion.

themselves converge into hillside ditches, the whole pattern resembling that of the twigs, branches, and trunk of a tree. Such a phenomenon is called incipient or finger gullying, and it represents normally an intermediate stage between sheet erosion and gullying.

Figure 7 is an aerial photograph of a wheat field in Kansas after a one-inch rain. It clearly shows the pattern of finger or "shoe string" gullies. All trace of these will be obliterated the next time the field is plowed or cultivated. Figure 8 is a ground view of the same phenomenon on the same field.

Gully Erosion.—Once water begins flowing in a definite channel the eroding power of a given volume on a given slope is greatly

Fig. 7.—Aerial photograph of a field of young wheat in Kansas showing the effect of a one-inch rain. A typical example of finger gullying.

Fig. 8.—View of the same field from the ground.

increased, in accordance with certain laws of hydraulics to be treated later. On fields where erosion has been allowed to remain unchecked long enough for this to happen, not only are losses accelerated but the expense and difficulty of reclamation and control are greatly augmented. When finger gullying has progressed to the point where the water channels are no longer interchangeable or easily obliterated, a state of gully erosion is said to have taken place.

Fig. 9.—Aerial photograph of an area in Northern Missouri. The white square encloses a 160-acre farm. (*Courtesy Soil Conservation Service, U. S. Dept. Agr.*)

The rapidity with which gullies can ravage a whole countryside is indicated in Fig. 9, which is an air view of an area four miles wide by three miles long located in northern Missouri. Note how the gullies are advancing into the remaining farm land by lengthening, by enlargement, and by the development of numerous side branches. Figures 10 and 11 might fairly be considered typical ground views of the gullies shown in Fig. 9. Quite frequently gullies such as these attain a depth of 50 feet or more, with proportionate width, in a remarkably short time; and their encroachment on good land is not necessarily preceded by finger gullying. This is particularly true where the surface soil becomes loosened, and overfalls develop in natural drainage depressions.

The following apt description of gully erosion is taken from a mimeographed handbook prepared by the technical staff of the U. S. Forest Service at Milwaukee, Wis.

FIG. 10.—Representative ground view of any one of the gullies shown in Fig. 9.

There are two general types of gullying. Ditch erosion occurs where head and sides of the gully are usually sloping and erosion occurs at the head, sides and bottom of the gully in varying degrees by the action of water, freezing and thawing. Waterfall erosion is caused by water falling over the edge of a gully or ditch bank and is often responsible for many of the deepest gullies. The falling water undermines the edge of the bank, which caves in, and the waterfall moves upstream. The undermining action of the waterfall goes on rapidly if the subsoil is an easily eroded type. Gullies formed by waterfall erosion may extend back through almost level land, as their growth usually depends on the fall, type of soil and size of drainage area furnishing water, rather than upon the slope of the land. Both types of gully erosion are often found in the same gully. Lateral gullies tend to form from the main gullies and ultimately a network of gullies develops.

Gully erosion is much more noticeable than sheet erosion, and for this reason is generally considered more serious than sheet erosion. This, however, is a false impression because the first and most serious damage results from sheet erosion. The formation of gully erosion can be retarded and controlled to a large extent by preventing excessive sheet erosion.

Fig. 11.—Representative ground view of any one of the gullies shown in Fig. 9 near its upper end.

Figure 12 is a ground view of a field ravished beyond hope of recovery for cultivated crops by sheet and gully erosion. Left to its fate, it will rapidly degenerate further to the condition shown in Figs. 2 and 3.

Stream Erosion.—Erosion of valley streams and drainage channels usually takes the form of bank cutting, but bottom scour also occurs when gradients are excessive or when the volume of flow is increased. A rearrangement of tributary flow on the upper reaches of a watershed by means of terraces or diversion channels may start erosion in a stream that formerly had stable sides and bottom.

Bank cutting is by far the most common form of stream erosion and is particularly noticeable on the outside bank at the beginning of bends in meandering streams. Frequently, in flowing around a bend, spiral cross currents develop that tend to eat away the outer bank and deposit silt or sand bars on the inside curve as the result of a clockwise rotation. As erosion continues and the curves become sharper the process grows more and more severe, until eventually the stream changes its course by cutting across the narrow necks and leaving long loops or horseshoe lakes to mark the site of the former bends.

WIND EROSION

Although wind action in the remote past is responsible for the formation of large areas of present-day farm land, it might

FIG. 12.—"An American tragedy" depicting the destiny of 75 per cent of all cultivated land in the United States unless erosion is controlled. (*Courtesy The Austin-Western Road Machinery Company.*)

seem that modern climatic conditions are not such as to permit wind erosion to attain major significance. Nevertheless, the dust storms attendant upon the drought of 1933–1934 reached terrific proportions, as evidenced by the photograph shown in Fig. 13, and are likely to be repeated often as long as the conditions largely responsible for their cause remain uncorrected. Regardless of rainfall, it is becoming a matter of common experience for a zone of transition from humid to arid regions, extending westward from and including parts of Oklahoma, Missouri, Iowa, and Minnesota, to suffer dust storms of increasing frequency and severity.

A return to normal rainfall together with timber and shrub shelter belts, the planting of semiarid crops in alternating strips, the cessation of fall plowing in affected areas, and less intensive grazing all will help, but the problem can only be solved completely by modifying agricultural practices materially in semiarid regions, *i.e.*, reducing the proportion of total land area in annual cultivation and careful maintenance of adequate herbaceous cover on the rougher grazing lands.

Fig. 13.—Aftermath of a dust storm in South Dakota.   Note almost complete submergence of fence.   (*Courtesy Soil Conservation Service, U. S. Dept. Agr.*)

Wave Action.—Erosion of ocean and lake shores by wave action is due, of course, to high winds whipping large bodies of water into a turbulent condition.   The judicious use of vegetation in conjunction with sea walls or piling will go a long way toward providing protection.   The subject is discussed more fully in Chap. XIII.

COMBATING AGENCIES

Until the advent of 1933, about the only agencies primarily concerned with soil erosion on farm lands, and its control, were a few individuals, the extension services of the land-grant colleges, and coworkers in Washington, D. C.   Considering the limited support accorded and the up-hill fight they waged, a great deal was accomplished by these pioneers.   In addition to innumerable public meetings and demonstrations of the value of fertility maintenance by proper culture, crop rotations, and soil management, the records show that over a period of 19 years 18,000,000 acres were protected by terraces and soil-saving dams. Of this area 16,000,000 acres are estimated as cultivated land on which terraces were built. The value of the terraces was usually reinforced by contour farming, legume cover crops, and soil improvement practices, including liming where needed.

As early as 1903, the Office of Experiment Stations of the U. S. Department of Agriculture undertook field studies of hillside drainage with a view to devising means of reducing erosion. A carefully planned field investigation of terracing was started in 1914 and was continued under the Bureau of Public Roads and the Bureau of Agricultural Engineering until this work was taken over by the Soil Conservation Service in 1935.

In 1917, some of the earliest experimental work was undertaken by the Agricultural Experiment Station of the University of Missouri, where runoff and soil losses were measured from a series of study plots that were subjected to different methods of surface treatment and crop rotations. This was followed, in 1926, by other similar experiments at Spur, Tex., and Guthrie, Okla., where some of the variable factors involved in terracing were introduced.

In 1929, a growing realization of the danger led the Congress of the United States to appropriate an initial sum of $160,000 for the establishment of federal experimental erosion farms to be operated as a joint venture with the various states. The administration of this work was entrusted to the Forest Service, the Bureau of Chemistry and Soils, and the Bureau of Agricultural Engineering, all of the Department of Agriculture. The Forest Service was given charge of erosion studies in the national forests, and the work on farm lands was divided between the two other bureaus. For the latter experiments, 10 farms[1] of 140 to 300 acres each were selected and established near the following places in the order named: Guthrie, Okla.; Temple, Tex.; Hays, Kan.; Tyler, Tex.; Bethany, Mo.; Statesville, N. C.; Pullman, Wash.; Clarinda, Ia.; La Crosse, Wis.; and Zanesville, O. The locations were chosen in erosive areas to represent wide

[1] Now (1936) increased to 13 by the establishment of additional stations at Spur, Tex.; State College, Pa.; and Ithaca, N. Y.

differences in soil, climate, topography, and farming conditions and practices (see Chap. XIV for detailed descriptions).

To the Forest Service goes the credit of making the first attempt to measure *quantitatively* the soil loss and runoff from limited areas. This work was carried on in 1915 in the Manti National Forest, Utah, and the appropriation of 1929 enabled such experiments in forested areas to be continued and extended.

Although the congressional appropriations begun in 1929 were continued and enlarged, the real "break" in anti-erosion activities did not come until March 31, 1933, when the Act for the Relief of Unemployment became a law. This Act provided for the establishment of a large number of Civilian Conservation Corps camps to do many kinds of emergency conservation work, the erosion control phases of which were placed under the direction of the Forest Service.

A short time later the Soil Erosion Service was set up in the Department of the Interior through the use of emergency funds, and this organization began to establish demonstrational projects on entire watersheds located largely in the same general areas occupied by the experimental farms (see Chap. XIV for a list of projects).

In April, 1935, the Soil Erosion Service was transferred to the Department of Agriculture; and all erosion activities of the various federal agencies, including the CCC erosion camps, were consolidated in a new bureau called the Soil Conservation Service. The present organization of the SCS contemplates a three-way division of the work into research, as exemplified by the erosion farms, demonstrational projects, and CCC work in outlying areas. The outlying area activity consists primarily of cooperation with County Conservation Associations, which are voluntary organizations composed of local public-spirited citizens who wish to perpetuate the benefits of erosion control for their respective communities. Efforts are being made to reestablish close relations with the State Extension Services in carrying on this work, and new demonstration areas are contemplated to supplement or perhaps supplant the local associations.

Various other erosion control programs have been set up from time to time, such as the one the author was called upon to plan and direct for the Iowa Emergency Relief Administration in 1934. While the accomplishments were creditable and effective, the program was short-lived because it was devised to meet a temporary need for employment of rural relief workers.

By and large it would seem that at last a beginning has been made in attacking the erosion menace on a scale somewhere nearly commensurate with the need. Let us hope that the substantial features of the current emergency conservation adventures will survive and find their way into the hegemonic structure of our federal and state governments.

> Hordes of gullies now remind us,
> We should build our lands to stay;
> And departing leave behind us,
> Fields that have not washed away.
> Then when our boys assume the mortgage
> On the land that's had our toil,
> They'll not have to ask the question,
> "Here's the farm, but where's the soil?"
>
> —Anonymous
> With apologies to Longfellow

CHAPTER II

FACTORS AFFECTING RATE OF EROSION

Aside from soil shifts due to seismic disturbances, such as earthquakes, landslides, upheavals, etc., which cannot strictly be classed as erosion, the causes of practically all excessive rates of erosion can be laid at the door of man. The only important exceptions are the destruction of forest and grass cover by lightning-set fires, snow slides in mountainous regions, and perhaps certain kinds of landslides.

For the purposes of this book it can be said that without water, wind, and soil there will be no erosion. These are the essential elements. Hence an understanding of the process and of the causes of excessive rates resolves itself into a study of the degree of unbalance between the resisting power of the soil and the eroding power of wind or water. Virgin soil in arable areas would not exist if, during the formative period, its resisting power plus its power of reproduction had not exceeded the power of water to erode. The cause or causes of excessive erosion are therefore to be sought in anything that lessens resisting power and thereby automatically increases eroding power. On cultivated fields, tillage, which of necessity destroys protective cover, exposes bare soil, and reduces the vegetal friction offered to flowing water, is chiefly responsible for bringing about such a condition.

Erosion, then, can be thought of partially as a function of the amount and rate of runoff considered in relation to the physical and chemical characteristics inherent in the soil. Inherent soil properties determine the degree of resistance to dislodgment of bare soil and fix to some extent the amount and rate of runoff resulting from a given rain. Other factors having an important influence on the amount and rate of runoff are:

1. Prevailing degree and regularity of land slopes (topography).
2. Size and shape of watershed (drainage area).
3. Kinds of vegetation and extent of coverage.

20

4. Presence or absence of well defined channels for surface drainage and hydraulic properties of same.

5. Permeability or imperviousness of subsoil and geological substrata.

Of all the factors mentioned, rainfall and land slopes are the only ones that cannot be modified to a greater or less extent by acts of man. Hence the analysis of a practical problem concerns itself largely with the extent of modification physically possible and economically feasible of all the controllable factors, and this will determine the proper use of land within definite slope limits and rainfall conditions to insure reasonable perpetuity of fertility.

Since surface runoff may occur without erosion but never erosion without runoff, we may consider the effect of the various factors on runoff as an indirect measure of their effect on erosion.

EFFECT OF RAINFALL ON RUNOFF

The amount, intensity, and duration of rainfall have profound effect on the amount and rate of the resultant runoff, as does the elapsed time since the preceding rain. Rainfall, being uncontrollable, the only fruitful procedure is to subject all existing records to critical study for the purpose of determining for a given locality, (1) the most damaging combination of characteristics, (2) the frequency of recurrence of storms with damaging characteristics, and (3) that storm with a recurrence frequency against which it is economically feasible to protect. Downpours of high intensity and comparatively short duration invariably cause maximum runoff on lands subject to erosion, and such storms will be accorded special treatment in Chap. IV.

EFFECT OF LAND SLOPE ON RUNOFF

Slope affects runoff by imparting velocity in accordance with the well-known law of falling bodies as modified by environmental conditions. It is apparent that the steeper the slope, other things being equal, the less time there will be for absorption and the faster the runoff will flow. From theoretical considerations, with some experimental support, it can be shown that the following laws of hydraulics are approximately true.

1. According to the law of falling bodies, velocity varies as the square root of the vertical drop. On sloping lands the vertical drop is measured as the fall in feet per foot or the total drop divided by the total length of slope

between the two points considered. Therefore, if the land slope is increased four times, the velocity of water flowing over it is about doubled.

2. If the velocity is doubled, the erosive or cutting capacity, as represented by kinetic energy, is increased about four times. (Kinetic energy varies with the square of the velocity or, more exactly, as $*V^2/2g$.)

3. If the velocity is doubled, the quantity of material of a given size that can be carried is increased about thirty-two times. (Amount varies with fifth power of velocity.)

4. If the velocity is doubled, the size of particle that can be transported by pushing or rolling is increased about sixty-four times. (Size of particle varies with sixth power of velocity.)

5. There is a definite limit to the amount of silt that can be carried in suspension, due to the action of cross eddies and upward components in water flowing at a given velocity and depth. When this limit has been attained, more material cannot be picked up, no matter how erosive it is, without increasing the velocity or depth. Any reduction in velocity or depth will result in deposition.

6. For a given volume of water the depth depends on the extent of lateral irregularity in slope and in erosive properties of the soil. When water flows in rather definitely defined channels, due to such irregularity, there is a reduction in friction and a still greater increase in velocity.

From greenhouse and field experiments, where the degree of slope was controlled, Duley and Hays[1] report that runoff increases rapidly from 0 to 3 per cent slope and then is relatively slight for each 1 per cent additional increase in slope. Soil losses increase gradually to about 4 per cent slope, then increase more rapidly to between 7 and 8 per cent, beyond which the rate of increase is still more rapid. The effect of slope is complicated by so many other variable factors of soil, cover, etc., that it is difficult to apply experiments such as these to any other than the particular conditions under which they were conducted. For instance, in these experiments, a silty clay loam suffered greater soil loss than a sandy loam on moderate slopes, but on steep slopes the loss from the sandy loam soil was larger.

The above discussion deals mainly with the influence of land slopes in imparting·velocity to runoff. The amount or volume of runoff also has an important bearing on erosion and this is fixed, for a given set of conditions, by the area of land contributing to the flow. Both the size and shape of the watershed area affect

* V = velocity in feet per second and g = acceleration of gravity, 32.2 feet per second per second.

[1] DULY, F. L., and HAYS, O. E., "The Effect of the Degree of Slope on Runoff and Erosion," *Jour. Agr. Research*, Vol. 45, pp. 349–360.

the amount of runoff at a given point and, on hillsides, the length of slope is more important than width.

Land slopes cannot be directly changed but can be modified in their effect on runoff by the use of transverse channels or terraces. By this medium, long slopes are divided into a series of short units, thus keeping velocity low; and the contributing areas are kept small, thus reducing the amount of runoff.

In regard to the effect of land slopes on gully erosion, the following quotation is of interest.[1]

In southern Ohio, Indiana, and Illinois the land in general is very rolling with short drainages feeding into the ravines. As a rule, the ravines have a fairly stable channel although there are a few exceptions. The gullying prevails on the short steep watersheds above and to the side of the ravines. The gullies are relatively short and usually extend from the ravine to the ridge tops. Numerous gullies parallel each other, and the watershed areas above the gullies usually range from practically nothing to only a few acres in area.

North and west of this area we find an area in Missouri, Iowa, northern Illinois, Indiana, and southern Minnesota where the topography flattens out and a different type of gullying prevails. In this area gully erosion is possibly in an earlier stage of development and numerous precipitous gullies are found in the valleys and ravines, eating their way through good agricultural land toward the heads of large drainage areas. The watersheds above the heads of the gullies vary in area from a few acres to several hundred acres, and the gullies are usually characterized by having a distinctly undercutting action from waterfall erosion at their heads.

EFFECT OF SOIL VARIABLES

It would seem from a cursory examination that the effect of soil variables on runoff and erosion could easily be determined; and so it could if size, gradation, and specific gravity of the soil particles, and the extent of their aggregation into granules were all that needed to be taken into account. Such physical characteristics as *texture* and, to some extent, *structure* are easily identified by soil type and, since all soils of the country have been classified into types, it might seem reasonable to assume that the erosional behavior of a soil would be completely known upon identification by type. Such is far from the case although the properties mentioned do have an important bearing on erosivity.

[1] *U. S. Forest Ser. Handbook*, Region 9.

The texture of a soil profile greatly affects but does not entirely determine the ease with which water is absorbed and hence the amount available for surface runoff. To be most effective the entire profile must have reasonably uniform texture so that percolation will continue after the soil becomes saturated. Palouse silt loam, Marshall silt loam, Colby silty clay loam, and Houston black clay are examples of uniform texture; whereas Kirvin fine sandy loam, Vernon fine sandy loam, and Cecil sandy clay loam are quite variable in texture within the profile.

Common soils are often open-textured in the surface or A-horizon and relatively impervious in the subsurface layers. This means that the surface layer quickly becomes saturated and a large portion of subsequent rainfall is precipitated down the slope as runoff, with disastrous results.

Soil structure, or the extent to which individual grains cling together into clusters and which is roughly related to the humus and lime content, is another determining factor of infiltration rates because of the relatively large pore spaces present.

That texture alone is not a sufficiently inclusive criterion on which to base erosivity is indicated by the following examples of soil and water losses from soils roughly comparable so far as texture is concerned. From a Cecil sandy clay loam cotton field on a 10 per cent slope in North Carolina, 43 inches of rainfall produced only 9 per cent runoff and soil loss of 14 tons per acre; whereas from an Abilene clay loam cotton field on a slope of only 2 per cent, 21 inches of rainfall produced 14 per cent runoff and soil loss of 8 tons per acre. In other words the soil loss from the flat slope was more than half that from a slope five times steeper and was produced by half as much rainfall.

A similar situation is revealed by the U. S. Bureau of Chemistry and Soils at their experimental farm near Tyler, Tex., where it was found that the soil loss from Kirvin fine sandy loam in cotton on an 8.75 per cent slope was three times as great, and the water loss 30 per cent more, than from Nacogdoches fine sandy loam in the same crop on a 10 per cent slope.

Some of the reasons for these differences have already been indicated as variations in the texture and structure of the profiles such as the occurrence, arrangement, and thickness of dense layers and the weight of the soil particles, but doubtless the shape and surface characteristics of the soil grains, their resistance to dispersion, and certain other properties must also be taken into account before a complete explanation can be reached.

Probably the most significant single quality inherent in a soil is its dispersion ratio or the readiness with which individual particles go into suspension in water. Soils in which silt predominates with a corresponding shortage in clay exhibit this property to a marked degree, as there is insufficient clay to serve as a binder. It should not be inferred from this, however, that a high percentage of clay is necessarily indicative of a nonerosive soil. On the contrary, if most of the clay particles are of colloidal size—0.002 to 0.005 millimeter or less in diameter—it is probable that excessive swelling will occur when the soil is wet and excessive shrinkage when dry. Swelling will tend to reduce infiltration and shrinkage will open surface cracks and tend to create fragments which are easy to dislodge.

Soil Tests.—A few years ago, H. E. Middleton of the technical staff of the U. S. Bureau of Chemistry and Soils undertook to make complete analyses of the physical and chemical properties of certain soils that had been observed in the field to be erosive and nonerosive,[1] for the purpose of discovering which properties were most significant in explaining erosional behavior.

Three groups of samples were selected as follows: one containing erosive and nonerosive soils of dissimilar texture taken from widely separated localities; one containing two soils of almost identical texture from the same locality but differing greatly in erosional behavior; and one group of three soils from erosion experiment stations, all erosive.

GROUP 1

Erosive—Memphis silt loam and Orangeburg fine sandy loam, both from Mississippi.
Nonerosive—Nipe clay from Cuba, and Aikin silty clay loam from Oregon.

GROUP 2

Erosive—Iredell loam from 14 miles east of Greensboro, N. C.
Nonerosive—Davidson clay loam from 9 miles north of Greensboro, N. C.

[1] To conform to the newly adopted terminology of the Soil Conservation Service, read "erodible" for "erosive," and "erodibility" for "erosivity" in the discussion that follows.

Group 3

Erosive soils from erosion experiment stations—
Cecil fine sandy loam, Raleigh, N. C.
Shelby loam, Columbia, Mo.
Miles clay loam, Spur, Tex.

Representative samples from various horizons in the profiles of all of these soils were subjected to exhaustive physical and chemical tests. Quantitative determinations were made of the following physical properties:

Percentage of sand, silt, and clay.
Colloid content (particles smaller than 0.002 to 0.005 mm.).
Moisture equivalent.
Lower liquid limit.
Maximum water holding capacity.
Specific gravity (weight).
Slaking value.
Briquettes at maximum density.
  Moisture content.
  Apparent specific gravity.
  Shrinkage.
  Pore space.
  Volume of voids.
Dispersion ratio.
Ratio of colloid to moisture equivalent.
Erosion ratio.
Ratio of silt to clay.

Of all the enumerated qualities only three seemed to have any pronounced correlation with erosional behavior as observed in the field. These were, (1) dispersion ratio, (2) ratio of colloid to moisture equivalent, and (3) erosion ratio. Since erosion ratio is a simple function of the two other ratios, in reality the three qualities to be determined by test are moisture equivalent, colloid content, and dispersion ratio.

It is apparent from a study of Table 1 that the dispersion ratio decreases as the resistance to erosion increases and is therefore a fairly consistent measure of erosional behavior, regardless of other properties. On the other hand the colloid-moisture equivalent ratio increases as the resistance to erosion increases. Since the dispersion ratio is a function of the mechanical composition and ease of dispersion of the soil particles, and the colloid-moisture equivalent has some relation to absorptive power and

TABLE 1.—PHYSICAL PROPERTIES OF EROSIVE AND NONEROSIVE SOILS[1]

Character and sample number	Soil type	Depth, inches	Mechanical analysis			Colloid, per cent	Moisture equiv-alent, per cent	Dispersion ratio	Ratio of colloid to moisture equivalent	Erosion ratio
			Sand, per cent	Silt, per cent	Clay, per cent					
	Group 1									
Erosive										
1	Memphis silt loam (Miss.)[2]	0–8	11.2	75.4	13.4	14.6	21.5	44.6	0.68	65.2
2	Memphis silt loam (Miss.)[2]	8–28	6.2	63.0	30.8	32.2	28.6	26.3	1.13	23.3
3	Memphis silt loam (Miss.)[2]	120–216	5.6	80.3	14.2	12.3	21.7	66.0	.57	115.8
4	Orangeburg fine sandy loam (Miss.)	0–16	64.0	26.1	9.9	11.6	15.0	39.2	.77	50.9
5	Orangeburg fine sandy loam (Miss.)	16–72	56.9	20.1	23.0	23.5	17.3	16.9	1.36	12.4
6	Orangeburg fine sandy loam (Miss.)	72–96	77.4	6.4	16.2	16.5	12.5	29.6	1.32	22.4
7	Orangeburg fine sandy loam (Miss.)	96–136	97.6	6	1.8	2.4	2.2	27.0	1.09	24.8
Nonerosive										
8	Nipe clay (Cuba)	0–12	20.4[3]	32.5	47.1	65.1	30.4	6.1	2.14	2.9
9	Nipe clay (Cuba)	12–24	23.4[3]	24.1	62.5	63.7	27.2	5.2	2.34	2.2
10	Aikin silty clay loam (Ore.)	0–20	11.7	28.8	59.5	52.5	30.3	15.1	1.73	8.7
11	Aikin silty clay loam (Ore.)	20–40	10.4	23.7	65.9	59.8	30.8	13.4	1.94	6.9

[1] *U. S. Dept. Agr. Tech. Bull.* 178.
[2] Based on wet volume.
[3] A considerable part consists of concretions.

TABLE 1.—PHYSICAL PROPERTIES OF EROSIVE AND NONEROSIVE SOILS.—(Continued)

| Character and sample number | Soil type | Horizon | Depth, inches | Mechanical analysis[1] | | | Colloid, per cent | Moisture equivalent, per cent | Dispersion ratio | Ratio of colloid to moisture equivalent | Erosion ratio |
				Sand, per cent	Silt, per cent	Clay, per cent					
					Group 2						
Erosive											
12	Iredell loam	A¹	0–5	36.2	38.4	16.4	24.7	30.5	19.6	0.81	24.2
13	Iredell loam	A²	5–10	37.3	45.6	16.4	15.0	18.1	13.0	.83	15.7
14	Iredell loam	B	10–20	11.2	23.9	63.1	63.9	45.9	20.9	1.39	15.0
15	Iredell loam	C	20–27	34.9	28.5	35.2	39.0	38.0	23.5	1.03	22.8
Nonerosive											
16	Davidson clay loam	A	0–9	31.9	39.9	23.8	27.3	25.1	13.3	1.09	12.2
17	Davidson clay loam	B¹	9–36	14.0	22.3	60.4	64.8	39.3	6.1	1.65	3.7
18	Davidson clay loam	B²	36–60	18.5	30.4	50.3	66.5	43.0	6.6	1.55	4.3
19	Davidson clay loam	C	60+	35.4	34.5	29.6	53.8	39.3	10.6	1.37	7.7
					Group 3						
Erosive											
20	Cecil fine sandy loam, N. C.		0–6	58.0	14.4	25.3	21.1	19.2	28.4	1.10	25.8
21	Cecil fine sandy loam, N. C.		6–24	28.4	12.3	58.6	53.9	32.9	9.8	1.64	6.0
22	Shelby loam, Mo.		0–7	11.9	61.4	24.3	19.5	23.6	31.0	.83	37.4
23	Shelby loam, Mo.		7–24	6.1	49.7	42.5	40.2	32.4	27.6	1.24	22.3
24	Shelby loam, Mo.		24–36	14.9	42.3	41.7	37.6	30.4	30.3	1.24	24.4
25	Miles clay loam, Tex.		0–8	30.1	33.1	34.0	31.4	25.2	27.4	1.25	21.9

[1] Determinations by L. T. Alexander.
[2] Based on wet volume.

infiltration, a combination of the two seems to give a fairly accurate and complete index of erosional behavior so far as physical soil properties are concerned. Such a combination is represented by the "erosion ratio," which is derived by dividing the dispersion ratio by the colloid-moisture equivalent ratio. The colloid-moisture equivalent ratio is of course simply the per cent of colloids in the soil divided by the moisture equivalent, which is also expressed on a percentage basis.

In Middleton's studies the dispersion ratio was measured as follows:

A sample of air-dry soil equivalent to 10 grams of oven-dry soil was placed in a tall cylinder of approximately 1200 cubic centimeter capacity fitted with a rubber stopper. Sufficient distilled water was added to make the volume a liter. The cylinder was closed with a stopper and was shaken end over end twenty times. The suspension was then allowed to settle until a 25 cubic centimeter sample, which was pipetted at a depth of 30 centimeters, consisted of particles of a maximum diameter of 0.05 millimeter. From the dry weight of the pipetted fraction, the total weight of silt and clay in the suspension was calculated. The ratio, expressed in percentage, of the silt and clay so determined to the total silt and clay obtained by mechanical analysis is called the dispersion ratio.

Several methods have been proposed and used for determining the colloid content of soils. None is entirely accurate and satisfactory, but the one used by Middleton seems to be considered among the best at the present time. It is based on the fact that colloids or "ultra clays," regardless of source, have nearly the same capacity to absorb water, i.e., an average "specific water absorption" of 0.298. The colloid is measured by determining under certain conditions the water absorption of the entire specimen—which is the difference between the weight of the material when saturated and when dried at 110 degrees—and dividing the result by the constant 0.298.

The moisture equivalent is defined as the maximum percentage of moisture that a soil can retain in opposition to a centrifugal force equal to 1000 times the force of gravity. Its determination is relatively simple in technique but requires special apparatus that is part of the standard equipment of every soils laboratory.

Middleton made a complete chemical analysis of the soils in Table 1 but was unable to discover any direct correlation between chemical characteristics and erosional behavior. On this point Middleton says,[1] "None of the chemical properties studied have been found useful in differentiating between erosive and nonerosive soils, though undoubtedly the dispersivity of a soil is influenced by the quantity and character of the exchange bases present (pH value), and the silica-sesquioxide ratio (molecular ratio of the silica to the combined alumina and iron oxide present in the colloid) is the determining influence on physical properties."

In a later publication in 1932, *U. S. Department of Agriculture Technical Bulletin* 316, the same author says:

The dispersion ratio and the erosion ratio are the only criteria that have been developed for estimating, in advance of actual measurement, the erosivity of a soil. . . . An analytical basis has been established, to which may be referred the future field behavior of these soils when it has been determined, so that a quantitative expression of anticipated behavior may (eventually) be developed.

In further explanation of the striking difference in erosivity of the soils in Group 2 of Table 1, J. F. Lutz remarks:[2]

The aforementioned data show very clearly that one of the principal differences between erosive and nonerosive soils is the degree of aggregation of the finer mechanical separates into large, stable granules. . . . The Davidson aggregates are friable and porous; those in the Iredell are plastic and compact. The high content of large porous aggregates in the Davidson is in marked contrast to the small, compact granules and dispersed condition of the Iredell. The size of particles, whether primary or secondary units, determines to a great extent the amount of erosion by any given quantity of runoff.

EFFECT OF VEGETATION

The role of plant life in soil and water conservation is one of transcending importance and is manifested in at least nine different aspects:

1. Direct dispersion, interception, and evaporation of falling rain drops by the foliage of trees and shrubs.

---

[1] MIDDLETON, H. E., "Properties of Soils Which Influence Soil Erosion," *U. S. Dept. Agr. Tech. Bull.* 178, 1930.

[2] LUTZ, J. F.: "The Physico-chemical Properties of Soils Affecting Erosion," *Univ. Mo. Research Bull.* 212, 1934.

2. Transpiration, through the body tissues and leaves, of vast quantities of moisture from the subsoil back into the air.

3. Protective shield afforded by close-growing grasses and cover crops against violent impact of rainfall.

4. Knitting and binding effect of root systems in surface layer of soil simulating a sponge-like condition.

5. Penetration of roots throughout soil profile, which decay and leave numerous tubular cavities to promote infiltration.

6. Improvement of soil structure by addition of organic matter, increases absorption, and keeps the soil in condition to support vigorous growth.

7. Increased surface friction reduces volume of runoff and decreases velocity of remainder.

8. Surface friction tends to keep water spread out laterally and thus delays the rate of concentration in tributary drainage ways.

9. Entrance of air is facilitated by adding humus to the soil, and a more favorable environment is created for the activity of beneficial bacteria.

The most noticeable single effect of the above phenomena is low density (as to silt content), small volume, and slow rate of runoff resulting from any rain.

Forests.—A thick stand of trees growing over areas of appreciable size affords one of the best possible protections against erosion. When trees are well established, a dense foliage canopy, a ground mat of leaf and litter mulch, and extensive root development make a combination that renders the soil practically invulnerable.

Because trees and shrubs are so effective they are commonly considered man's last line of defense to be prescribed when all other expedients have failed. While this is, in a sense, true, and trees are resorted to on lands so badly eroded as to be fit for nothing else, at the same time their economic value as merchantable timber should not be overlooked. There are doubtless many cases of exceptionally vulnerable crop land where an economic analysis will show tree growing to represent the most profitable use. Judicious cutting and marketing of adult trees will provide an annual income and at the same time allow for perpetual reproduction and for effective soil and water conservation. Trees, vines, and shrubs can insure practical immunity to erosion on even the steepest slopes, such as are found in mountainous regions.

A general idea of the relative holding power for water and soil of various kinds of trees, shrubs, grasses, and crops can be gained from Table 2, which was compiled by A. F. Dodge in

1932 as a result of field studies in Warren County, Ia. Plots $\frac{1}{200}$ acre in size were used. The figures shown are corrected for modal slope but are uncorrected for numerous other variable factors and are therefore of qualitative interest only.

TABLE 2.—QUALITATIVE COMPARISON OF HOLDING POWER OF VARIOUS KINDS OF VEGETATION

Average runoff corrected for modal slope			Average silt loss corrected for modal slope		
Relative rank	Plant	Unit index	Relative rank	Plant	Unit index
1	Hazel brush	0.48	1	Hazel brush	0.0
2	Oak-hickory	0.93	2	Oak-hickory	0.0
3	Timothy-clover	1.00	3	Sweet clover	0.013
4	Wheat, across slope	1.06	4	Timothy-clover	0.023
5	Sweet clover	1.18	5	Alfalfa	0.026
6	Barley	2.24	6	Ragweed	0.047
7	Alfalfa	2.89	7	Weeds after corn	0.048
8	Ragweed	3.54	8	Barley	0.078
9	Weeds after corn	4.2	9	Dog fennel grass	0.085
10	Corn	4.58	10	Wheat, across slope	0.11
11	Wheat, down slope	4.91	11	Oats	0.13
12	Sudan grass	5.25	12	Wheat, down slope	0.25
13	Soy beans	6.22	13	Sudan grass	1.58
14	Dog fennel grass	6.56	14	Corn	2.04
15	Oats	6.66	15	Sorghum	2.72
16	Sorghum	7.74	16	Soy beans	3.02

The average slope of the plots was 10.97 per cent, with a range of 8 per cent for the flattest to 16 per cent for the steepest. The left half of the table shows the sixteen plants arranged in order of effectiveness for holding moisture and the right half the order of the same sixteen for holding soil. Hazel brush and oak-hickory trees were most effective in each case. Sorghum was most wasteful of water but was slightly more effective than soy beans in holding soil. Corn ranks tenth in holding water but drops to fourteenth for holding soil. The relative rank in the case of dog fennel grass is almost the reverse; from 14 to 9. Apparently, if these results are representative, plants differ more than twice as much in ability to hold moisture as in ability to hold soil.

Perhaps the most significant conclusion to be drawn from this study is that plants vary in ability to prevent losses almost in direct proportion to the degree of their natural environmental adaptation.

Table 3 gives the result of plot experiments to show the effect of forest cover and grass on erosion and runoff, as measured on the Kirvin fine sandy loam in east Texas and on Vernon fine sandy loam in central Oklahoma. In both instances the ground cover of litter was decidedly light as compared with the average forest-floor litter of the country.

TABLE 3.—EFFECT OF FOREST ON EROSION AND RUNOFF, AS COMPARED WITH GRASS—TYLER, TEX., AND GUTHRIE, OKLA.[1]

Fine sandy loam	Mean precipitation, inches	Slope, per cent	Cover	Soil-loss, tons per acre	Water-loss, per cent of precipitation (runoff)
Kirvin..	44.4	12½	Forest	0.01	0.8
Kirvin..	44.4	12½	Forest, litter burned	0.19	2.6
Kirvin..	42.3	8¾	Bermuda grass	0.21	1.5
Kirvin..	48.8	16½	Bermuda grass	0.00	0.7
Vernon.	33.5	5⅕	Forest	0.017	0.13
Vernon.	33.5	5⅕	Forest, litter burned	0.22	5.06
Vernon.	32.9	7⁷⁄₁₀	Bermuda grass	0.04	1.5

[1] BENNETT, H. H., *Transactions, American Geophysical Union*, 1934.

These results show that forest as well as good stands of grass give practically complete protection from erosion on these very extensive and important soil types. The water losses also have been exceedingly small, especially where the ground cover of forest litter has not been burned. The difference between the effectiveness of grass and forest is seen to be very slight.[1]

In a joint publication of the U. S. Forest Service and Weather Bureau,[2] Bates and Henry describe a study of runoff and erosion from two mountain watersheds of about 200 acres each. Rainfall

[1] BENNETT, H. H., *Transactions, American Geophysical Union*, 1934, pp. 474–478.

[2] BATES, C. G., and A. J. HENRY: "Forest and Stream Flow Experiment at Wagon Wheel Gap, Col."

and discharge were carefully measured and eroded material caught in settling basins. Records covered about 15 years. Both watersheds were studied in their original condition for half the period, and then one was denuded. Annual precipitation throughout the period averaged 21 inches, half rain and half snow, which, coupled with the effect of an absorptive soil, resulted in light runoff and erosion. Conclusions were as follows:

1. Denudation increased runoff 15 per cent and flood flows 58 per cent.
2. Denudation increased erosion eight and one-half times.
3. Denudation increased the ratio of high to low stages, or vertical fluctuation of extreme high water to extreme low water, from 12:1 to 17:1.

Literature on the effect of forest cover on climate, floods, erosion, water supply, and recreation is voluminous. In another bulletin of the U. S. Forest Service in 1927, Zon[1] compiled a bibliography of 1100 such publications, which he digested and analyzed from a forester's viewpoint. His conclusions are, very briefly:

1. The total discharge of large rivers is practically independent of forest cover.
2. Forest cover distributes and equalizes stream flow but has little influence on large floods.
3. In mountainous country forests increase underground storage and seepage and conserve water for stream flow; in level country they aid drainage.

The apparent contradiction between Zon's conclusions and those of Bates and Henry can partially be explained on the basis of size of watershed. Zon had principally in mind very large areas, whereas the other study dealt with an area of less than one square mile, steep slopes, and flashy runoff.

Grass Cover Crops and Cultivation.—In considering the effect of cultivation on erosion it should again be pointed out that the natural condition of the land surface, in all except arid and arctic climates, is a vegetative cover of some kind, either forests, shrubs, or prairie grasses, or a combination of all three. It must be assumed that natural cover was effective in controlling erosion, else there would have been no layer of rich topsoil to exploit when these lands were first put under the plow.

---

[1] ZON, RAPHAEL: "Forests and Water in the Light of Scientific Investigations," *U. S. Forest Ser.*, 1927.

As noted in Table 2, all plants, including those grown as cultivated crops, have some anti-erosion value, but in varying degree and inevitably, tillage operations will cause bare soil to be exposed during times when erosive forces are usually most severe. The following tabulation indicates the average number of days each year that soil is left uncovered under various cropping plans.

Cropping System	Average Number of Days per Year Soil Is Uncovered
Continuous corn	207
Continuous wheat	91
Corn, soybeans, oats, cowpeas	259
Corn, oats, wheat, clover	95
Corn, wheat, clover	73
Corn, oats, clover	73
Corn, wheat, clover, timothy	18
Continuous bluegrass	0

Similar data for cotton or tobacco, with their supporting rotational crops, would show substantially the same extent of exposure. These figures should not be interpreted to mean that erosion loss is necessarily in direct proportion to days of exposure, but they do mean that with any cultivated crop and any rotation scheme there is more or less opportunity for excessive erosion to occur. It is interesting to note that a four year rotation of corn, soybeans, oats, and cowpeas exposes bare soil 52 days longer than does continuous corn.

A very good measure of the effect of crops and cultivation is afforded by the data in Table 4, which gives the results of 14 years' plot measurements and observations at Columbia, Mo. The plots extended up and down a slope of 3.68 per cent and each was $\frac{1}{80}$ acre in size, being 6 feet wide and 90.75 feet long. The soil was a Shelby loam of "rather poor quality." Since the figures shown are averages over a considerable time period, they have quantitative value as representing the relative effect of fallow ground, bluegrass pasture, wheat, corn, and a three-year rotation of corn, wheat, and clover on soil and water losses for the particular soil type and slope stated. These valuable experiments will be considered more in detail in the following chapter.

Losses from experiments on a series of four plots on Cecil fine sandy loam in North Carolina have been measured over a period of 3 years by F. O. Bartel. The plots were 75 feet long on a slope of 9 per cent and were cropped respectively to grass sod, cotton annually, corn annually, and bare (hoed just enough to keep down weeds). The annual loss of soil per acre from the bare plot was 21 tons, from the cotton plot 20 tons, from the corn plot 13.5 tons and from the sod plot 0.42 ton. Although the slope is much steeper than on the Missouri plots the soil loss is

TABLE 4.—GENERAL SUMMARY OF RUNOFF AND OF SOIL ERODED PER ACRE DURING FOURTEEN YEARS AT COLUMBIA, MO.[1]

	Cultural and cropping systems					
	Plowed 4 in. fallowed	Plowed 8 in. fallowed	Continuous bluegrass	Continuous wheat	Rotation— corn, wheat, and clover	Continuous corn
Average No. tons soil eroded per acre annually.	41.64	41.08	.34	10.10	2.78	19.72
Surface inches of soil eroded annually.	.291	.287	.0023	.070	.019	138
Average No. cu. ft. runoff per acre annually.	46,132	45,836	18,379	35,209	21,129	44,524
Average per cent runoff annually.	30.7	30.3	12.0	23.3	13.8	29.4
Pounds runoff required to erode 1 lb. soil.	34.4	34.8	1,666.9	109.1	236.5	70.3
No. years to erode 7 in. of soil.	24	24	3,043	100	368	50

[1] *Mo. Agr. Exp. Sta. Research Bull.* 177.

less. The rainfall is a little more in North Carolina, 41 inches, while in Missouri it is 37 inches annually. This is further evidence of the great variation to be expected due to differences in erosive characteristics of soils.

EFFECT OF FROST ACTION

The degree of erosion suffered by soil when left bare or under crops is modified materially by temperature. In southern latitudes where winter precipitation is almost exclusively in the form of rain, and the soil seldom freezes, the opportunity for erosion is greater than where snow is the rule in winter and the ground remains frozen for several months each year. If snow accumulates in deep drifts, however, (as in the winter of 1935–1936) and melts quickly in the spring when frost is leaving the ground, local losses may be more severe than they would have been had the soil remained open.

Another frost phenomenon often overlooked is the possibility of drawing up large quantities of water through a highly colloidal soil profile by molecular cohesion and storing it in the form of ice lenses near the surface where it is released during spring thaws. The work of Stephen Taber of the University of South Carolina showed that the upward heave is equal to the combined thickness of the ice layers and may often be as much as 2 feet. The force exerted is much greater than capillarity and, under favorable conditions, may pull water from a depth of 15 feet or more. Apparently the phenomenon is most active in soils with grain diameter of one micron or less and where unlimited water is available from the subsoil. Taber's results were reported in the *Journal of Geology*, Vol. 38, No. 4, pp. 303–317, from which Fig. 14 is taken.

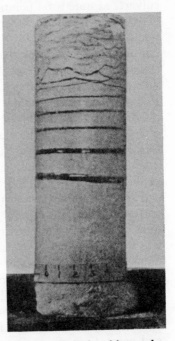

Fig. 14.—Cylinder of frozen clay showing layers of free ice formed by uplift of water. Note symmetry and relation between thickness of layers and distance apart. Scale in centimeters.

Frost does not usually leave the ground by continuous melting but through a succession of alternate freezes and thaws. Gullies formed by this means may extend in all directions without any particular relation to land slopes. Alternate freezing and thawing loosens the soil, which sloughs off in lumps and is carried away by subsequent rains.

MISCELLANEOUS FACTORS

Among the miscellaneous factors affecting the rate of erosion, in addition to those touched upon in Chap. I, may be mentioned the diversion of natural drainage courses by highway and railway embankments and culverts. Unless careful attention is given to the problem, the delivery of water through poorly installed culverts at unnatural points may result in gullies. The disposal of roadway drainage water, both down fills and through cuts, frequently is accompanied by erosion. With proper design, however, not only can this kind of erosion be prevented but embankments can be combined with drop-inlet culverts to provide a highly useful service.

Not infrequently gullies start from a chance wagon track or by dragging an implement down a slope, especially when the ground is soft. This breaks the surface and forms a depression down which water may travel in increasing quantities and gradually cut out a gully. Other adventitious causes are mole, gopher, or groundhog holes and livestock paths.

There are certain powerful economic factors such as the system of farming practiced, debt, size of farm, and landlord-tenant relations that sometimes force injudicious use of land regardless of consequences. Consideration of this kind of maladjustment is reserved for a later chapter.

To fix in mind the natural variables having a vital effect on the rate of erosion the following equation has been proposed. It is in no sense homogeneous and merely states in symbol form that erosion varies as some function of rainfall, topography, soil, and vegetation.

$$E = f(RGSV)$$

Where E = rate of erosion

R = a factor depending on the amount and intensity of the rainfall

G = a factor depending on the slope and area of the land

S = a factor depending on the physical and chemical properties of the soil

V = a factor depending on the extent and nature of the vegetal cover.

CHAPTER III

METHODS OF CONTROL

After considering the four variables and numerous sub-variables discussed in Chap. II, and the almost infinite number of ways in which they can combine, it is apparent, for the present at least, that the best control measure or measures for a given set of conditions can hardly be reduced to the precision standard of a mathematical formula. Laboratory tests and plot measurements are necessary and extremely valuable indicators but the ultimate guide to good practice must be actual field experience. At the same time a thorough theoretical knowledge of the various factors involved is required before field experience can properly be evaluated and probable improvements suggested.

Remembering that erosion cannot be prevented in an absolute sense and that the normal rate of runoff and erosion is that resulting from natural conditions of cover, the problem of control is largely a determination of where and how natural protection can be destroyed by tillage without inviting disastrous losses.

The first step in any rational solution is to restrict open cultivated land to slopes and conditions where erosion can be held within predetermined limits. This means that there will be certain slopes best suited for cultivated crops, steeper slopes best suited for permanent pastures, and still steeper slopes best suited for forests. The division between these three uses will not be a thin line but a border zone of considerable width and flexibility to allow for local variations.

This chapter will be concerned principally with ways and means of keeping erosion under control on slopes suited for cultivated crops. The difficulty of control is one factor that fixes the upper slope limit for crop land. Since soils vary in erosivity and since plants differ in holding power, it is evident that the maximum slope for a rate of loss considered tolerable will vary with the soil type and crop.

39

A control measure may roughly be evaluated and judged by asking the following questions:

How much is absorption increased and per cent of runoff reduced?

How much protection is afforded against damage by the residual runoff?

How much does it cost and how much is added to the inconvenience of tillage and annual cost of production?

How will the measure affect the cash income from the land?

How thoroughly has it been tested both experimentally and in actual practice?

The final practical answer to these questions pertaining to a particular farm will come as a result of field experience on that farm over a term of years. In most cases a combination of all recognized control methods will be needed for adequate protection.

All control measures now in common use seek to accomplish the results indicated in the first two questions. Absorption may be increased by improving the infiltration rate of the soil and by impounding the water where it falls, thus increasing the time of contact or the absorption opportunity. Under exceptionally favorable circumstances it may be possible to induce absorption of the entire rainfall, in which case there will be no runoff and no need to consider the second question.

ABSORPTION RANGE OF SOILS

That such a possibility is within reason in humid regions has been demonstrated by the experiments of G. W. Musgrave[1] who by the use of lysimeters and experimental plots measured the infiltration rates of two soils in their natural undisturbed state. Marshall silt loam and Shelby silt loam were the two types studied, and all the natural vagaries to which soils are subject, such as nonuniform texture, varying structure and the presence of root cavities, worm holes, etc., were taken into account. The lysimeter assembly used in these experiments is shown in Fig. 15. Each cylinder contains undisturbed soil that was carefully excavated and moved *en bloc* from its original habitat. The observation tunnel, to which all of the cylinders are connected, contains equipment for measuring both the amount and rate of surface runoff and the amount and rate of percolation through

[1] MUSGRAVE, G. W., "The Infiltration Capacity of Soils in Relation to the Control of Surface Runoff and Erosion," paper before Amer. Soil Survey Assoc., 1934.

the cylinders. Surface runoff is collected through the funnel pipes shown in the picture and similar connections to the tunnel exist at the bottoms of the cylinders for percolated water. Great care is exercised to seal the inner surfaces of the cylinder containers against leakage.

Musgrave's results are shown graphically in Fig. 16. An analysis of Fig. 16 shows that in the first 15 minutes the infiltration rate upon the Marshall exceeded that upon the Shelby

Fig. 15.—Lysimeter assembly used in Musgrave experiments.

silt loam by 0.37 inch. In the first 30 minutes the difference was 0.62 inch; 45 minutes, 0.88 inch; 1¼ hours, 1.30 inch; and within 5½ hours the difference was 3.82 inches. Assuming that 1.5 inches of rain can be held on the surface where it falls by contour listing or basins and that the critical rainfall rate is as indicated, the chart shows that excess runoff will occur on Shelby silt loam after about 20 minutes (where the rainfall curve intersects the Shelby curve) and will continue at an increasing rate for the duration of the rain; whereas on the Marshall there will be no runoff because, after an initial "boost" of 1.5 inches, the infiltration rate exceeds the rainfall rate throughout. The total amount of runoff on the Shelby, in this hypothetical study, is represented by the area included between the rainfall curve and the Shelby curve and the total reserve capacity of the Marshall is similarly represented by the area between the Marshall and rainfall curves. Likewise the total difference in absorptive capacity for the 6-hour period is the area between the Marshall and Shelby curves.

For easy figuring Musgrave recommends that 0.75 inch per hour be taken as the infiltration rate for Marshall silt loam and

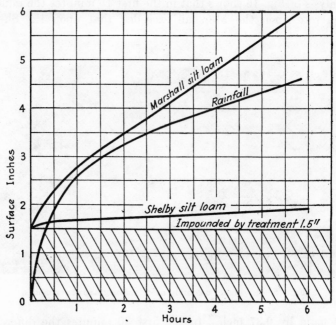

FIG. 16.—Protection provided against runoff on Marshall and Shelby silt loam for rain of rare intensity and duration.   Infiltration rates determined on soil of normal structure, moist, sod removed.   Rates determined by: (*a*) Horton's method; (*b*) lysimeters; (*c*) by direct measurement from added water.   All three methods gave like orders of magnitude.   (*Data from Soil Erosion Exp. Sta., Missouri Valley Loess Region, Clarinda, Iowa.*)

0.10 inch per hour for Shelby silt loam.   These rates represent about the extremes in perviousness and imperviousness likely to be encountered anywhere.

USE OF VEGETATION

A general summary of runoff and of soil eroded per acre during 14 years at Columbia, Mo., has already been presented in Table 4 of Chap. II.   That the cropping system has a decided effect on both runoff and erosion is clearly evident, but not in like proportion. The reduction in soil loss by crop rotation is invariably more pronounced than the reduction in runoff. This, as well as the seasonal distribution of losses, is shown in Fig. 17, with runoff on the left and soil loss on the right. It is easy to trace from this diagram the action of spring and summer rains and, somewhat more obscurely, the periods when the soil is

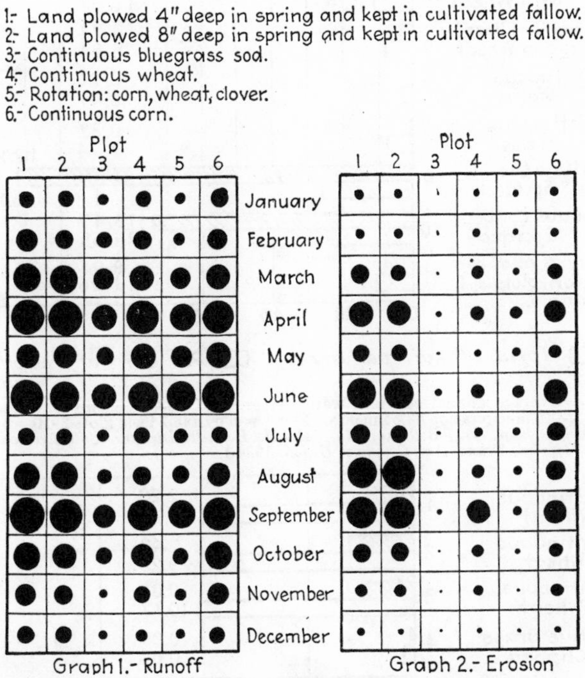
1:- Land plowed 4" deep in spring and kept in cultivated fallow.
2:- Land plowed 8" deep in spring and kept in cultivated fallow.
3:- Continuous bluegrass sod.
4:- Continuous wheat.
5:- Rotation: corn, wheat, clover.
6:- Continuous corn.
Plot
1 2 3 4 5 6
January
February
March
April
May
June
July
August
September
October
November
December
Graph 1.- Runoff
Graph 2.- Erosion

FIG. 17.—Relative average monthly runoff and erosion losses. Plot experiments 1918–1931. (*Agr. Exp. Sta. Columbia, Mo. Mo. Res. Bull.* 177.)

bare in the cropping cycle. Apparently, deep plowing has a negligible effect as compared with shallow plowing, at least under the particular conditions of these experiments.

More data of the same nature from three of the federal erosion stations are shown in Figs. 18, 19, and 20. These charts are quite complete in themselves and require very little additional discussion to make their meaning clear.

Figure 21 shows the effect of a single rain of 3.71 inches at Bethany, Mo., 3.30 inches of which fell at the rate of 2.36 inches

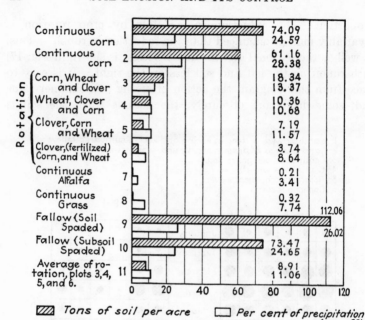

Fig. 18.—Average annual soil and water losses, 1931–1933. Shelby silt loam, slope 8 per cent; mean precipitation 33.54 inches. Plot 1 = 6 by 145.7 feet; Plots 2–10 = 6 by 72.85 feet. (*Erosion Exp. Sta., Bethany, Mo. H. H. Bennett, Director, Soil Erosion Service, Dept. Int., Reprint, Trans. Am. Geophys. Union, 1934.*)

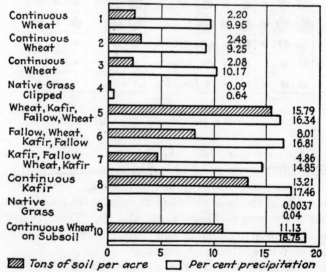

Fig. 19.—Average annual soil and water losses, 1930–1933. Colby silty clay loam, slope 5 per cent; mean precipitation 22.18 inches. Plot 1 = 6 by 36.3 feet; Plot 2 = 6 by 145.2 feet; Plots 3–10 = 6 by 72.6 feet. (*West. Kansas Plains Sta., Hays, Kans. H. H. Bennett, Trans. Am. Geophys. Union, 1934.*)

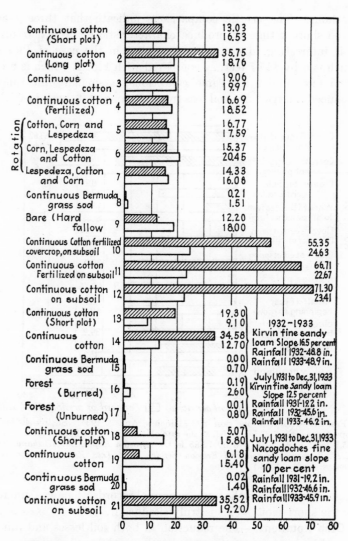

Tons of soil per acre ☐ **Per Cent precipitation**

FIG. 20.—Average annual soil and water losses, 1931–1933 inclusive. Kirvin fine sandy loam, slope 8.75 per cent; mean precipitation 42.31 inches; Plots 1, 13, 18 = 6 by 36.5 feet; Plot 2 = 6 by 145.8 feet; Plots 3–12, 14–17, 19–21 = 6 by 72.9 feet. Results on Plots 13–21 for years, slopes, and rainfalls as shown. (*Erosion Sta. Tyler, Tex. H. H. Bennett, Trans. Am. Geophys. Union*, 1934.)

per hour. The erratic comparisons indicate that three years is too short a time to produce characteristic or typical results. It is interesting to note, however, that in the case of Plot 1, which is 6 by 145.7 feet,.as compared with Plot 2, which is 6 by 72.85 feet, under the same conditions, a smaller unit runoff produced a larger unit soil loss from the long plot, both from the

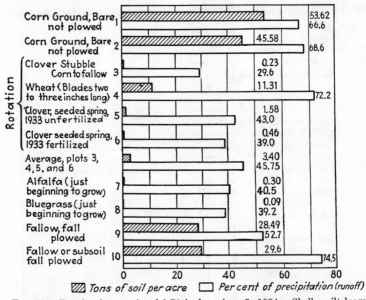

FIG. 21.—Result of one rain of 3.71 inches, Apr. 3, 1934. Shelby silt loam, slope, 8 per cent; 3.30 inches fell at the rate of 2.36 inches per hour; Plot 1 = 6 by 145.7 feet; Plots 2–10 = 6 by 72.85 feet. (*Erosion Exper. Sta., Bethany, Mo. H. H. Bennett, Director, Soil Erosion Service, Dept. Int., Reprint, Trans. Am. Geophys. Union, 1934.*)

single rain and from the average annual records, than was suffered by the short plot. This is truly significant.

Crop Rotations.—The reduction in both soil losses and runoff brought about by various rotations on different soil types is apparent from a comparison of some of the data in Table 5 and Table 6.

Another very striking angle to the effect of better structure assured through rotation is presented in Table 7, which is taken from *Agricultural Experiment Station Research Bulletin 177, University of Missouri.*

TABLE 5.—COMPARISON OF SOIL AND WATER LOSSES UNDER CROP ROTATIONS ON EIGHT IMPORTANT SOILS[1]

Location	Soil	Slope, per cent	Rotation	Mean precipitation, inches	Soil loss, tons per acre	Water loss, per cent of precipitation (runoff)
Bethany, Mo.......	Shelby silt loam	8	Corn, wheat, clover	34	10	11
Columbia, Mo......	Shelby loam	3.7	Corn, wheat, clover	40	10	24
Hays, Kan.........	Colby silt clay loam	5	Wheat, kafir, fallow	22	10	16
Guthrie, Okla.......	Vernon fine sandy loam	7.7	Wheat, sweet clover, cotton	33	6	12
Temple, Tex........	Houston Black Clay	4	Cotton, corn, oats	27	6	5
Tyler, Tex.........	Kirvin fine sandy loam	8.75	Cotton, corn, lespedeza	42	16	18
LaCrosse, Wis......	Clinton silt clay loam	16	Barley, corn, clover	29	21	13
Statesville, N. C....	Cecil sandy clay loam	10	Corn, wheat, lespedeza, cotton	43	7	10

[1] BENNETT, H. H., *loc. cit.*

Interpretation of Plot Data.—In arriving at correct conclusions from data obtained by plot measurements, certain definite limitations should be carefully considered:

With the exception of one plot at each federal station which was 145 feet, all of the plots were less than 100 feet long.

All plots were only 6 feet wide, which precludes the possibility of lateral accumulation.

Losses are computed and reported on an acre basis, but were measured on plots $\frac{1}{80}$ to $\frac{1}{100}$ acre in size. In other words, the losses actually measured were multiplied in the tables on the assumption that unit losses in the plot would be the same as unit losses in a large field. According to laws of similitude between models and prototypes that have been carefully worked out in other types of investigations, this is highly improbable.

In regard to the limitations on interpretation imposed by the length of plots, the authors of *Missouri Research Bulletin* 177 have this to say:

It is of importance to consider, too, that the length of slope used in this investigation is about the interval which, with the existing grade, would be recommended between terraces on this soil type. In case the land were terraced, therefore, the eroded soil would be washed into the terrace channels under the different cropping systems. In case the terraces had only a slight grade, the soil would largely remain in the

TABLE 6.—COMPARISON OF SOIL AND WATER LOSSES BY SURFACE RUNOFF AT SEVERAL OF THE SOIL-EROSION EXPERIMENT STATIONS[1]

Area—soil type—inches rainfall	Plot treatment	Soil loss, tons per acre	Loss of rainfall (run-off), per cent
Upper Mississippi Valley, La-Crosse, Wis. Clinton silt loam. 16% slope. (1933 only) rain, 29.11.	Bare soil, uncultivated	51.5	15.9
	Continuous corn	59.9	19.2
	Continuous barley	12.0	17.8
	Continuous bluegrass	0.003	2.9
Mo.; Ia.; Bethany, Mo. Shelby silt loam. 8% slope. (Av. 3 yrs. 1931–1933.) Av. annual rain 33.53.	Bare	112.48	25.98
	Continuous corn	61.16	28.38
	Continuous bluegrass, timothy	0.36	7.72
	Continuous alfalfa	0.22	3.40
Red Plains; Guthrie, Okla. Vernon fine sandy loam. 7.7% slope. (Av. 4 yrs. 1930–1933.) Av. annual rain 32.92.	Bare	14.59	26.04
	Continuous cotton	28.05	14.18
	Bermuda grass	0.04	1.51
Tex.; Ark.; La. sandy lands region; Tyler, Tex. Kirvin fine sandy loam. 8.75% slope. (Av. 3 yrs. 1931–1933) Av. annual rain 42.31.	Bare	12.20	18.20
	Continuous cotton	19.06	18.00
	Bermuda grass	0.20	1.50
Central Piedmont, Statesville, N. C. Cecil sandy clay loam. 10% slope. (Av. 3 yrs. 1931–1933) Av. annual rain 42.9	Bare	65.3	32.0
	Continuous cotton	14.0	9.7
	Continuous grass	0.8	5.2

Note: All plots 72.6 feet long, 6 feet wide—$\frac{1}{100}$ acre.
[1] *U. S. Yearbook of Agr.*, 1935, p. 302.

terrace channels and would later be thrown on the terraces during the course of terrace maintenance. The terraces would therefore delay the time when the soil would leave the field. On the other hand, if the terraces had a grade which provided for a self-scouring channel, this soil would largely be removed from the field through the terrace outlet. *The data therefore show what losses may be expected between the terraces under the cropping systems followed.*[1]

In other words, the savings in soil and water to be derived from crop management, as set forth in the foregoing plot data, are applicable only to fields upon which terraces have been constructed, if the length of slope exceeds the length of the

TABLE 7.—AVERAGE RUNOFF AND EROSION FROM THE PLOT IN CONTINUOUS CORN AND THE ROTATION PLOT FOR THOSE SEASONS WHEN THE ROTATION PLOT WAS IN CORN—1920, 1923, 1926, AND 1929

The Data Are Summarized for the Months of the Corn-growing Season in Each Case from Missouri Plot Experiments, 1918–1931

Month	Corn in rotation		Continuous corn	
	Runoff, cu. ft. per plot	Erosion, lb. per plot	Runoff, cu. ft. per plot	Erosion, lb. per plot
April	180.3	18.1	525.9	471.7
May	96.8	17.4	325.9	95.9
June	108.5	80.6	347.8	502.6
July	47.6	64.9	151.7	208.4
August	78.0	53.1	110.6	72.2
September	152.5	82.8	235.3	144.1
Total	663.7	316.9	1697.2	1494.9

Mo. Research Bull. 177.
Runoff from continuous corn = 2.5 times that from corn in rotation.
Erosion from continuous corn = 4.7 times that from corn in rotation.

plots. Undoubtedly important benefits will accrue from good cropping practices on unterraced fields, but the extent of such benefits cannot reliably be estimated solely from data secured on small experimental plots.

CONTOUR FARMING

When row crops are planted crosswise of a slope rather than running up and down, the rows act as miniature terraces and tend to hold rain water where it falls, thus increasing absorption and reducing runoff. If the rows are run up and down the slope, as is customary in many localities, each plow or cultivator furrow serves as a channel for rapid flow and results in gully cutting.

[1] Italics supplied by author.

In a series of experiments at the Alabama Agricultural Experiment Station, Nichols found that a rain of one inch in 9 minutes

TABLE 8.—SOIL AND WATER LOSSES FROM FOUR IMPORTANT SOILS UNDERGOING DIFFERENT MECHANICAL TREATMENTS[1]

Treatment	Slope, per cent	Rainfall, inches	Soil loss, tons per acre	Water loss, per cent of rainfall (runoff)
Spur, Tex.—Abilene clay loam				
Cotton, level terraces closed at ends......	0.5	18.5	0.0	0.0
Cotton, contoured rows.................	0.5	18.5	.....	6.8
Cotton, rows down slope...............	0.5	18.5	.....	8.8
LaCrosse, Wis.—Clinton silt loam				
Corn, ordinary cultivator on contour.....	16	14	0.7	4.1
Corn, cultivated on contour with hole digger............................	16	14	0.09	0.02
Corn, rows sloped 5 %, ordinary cultivator.	16	14	4.9	9.1
Corn, rows sloped 5 %, cultivated with hole digger............................	16	14	0.4	2.5
Guthrie, Okla.—Vernon fine sandy loam				
Cotton, rows down slope...............	6.8	35	59.	13.7
Cotton, rows contoured...............	6.9	35	21.	11.3
Hays, Kan.—Colby silty clay loam				
Fallow, double-disc....................	4.	14	2.8	10.8
Fallow, hole digger...................	4.	14	0.6	3.9
Fallow, duckfoot down slope............	4.	14	3.4	13.9
Clarinda, Ia.—Marshall silt loam				
Corn, rows down slope (Plot 42′ × 530′)..	8.4	26	34.5	9.4
Corn, rows down slope (Plot 42′ × 315′)..	8.4	26	20.	9.5
Corn, rows down slope (Plot 42′ × 157.5′).	8.4	26	11.	11.5
Corn, rows on contour (Plot 42′ × 157.5′).	8.4	26	0.0	0.0

[1] BENNETT, H. H., *loc. cit.*

(a rate of about 6 inches per hour) produced a very small soil loss on fields up to 10 per cent slope when the rows were across, but with rows paralleling the slope the loss approximated one ton per acre. On steeper slopes the rate of loss continued to increase rapidly and, on a slope of 20 per cent, amounted to 30 tons per acre from rows on the contour and 60 tons per acre from rows with the slope.

Table 8 gives a summary of other experimental data on the effect of various mechanical treatments on soil and water losses. The data should be considered as qualitative rather than quantitative because of the short-time measurements and other

Fig. 22.—Basin lister-planter. Corn is planted in basins 12 by 36 inches, 8 inches deep, spaced 4 feet apart. (*Iowa State College Photo.*)

limitations. It is interesting to note, however, the apparent effectiveness of "hole-diggers" at LaCrosse and Hays, and that there were no losses of either soil or water on Marshall silt loam in corn that was listed on contours. These experiments are also of interest as introducing plots of greater width and length than those heretofore used.

Basin Forming Machine.—Figure 22 shows a new type of basin forming machine to be attached to a standard lister or other implement for the purpose of making basins about 1 by 3 feet, 8 inches deep, and spaced about 4 feet apart. This machine was developed at Iowa State College and is intended to impound as much as 1.5 inches of rainfall on the surface where it falls. It is being tried out experimentally on moderate slopes and absorp-

tive soils. It is conceivable that the use of this machine may
have a deleterious effect during rains of extraordinary intensity
by holding back temporarily a part of the early rainfall and then
releasing it suddenly, when the basin rims are overtopped. On
the other hand, when dealing with soils such as Marshall silt
loam there is every indication that runoff may be entirely prevented from all but the rarest rains (see Fig. 16).

Fig. 23.—Five-foot chisel cultivator. (*Courtesy Killefer Manufacturing Corpo-
ration.*)

Chisel Cultivator.—The chisel cultivator shown in Fig. 23 is
quite popular in arid regions where it is used after harvest to
provide moisture storage during the winter. The 5-foot machine
will open the soil to a depth of 15 inches using a three- or four-
plow tractor for power, depending on the number of chisels used.
The machine can be had with chisels spaced 12, 15, or 20 inches
apart. Variations of this machine with a single chisel can pene-
trate to a depth up to 48 inches. Sometimes a steel nose,
attached at the chisel bottom, can be used under certain conditions to provide an underground channel for drainage.

Where subsoil conditions are favorable this machine may be
used between terraces to promote rapid infiltration and increase
absorption (see Fig. 24).

Explosives.—Dynamite has been used to a limited extent to accomplish the same purpose by breaking up tight, impervious subsoils. Subsoiling by this method is rather expensive and is economical, as a rule, only in special cases where an impervious layer of hard pan or similar material is underlaid by relatively pervious strata. Unless this condition prevails the explosive

Fig. 24.—Ten-foot chisel cultivator operating on land between terraces in Kansas.

will probably blow out jug-like cavities surrounded by highly compressed material that is water-tight.

STRIP CROPPING

By "strip cropping" is meant the practice of growing inter-tilled crops in alternating bands or strips with close-growing hay or small grain running crosswise of the slope and laid out to follow the contour of the land as nearly as possible. While not entirely new in some localities, practically no experimental data have yet been collected.

The practice is best suited to gently rolling land with uniform slopes but may occasionally be used on slopes quite steep. Usually strips of densely growing or fibrous rooted crops, such as oats, wheat, barley, sorghums, alfalfa, clover, or grasses are planted between strips of clean-tilled crops, such as corn, cotton, tobacco, soy beans, etc. The wider and closer together the strips of nonerosive crops are placed the more effective they are in

checking erosion from the entire field, the object being of course
to slow down the runoff velocity, filter out the soil, and increase
absorption.

Strip cropping is of such recent origin as an erosion control
measure that considerable divergence of opinion .exists among
specialists as to how best to apply it. For this reason it is
thought advisable to quote in some detail customary practice
in three representative localities, Texas, Missouri, and Wisconsin.

Texas Practice

The following discussion is adapted from mimeographed
instructions issued by Texas specialists:

Where land is not terraced, a rotation system should provide
for erosion-resisting crops to be planted in strips that would
occupy at least one-third of the land the year round. This is
considered necessary, in order to control erosion in Texas, even
on slopes of about 1 per cent. Such a program, to be fully
effective, calls for a rotation system providing for 30 to 50 per
cent of the land to be in such close-growing crops as those mentioned above and Hubam clover.

Width of Strips.—The strips of closely-planted crops on unterraced land should be from 30 to 50 feet in width and row crops
from 60 to 100 feet in width. The field should be laid off in
permanent contour lines spaced 30, 40, or 50 feet apart, depending
upon the width of the strips needed for erosion control. The
spacing of these lines is governed by the slope of land, character
of soil, and type of farming. The steeper the slope and the more
easily the soil erodes, the closer the strips should be spaced.
If 40-foot strips are to be spaced 80 feet apart, the contour lines
are spaced at 40-foot intervals across the slope. This provides
an easy method for determining the location for the strips.
This method is illustrated in Fig. 25. (Note the way the rows
are laid off and how the strips are rotated for a three-year
period.)

Permanent Contour Markers.—The contour lines for strip
cropping are run on a level, and are spaced by measuring the
steepest part of the slope. After the contours are run, they
should be marked by backfurrowing. Throwing two or three

rounds together with an ordinary plow is usually sufficient. Permanent markers (stakes) should also be placed at each end of the lines, which, together with the backfurrowing, should assure the permanency of the contours and eliminate the necessity of re-running the lines each year.

Protection of "Washes" or Gullies.—In some fields there may be small depressions or washes where water will collect. These should be planted to some erosion-resisting crop to prevent further

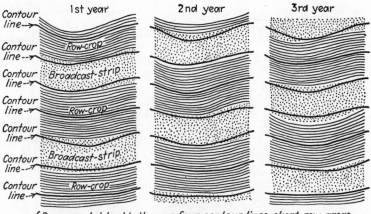

(Rows are laid out both ways from contour lines,-short-row areas are taken up in broadcast strips)

FIG. 25.—Strip cropping without terracing. Showing a section of a field and the rotation possible during 3 years.

washing. Bands of non-noxious permanent grass may be planted up and down these depressions. These grasses may be started by planting in bands 2 feet wide and about 10 feet apart, beginning at the head of the depression or gully and stripping the entire length of the depression or gully. Between these bands, a temporary, quick-growing cover, such as rye grass, Sudan grass, or sorghum cane should be sown to assist in holding the soil until the permanent grass completely covers the gully or wash. If the draw or gully is not too narrow and deep, this will prevent further washing and will cause soil to be deposited, tending in time to fill the draw. Where a field having a considerable slope borders a road, there is often a tendency for bad gullies to form,

extending from the road ditch up into the field.   This condition
may often be overcome by sowing a strip of permanent grass,
oats, cane, Sudan grass, or similar crops along the edge of the
field.

Strip Cropping with Terraces.—Strip cropping alone is not
recommended on badly gullied fields or on fields with more than
3 or 4 per cent slope.   On fields having a greater slope, a combination of terracing and strip cropping is recommended.   Ter-

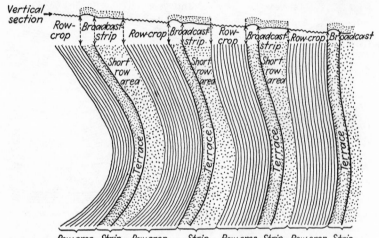

Fig. 26.—Combination strip cropping and terracing? Plan No. 1.   Thirty to
forty per cent in close-planted crops.

racing alone is not sufficient to completely control erosion, but
planting broadcast crops in strips on or between terraces helps
to reduce erosion to a minimum.   Strip cropping used with
terraces presents an excellent opportunity to eliminate one of
the objections to terracing, that of point rows.   This combination
system also does away with one of the disadvantages of strip
cropping alone—that of leaving the land more or less unprotected
at certain periods of the year.   Terraces are permanent and,
therefore, give protection the year round.

There are several combinations of strip cropping with terracing that may be used very effectively to help decrease erosion.
These plans are illustrated in Figs. 26, 27, 28, 29, and 30.

The first plan is shown in Fig. 26, Plan No. 1, where each terrace is covered with a thickly planted, erosion-resisting crop that extends below the terrace 12 feet or more, including point rows. In this plan there are no point rows, and the terrace is protected the first year and given time to settle before it is worked in row crops. This plan may be changed to include the point rows above the terrace instead of below, the advantage being that excess water breaking over the rows above will deposit its load when it hits the close-planted strip. The advantage

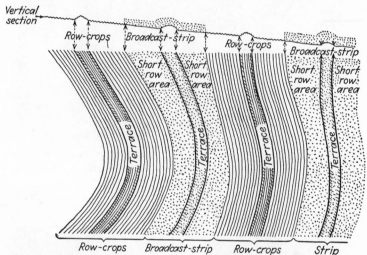

Fig. 27.—Combination strip cropping and terracing. Plan No. 2. Thirty to forty per cent in close-planted crops.

of leaving the strip to extend below the terrace is that the strip protects that part of a terraced field which is most susceptible to erosion. This method should be changed to Plan No. 2, Fig. 27, or alternated with Plan No. 4, Fig. 29, the second year, in order that row crops and broadcast strips can be rotated.

Plan No. 2, Fig. 27, is that of using every other terrace as a guide line for the rows and planting the strips on the other terraces including the odd areas. Under this plan every other terrace is protected by a strip of close-planted crop that extends above and below the terrace to include the point row intervals. The width of this strip might be increased or decreased, depending on the amount of feed required on the farm. This is a very good plan because it permits the row crops and strip crops to be rotated and may give protection to as much as half of each terrace interval.

Plan No. 3, Fig. 28, requires that each terrace be covered with a broadcast strip 30 feet wide with point rows in the middle of the terrace

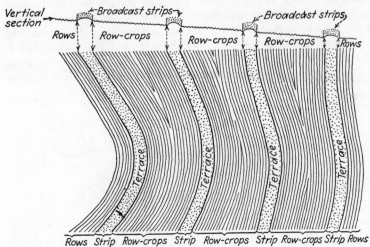

FIG. 28.—Combination strip cropping and terracing.   Plan No. 3.   Twenty-five per cent in close-planted crops.

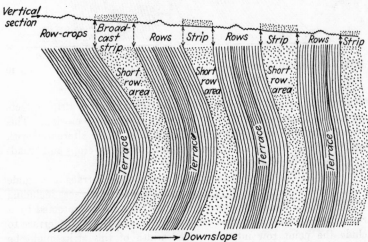

FIG. 29.—Combination strip cropping and terracing Plan No. 4.   Thirty per cent in close-planted crops.

interval. This plan, like Plan No. 1, is effective in holding terraces after completion, as it gives them time to settle the first year before working in rows. In order to rotate strips and row crops, Plan No. 2 or Plan No. 4 should be followed the next year.

Plan No. 4, Fig. 29, requires that intervals between terraces be stripped with a close-planted crop with a minimum width of 25 feet, including point rows within the strip. This plan does not permit rotation, and therefore it is advisable to alternate with Plan No. 1 or No. 3. Plan No. 4 can be used with No. 1 as shown in Fig. 30. This diagram

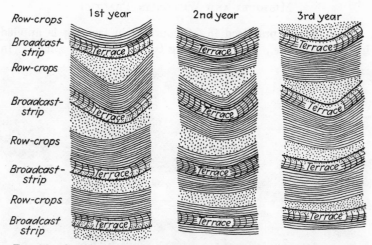

Fig. 30.—Combination strip cropping and terracing, showing a three-year rotation. Varying plan No. 1 first and third years, and using plan No. 4 the intervening year. Twenty-five to thirty-five per cent in close-planted crops.

illustrates rotation using both plans but varying Plan No. 1. The first year, begin at the center of the terrace and strip down about 15 feet, including point rows if desirable. The third year start in the middle of the terrace and strip above the terrace about 15 feet, including point rows if desirable. This gives a good rotation and permits a broadcast cover to be rotated so that in three years it will have covered the entire field. Plan No. 4 is used the second year in this rotation. All four of the above described plans may be varied somewhat to fit conditions found on different farms.

Strip Cropping to Facilitate Terracing.—Strip cropping may also be used as a prelude to terracing. When used in this manner the erosion-resisting crops are planted in bands 30 or more feet wide along the terrace lines which have been surveyed in the regular manner, usually with a grade. After the strips are harvested in the summer, the terraces can be built immediately, without damaging the principal crop in the field, while the summer work is slack and soil and weather conditions are favorable for terracing. This practice can be rotated from field to field until the farm is completely terraced.

Missouri and Wisconsin Practice

As generally practiced in Missouri, strip farming is applied in two ways, *i.e.*, "crop stripping" and "field stripping." In

Fig. 31.—Typical example of strip farming by the field stripping method. (*Courtesy Soil Conservation Service, U. S. Dept. Agr.*)

crop stripping, narrow strips of some close-growing crop are planted on approximate contours at about the spacing recommended for terraces. These strips generally fit into the rotation scheme so that they occupy the field for only one year at a time.

In field stripping, the entire field is divided into strips of nearly uniform width running crosswise of the slope, and the crops of a given rotation are so alternated that row crop strips are always separated by strips of close-growing crops. This practice is of course much more effective than crop stripping (see Fig. 31).

Width and Arrangement of Strips.—The following discussion is taken from the soil conservation handbook previously cited.

The width of the strips will be determined by the slope and regularity of the field, the type and erosiveness of the soil, the kind of rotation adopted, and the needs of the individual farmer. Ordinarily the strips in field stripping will vary in width from 60 to 120 feet.

Figure 32 shows a curve denoting the recommended width of.strips to use on various hillside slopes, which are not terraced and which are moderate in productivity and in their capacity to absorb water. These widths are slightly in excess of the conventional horizontal spacing of terraces. Where it is planned that the field will eventually be terraced, the strips should be given a regular, horizontal terrace spacing and be located so that the terrace line will fall somewhere near the center of the strip.

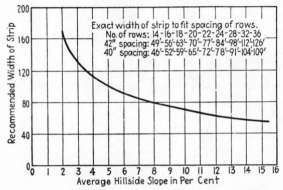

Fig. 32.—Recommended width of strips on field-stripped areas.

The location of base lines or contour lines is the first step in laying out a strip-cropping system. It is convenient to run the first base line along the lower edge of the top strip. If there are several slopes in the field the respective base lines should be on the same elevation, to facilitate the joining of the respective systems.

The irregularity of the slopes will cause lines parallel to and above a contour line to slope toward the ridges, and lines parallel to and below a contour line to slope to the waterways. Since it is desired to carry the water to natural waterways, the contour lines should mark the upper edges of the strips. However, putting the top of each strip on an exact contour would in most cases mean a correction area on every strip boundary. Slopes of 1 or 2 per cent may be allowed along the strip. In extreme cases it may be necessary to allow a greater slope along the bottom of the strip but only for very short distances.

Methods of carrying strips over long sloping ridges and of using correction areas are shown in Fig. 33. A typical field stripping system without the use of terraces is shown in Fig. 34. This represents an eighty-acre field in Harrison County, Mo. All strips are uniform in width. A three-year rotation is practiced on this field, the same rotation being followed on the larger, nearly level, portion marked "D" and on the strips. Portions marked "E" are left seeded permanently, some to alfalfa and others to timothy and clover. Some of the strips in this field are approximately one mile in length.

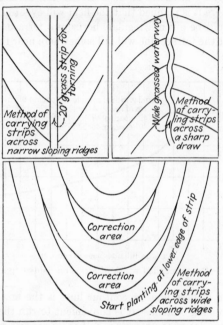

Fig. 33.—Methods of laying out strips for strip cropping.

Cultivated strips may be, and generally should be, kept nearly uniform in width by making the grass and small grain strips more variable or by seeding necessary correction areas permanently to a hay crop.

Whenever, in Missouri and in southern Iowa, correction strips or other odd shaped areas in strip-cropped fields are quite thin and so not well suited to alfalfa or clover, they may be seeded to oats and lespedeza. Each spring such areas are disced and reseeded to oats. No reseeding of the lespedeza will be necessary, as it will reseed itself.

Slopes of 8 per cent and greater that are to be cultivated should have terraces spaced from 45 to 60 feet apart, depending upon the steepness of the slope and upon the crops to be grown, when terraces alone are used. It is advisable wherever possible to keep terraces at least 50 feet apart, therefore, for slopes of 8 per cent or more, a combination of strip cropping and terraces is recommended.

Figures 35 to 38, inclusive, represent a method, described by Landon and Ryerson of Wisconsin in the February, 1935, issue of "The Land," by which benefits of terracing and strip cropping are combined with the elimination of objectionable point rows. A four-year rotation of corn—small grain—meadow—meadow is used on this field. An old meadow was plowed a strip at a time until the entire field was stripped. As shown here five irregular portions of the field are left permanently in grass. This is not essential, however, as these areas could occasionally be plowed and reseeded. Any one of the upper three small areas might be plowed when the strip immediately below it is in corn. When this is done the rows of corn should be run in such a manner that the point rows are left

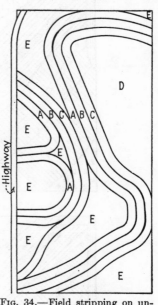

Fig. 34.—Field stripping on unterraced field.

on the lower side of the strip and may drain their extra water directly into the terrace channel.

When it is impossible to establish a strip-cropping system on an old meadow, small grain with clover and timothy seeded in it may be substituted for the meadow strips, with the exception of the one to be plowed the following year for corn. It should be sown to small grain with the grass seeding omitted. Sweet clover might be grown in the small grain, however, and then turned under as a green manure crop the following spring.

Instructions for following this system are very simple. The number of the terrace or strip to be planted to corn, and the number of rows of corn to be planted on it, are all that is necessary. The strip that is in corn any one year is then seeded to small grain and new meadow the next.

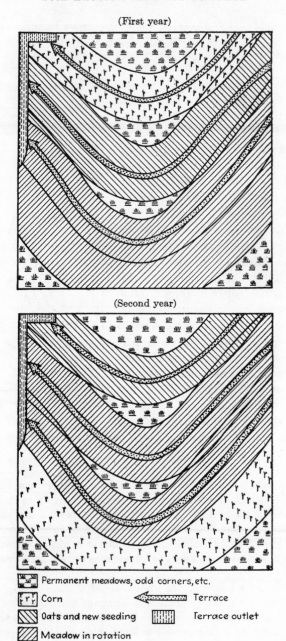

(First year)

(Second year)

Permanent meadows, odd corners, etc.

Corn — Terrace

Oats and new seeding — Terrace outlet

Meadow in rotation

FIGS. 35, 36.—Combination field stripping with terraces. Four-year rotation,

(Third year)

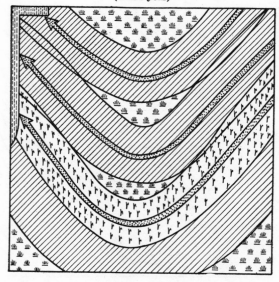

(Fourth year)

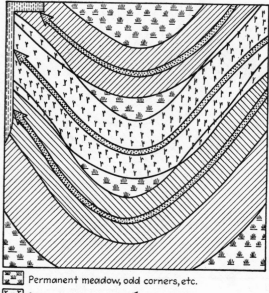

Permanent meadow, odd corners, etc.

Corn   Terrace

Oats and new seeding   Terrace outlet

Meadow in rotation

FIGS. 37, 38.—Combination field stripping with terraces. Four-year rotation.

(First year)

(Second year)

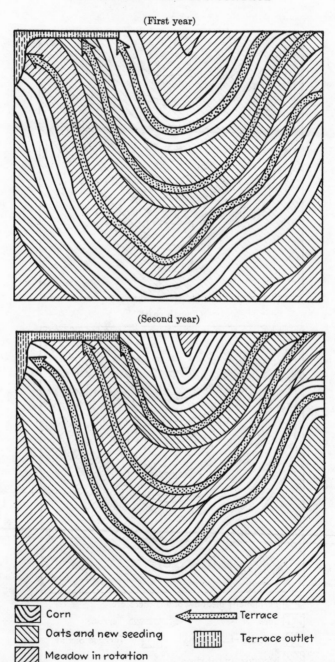

Corn

Oats and new seeding

Meadow in rotation

Terrace

Terrace outlet

FIGS. 39, 40.—Combination of field stripping and terraces.   Three-year rotation.

To determine the number of corn rows to be planted along any one terrace, take the weighted average width of the two terrace intervals and, with this width known, determine the nearest even number of corn rows possible. If the two adjacent spacings are equal or nearly so in width, half of the corn rows may be planted on each side of the center of the terrace ridge. However, if the two terrace intervals are of greatly uneven width, the number of rows on the side of the narrowest interval should never be so great as to extend to the next terrace at any point.

The strips should be so arranged that corn will always fall on the lower side of the strip of old meadow, while the strip of new meadow

Fig. 41.—Combination of contour farming, strip cropping, and terracing as practiced on steep slopes and erodible soils in Wisconsin. The men are standing on two adjacent terrace banks.

should be above the old meadow strip. Should corn be placed above the old meadow, the old grass growing in the terrace channel might so slow up the flow of the water as to cause terrace overtopping.

Figures 39 and 40 represent two years of a three-year rotation on a terraced field. The corn strips are kept uniform in width each year. A larger portion of the upper center part of the field might if desired be left permanently in grass.

Crop Stripping.—Crop stripping also may be used alone or in connection with terracing. It may be used on fields intended to be terraced, but where it is impossible to build the terraces before seeding or planting time. The terrace lines may be staked out and a strip 25 to 40 feet wide along the terrace line be seeded to some early maturing crop such as sudan grass, oats, or spring barley. It is very desirable that the crop used for this purpose be close-growing for erosion resisting purposes. When this crop is removed the terraces can be built with but little or no injury to the remaining crop on the field.

Figure 42 represents an unterraced field on which area stripping is used the year of the rotation that the field is in corn. Strips here are about 30 feet wide at the narrowest places. The two lower corners are left seeded permanently to meadow. More point rows could be eliminated by increasing the width of the center strips near the middle of the field.

Figure 43 represents crop stripping used on the same field shown in Fig. 42 only after terraces have been built. In this case the strips of close-growing crops are so located between the terraces as to eliminate all point rows. These strips extend entirely across the field, so the hay crop can easily be harvested. Another strip could be planted some distance below the lowest terrace, if it is desirable to still further break the slope.

Advantages of Strip Cropping.—Strip cropping costs but little and can be put into immediate practice. As a matter of fact it usually costs no more than does the inauguration of a regular good rotation. No surveying is necessary, though it may be advisable. If the lines are surveyed this may be done by anyone who understands the use of an ordinary farm level [see Chap. VI for instructions in use of level]. There is no labor necessary other than that required for the production of the crops being grown. There are no obstructions to interfere with the use of any type of farm machinery. There is no appreciable upkeep required. The length of rows may actually be increased in many cases, and since these rows run more or less on the level the draft in pulling farm tools will be greatly reduced. This point was nearly always stressed by farmers near LaCrosse, Wis., where strip cropping is a common practice. Strip cropping does not materially interfere with any cropping system determined as best for a farm. It may be used with or without terraces and is a valuable supplement to terracing on fields of 8 per cent slope or greater.

Disadvantages of Strip Cropping.—Strip cropping is difficult to lay out on very irregular or badly cut up fields. It is not likely to prove satisfactory where at least a good portion of the strips cannot be made nearly uniform in width throughout their length. A considerable amount of irregularity, however, can be taken care of by seeding permanently to grass, alfalfa, etc., the odd shaped correction areas, or by increasing the width of the small grain or sod strips so as to include these irregular portions as indicated below.

In strip cropping, as in all contour farming, it is not possible to have straight rows or checked corn. These objections are generally more imaginary than real, however, on fields that are really suitable for stripping. It is usually not so necessary to check corn where rotations are practiced, as weeds are not likely to be serious, and a better control of weeds is about the only valid reason for checking.

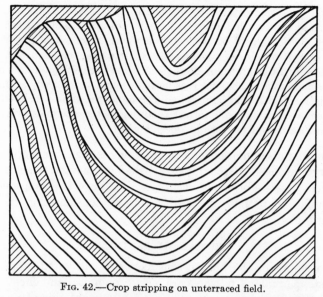

Fig. 42.—Crop stripping on unterraced field.

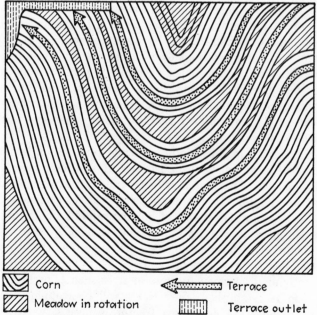

Corn   Terrace

Meadow in rotation   Terrace outlet

Fig. 43.—Crop stripping with terraces.   Three-year rotation.
(Third year)

Some pasturing of meadow aftermath may be lost if strips cannot be fenced, and such fencing is usually not practicable. Even this objection can largely be overcome, however, where it is possible to strip crop two fields of similar size. In this case corn and first year meadow might be grown in alternate strips in one field and in the other field small grain and second year meadow might be similarly arranged. The latter field should be pastured as soon as the grain and hay crops are removed, while in the former pasturing of the aftermath would be delayed until after the corn had been husked.

Another disadvantage of strip cropping is that its effectiveness has not yet been thoroughly established (as has terracing) either by field practice or experimentally. It is nevertheless a method of sufficient promise to justify serious consideration in any control plan.

PERMANENT PASTURES

On slopes in the border zone between cultivated crops and forests, permanent pastures are most economical and effective as erosion control measures. The most important thing to watch, where the grass is depended on to control erosion, is overgrazing. Many areas, not only in the range lands of the west, but also in pasture lands of humid regions, have suffered serious losses to the point of exhaustion without ever having been plowed. A part of such land will restore itself naturally if permitted an opportunity but much will require heavy fertilization and manuring plus some form of mechanical treatment to conserve moisture, prevent floods, and protect against loss of expensive fertilizer applications.

Terracing in a modified form is very helpful and, of late, other mechanical means of assuring surface storage have been developed. One such machine now being tried out experimentally is shown in Fig. 44. It was developed by E. V. Collins of Iowa State College and is capable of holding rainfall amounting to 3 inches in pockets $3\frac{1}{3}$ by 8 feet and 12 inches deep. These pockets are of such dimensions and are spaced so that they can be straddled by a wagon or motor truck. They are practical only on lands in permanent grass or trees such as orchards and, after sod is established, they can stand overtopping without serious damage. A four-plow tractor is necessary to furnish power for this machine.

Grass Lands.—On vast areas of western range lands excessive numbers of livestock, unevenly distributed, have so impaired the vigor of plants that the sparse and sickly vegetation is no longer effective in controlling either runoff or erosion. Neither does it provide sufficient nourishment, so that the animals themselves suffer. Improvident grazing sets up a vicious cycle no less harmful in its all-round effects than improvident husbandry of cultivated lands in humid regions.

Fig. 44.—Experimental machine for making large pockets for surface storage of water in permanent pastures, range lands, and orchards. (*Iowa State College Photo.*)

An excellent analysis of this situation is contained in *Technical Bulletin* 220 of the U. S. Forest Service, which reports the results of fifteen years' measurements of precipitation, surface runoff, and erosion from summer rains, and seven years' measurements of melted snow runoff and erosion from two experimental watersheds in central Utah—one 11⅓ acres in extent and the other 9 acres. On one of the areas losses, when 16 per cent of the surface was covered with vegetation, are compared with losses when the coverage was 40 per cent and with the second area which was under 40 per cent cover throughout the 15 years of the investigation. In summarizing his results the author, C. F. Forsling, says:

Only 4.6 per cent of the average annual surface runoff was caused by summer rainstorms when there was a 16 per cent cover of vegetation; but this runoff caused 84.5 per cent of the erosion. The remainder of the runoff, which was melted snow, caused far less erosion. After the vegetation had increased to 40 per cent of a complete cover, only 1.3 per cent of the annual runoff was from summer rains. The increase in the density of the vegetation from 16 to 40 per cent of a complete cover, and the replacement of certain plants by others with more extensive and more fibrous root systems, reduced the rainfall surface runoff 64 per cent and rainfall erosion 54 per cent. It reduced melted snow erosion 57 per cent but did not influence melted snow runoff.

The results of these experiments show the importance of herbaceous vegetation in reducing rainfall runoff and floods and in controlling erosion. They also show the need for regulating grazing to prevent depletion of the herbaceous cover on sloping lands subject to torrential rainfall; because the more complete the plant cover, the more adequate is the protection against erosion.

Because of the evil consequences of overgrazing, the grazing of livestock on watershed lands should be so managed as not to interfere with the function of the herbaceous cover in controlling surface runoff and erosion. Studies and detailed observations of adjacent watershed areas in various stages of plant depletion and erosion have shown that under the conditions of soil, relief, and climate affecting the present experimental areas measures that will restore and maintain the maximum plant cover for grazing purposes will also insure adequate watershed protection, except in some of the more extreme cases. Acts which reduce or destroy the cover on watersheds also reduce or destroy the productive capacity of the range itself. The more important particulars of improved range management, as worked out by various investigators, are as follows: The application of deferred and rotation grazing, or other methods which will promote the reproductive functions of the vegetation; regulation of the season of grazing so as to prevent injury from too early grazing in the spring and to avoid too close utilization in the fall; stocking the range within the limits of the carrying capacity; handling of livestock on the range to obtain even distribution over the range and to prevent overgrazing of local areas, trailing, or excessive trampling; and the control of range-destroying rodents.

Badly depleted watersheds and other special conditions will require extra measures to provide the maximum possible seed crop each year and the leaving of sufficient vegetation to insure rapid building up of the soil. It may be necessary to defer grazing until all the plants have scattered their seed each year and then to graze only lightly for a sufficient number of years to restore an adequate plant cover and to increase the obstruction to surface runoff. Light grazing late in the season ordinarily is more desirable than no grazing at all, since the trampling by livestock at that time of the year will aid in planting the seed which has been scattered on the ground. Or, grazing may have to be greatly restricted or excluded entirely to safeguard watershed values. Very steep slopes, easily erodible soil, or areas where livestock are likely to make trails which will result in erosion channels, require special attention.

When overgrazing and erosion are checked on a depleted area, the vegetation present will gradually spread, slowly increasing the vegetable matter and plant foods in the soil. Short-lived species will be replaced naturally by perennials and better soil-binding plants.

Contour Ridging.—A practice known as "contour ridging" has recently come into favor in the development of permanent pastures on steep slopes to be retired as submarginal land and in the improvement of old pastures that have been damaged by drouth and overgrazing.

Development of pastures on such areas frequently entails removal of brush, weeds, sprouts, and other scattering growth of grass and afford very little protection to the soil during heavy rains.

In preparing a pasture for contour ridging the following sequence of steps should be observed:

Remove stumps, and deaden and remove undesirable trees.
Rid pastures of weeds by mowing, pulling, or hoeing.
Level old beds or terraces.
Plow in gullies.
If contour ridges are to be built on land being retired from cultivation, the sowing of oats or other small grain in advance of the construction of the ridges is recommended.

When laying out and constructing the ridges, the work should be done in the following order:

Check level and be sure it is in adjustment. (See Chap. VI.)
Set up level and run first contour line near top of slope. (Set stakes at 25-foot intervals.)
Step 12 feet downhill at the point of the steepest slope and run second line on level. Continue until all lines are run.
Walk out each contour line and mark the lines with a plow. A shovel plow is best suited for this purpose.

Plow one round with a 12-inch turning plow beginning 6 to 8 feet below contour line and throwing the soil downhill first.

Turn furrows up at each end, and *do not* cross depressions or gullies. Turn furrows uphill, and stop at the point where the land begins sloping off into a depression or gully.

Complete ridge by making one or more rounds with a long-winged terracing plow, beginning on the downhill side and throwing the soil uphill first. In completing the round on the uphill side start the terracing plow on true

Fig. 45.—Air view of pasture contour ridges made with long-winged terrace plow at College Station, Tex.   (*Courtesy G. A. Kelly Plow Company.*)

contour line, which was marked off with a plow as stakes are removed.   (If a long-winged terracing plow is not available, one may be made by wiring a 1 by 6 inch board 30 inches long to the plow wing.)

In order to prevent water from concentrating in possible low places in contour ridging and causing breaks, each contour ridge should be blocked off every 25 feet on each side of any depression, by making a small dam across the channel with a few shovelfuls of earth.

FORESTS AND WOOD LOTS

Aside from efficacy in conserving soil and water a thick growth of trees provides excellent cover for game animals and has high recreational value. Nor should the economic returns from a good stock of growing timber be overlooked although this need not be a primary consideration. Conservative estimates indicate that, once the stock is established, each acre may be expected to produce annually about one cord of fuel wood, or 150 board feet of saw timber, or the equivalent in fence posts.

From the standpoint of this book, however, it is in connection with the restoration of badly gullied areas and protection from sheet erosion of other areas that forests have major significance. Two aspects must be considered: (1) care and improvement of existing wood lots, and (2) new plantings in additional areas.

Fig. 46.—Poor forest practice induces gullying, loss of soil, and floods. Scene in Colorado. (*Photo by U. S. Forest Service.*)

The necessary care and improvement of existing forested areas involve the prevention and control of fires, the exclusion of grazing, and selective cutting. The last aims to improve the forest through leaving thrifty stock and through removal of defective timber and inferior species. For maximum erosion control benefits it is desirable to maintain the forest cover as nearly intact as possible. Cutting should, therefore, be light. A timber area that is graded, or burned over, or both, will not perpetuate itself, does not provide shelter for game animals, nor does it give the desired protection against runoff and erosion losses. This is particularly true on the steeper slopes where the exclusion of fire and grazing is essential in securing adequate control of erosion through forestry. Too often forested areas or wood lots are used for grazing with the idea that they will also provide satisfactory erosion protection as well as wood or timber. They cannot be used for both purposes satisfactorily and grazing can usually be supplied to better advantage by using native grasses or areas planted to grasses for this purpose. If wood production is not an important factor, controlled grazing can sometimes be practiced when necessary on the flatter wooded

Fig. 47.—Good forest practice. Trees cut low, brush piled, and young trees left to insure future crop of timber. Scene in Black Hills National Forest, S. D. (*Photo by U. S. Forest Service.*)

areas without harmful erosion, but it is not desirable unless necessary.

The planting of new forests for erosion control purposes has two objectives, (1) the establishment of a protective cover on areas where other erosion control practices cannot be used more economically, and (2) planting of a timber crop as a means of making productive use of areas which it is advisable or necessary to remove from tillage or pasture use. Where the grasses and other cover often establish themselves abundantly when protected from grazing and fire, the planting of trees is not always needed to provide satisfactory erosion control. On certain areas where natural cover will not establish itself satisfactorily, planting is necessary. On such areas trees can be planted for the purpose of keeping the land productive as well as checking erosion, since there are few other crops than timber that can be raised and harvested without pasturage or tillage. This subject is accorded detailed treatment in Chap. XIII.

USE OF TERRACES

The control of erosion by terracing is primarily a problem of surface drainage somewhat analogous in principle to the removal of storm water from city streets by curbs, gutters, catch basins,

FIG. 48.—Diagram illustrating the use of modern terraces as commonly constructed on cultivated hillsides.

and sewers. As shown by Figs. 48 and 49, modern terraces are nothing more than a series of broad flat undulations thrown up at intervals across a hillside and usually built with a slight longitudinal grade to carry the excess water off the field at low velocity. In effect each terrace acts as a shallow diversion ditch that intercepts the runoff from its individual catchment area and leads it away slowly before the water has a chance to attain harmful velocity or volume.

Inasmuch as terraces must be carefully planned and constructed according to definite standards, the discussion in this chapter will be limited to general phases, leaving the details for later treatment.

On cultivated lands subject to erosion, terracing is one of the very few control measures of widespread adaptation that has been thoroughly tested and found acceptable under actual farm conditions. This is not to be wondered at in view of the fact that growing cultivated crops on sloping hillsides exposes bare soil to the elements and is essentially an unnatural or artificial practice that would logically require some form of unnatural or artificial control as a counter agent.

Looked at from this point of view, terracing is regarded as a desirable concomitant of contour farming and the use of such

FIG. 49.—Aerial photo showing terraces protecting a field of young wheat in Kansas.

soil-building and soil-holding crops as can be grown most satisfactorily in a rotation and is not to be considered as an optional method of control except in special cases. As developed to suit modern field cultivation practices, terraces can and do save rich top soil in the magnitude order of 30 to 40 tons per acre per year when fields are in clean-tilled row crops and half as much when in small grain.

The exact figures for both soil and water savings so far as available for five of the federal erosion experiment stations are given in Table 9. While these data are not conclusive as to the causes of variations between the stations and as to runoff eccentricities, they are remarkably consistent in showing large savings of soil due entirely to the terraces. Attention is invited particularly to the 1932 figures for the Red Plains Station near Guthrie,

TABLE 9.—ANNUAL RUNOFF AND SOIL LOSSES FROM TERRACED AND UNTERRACED LAND[1]

Station and year	2 Rainfall	3 Treatment	4 Slope	5 Soil loss	6 Per cent	7 Runoff	8 Crops
Guthrie, 1931...	27.3	Terraced	5.5	1.25	2.8	10.7	Young oats, mature[a]
		Unterraced	5.1	43.90		22.7	cowpeas, fallow
Guthrie, 1932...	36.2	Terraced	5.5	4.06	4.6	23.3	Fallow, cotton, winter
		Unterraced	5.1	88.06		30.8	wheat
Guthrie, 1933...	30.4	Terraced	4.6	1.33	2.2	21.9	Winter wheat, cotton,
		Unterraced	5.1	60.39		14.1	later grass in cotton
Average......⎫ Guthrie......⎬	31.3	Terraced		2.21	3.4	18.6	
		Unterraced		64.12		22.5	
Tyler, 1933.....	45.7	Terraced	5.8	4.55	11.1	14.0	Cotton followed by fall
		Unterraced	7.5	41.03[b]		16.5	oats
LaCrosse, 1933..	26.8	Terraced	12.7	2.23	7.0	4.9	Barley followed by
		Unterraced	13.1	31.70		8.9	clover
Bethany, 1933..	31.7	Terraced	8.3	3.19	11.8	18.7	Corn followed by sweet
		Unterraced	6.7	27.09		19.2	clover; winter wheat following peas
Pullman, 1932..	24.4	Terraced	20[c]	2.85	12.6	10.0	Winter wheat
		Unterraced	20[c]	22.53		24.8	Winter wheat stubble
Pullman, 1933..	28.8	Terraced	20[c]	3.53	31.3	12.4	Winter wheat stubble,
		Unterraced	20[c]	11.26		37.3	fallow
Average......⎫ Pullman......⎬	26.6	Terraced		3.19	22.0	11.2	
		Unterraced		16.90		31.0	

[1] RAMSER, C. E., *Bureau of Agr. Eng., U. S. Dept. Agr. Soil Erosion Exp. Sta.*

[a] Crops for terraced area. Unterraced area winter rye, mature cowpeas and winter wheat. For others years and all other stations the terraced and unterraced areas were similarly cropped as shown.

[b] Gullies and watercourse protected by brush dams.

[c] Approximate.

Col. 2. Annual rainfall in inches.
Col. 4. Slope in feet per 100 feet.
Col. 5. Soil losses in tons per acre.
Col. 6. Terraced loss in per cent of unterraced.
Col. 7. Runoff in per cent of rainfall.

Okla., where a saving of 84 tons per acre was recorded for the terraced field over that for the unterraced on a moderate slope of 5 feet per hundred. Both fields were fallow until May 15; in cotton from May 15 to October 15; and in winter wheat for the rest of the year.

In the 1934 *Yearbook of the U. S. Department of Agriculture* there is reported a loss of 150 pounds per acre from terraced land in barley at La Crosse, Wis., whereas an unterraced field, similarly cropped, lost 7120 pounds per acre. Both losses were occasioned by two rains totalling 3.5 inches.

At Bethany, Mo., a single rain of 1.17 inches on a field of wheat produced a loss of 2100 pounds per acre from the unterraced portion and only 60 pounds from the terraced part. According to C. E. Ramser, until recently in charge of the engineering investigations at all the federal stations, the two portions of this field are comparable in every practicable way, including the total number of years that each has been in cultivation.

All losses of soil and water from both the terraced and unterraced fields at all of the stations were carefully and accurately measured in silt boxes and flumes equipped with automatic recording instruments (see illustrations in Chap. XIV). In the case of unterraced fields large boxes were placed at the lower side in such a position that all water and soil leaving the field is forced to enter and be measured. On terraced fields the flumes and silt boxes were placed at the outlet of each terrace.

Since the distance between terraces is about the same as the length of the experimental plots previously discussed it might seem that there would be some relation between the unit losses measured at the terrace outlet and the plot measurements for similar soil, slope, and crop. Undoubtedly there is, but it is complex due to similitude effect between narrow plot and wide field and to a multitude of minor dissimilarities. Certainly, if the soil passing the terrace outlet is less in amount than that measured from a comparable plot, there would seem to be little basis for assuming that the difference eventually escapes from the field without being measured. Elevations taken every foot along profile lines at right angles to the terraces at least once a year do not show progressive soil movement down the slope, or at least it is so slight as to be negligible. While not conclusive, results so far show little difference between terraced and unterraced land in this respect. Even if the channel did silt half full, proper plowing with a dead furrow in the channel would leave only part of the silt to be thrown on the bank where, being exposed only to rain that falls directly upon it, it is in a much less vulnerable position than it would be if similarly located on unterraced ground. Furthermore, since the clean-out soil is seldom if ever lifted clear over the crest of the bank, such washing as does occur will be back into the channel.

The disadvantages of terraces are of course that they are somewhat costly to build and troublesome to maintain; they may require abrupt changes in traditional farming practice; damage may be caused by diversion and concentration of water at unnatural exits; on thin land subsoil may be exposed in the terrace channels; and, finally, unless they match the ground perfectly and are inspected and repaired if necessary after each rain for the first year or two, they may do more harm than good. Terraces emphatically are not a cure-all and are dependent upon the mutual support of good farming and cropping practices to produce best results.

On the other hand none of these disadvantages are especially difficult to overcome if one is really conservation minded, and the alternative in most cases is complete exhaustion and abandonment of the land after a few years of exploitation. The advantages of soil insurance; moisture conservation (in regions of low rainfall and open soils, terraces are built level with closed ends); consolidation of gains from lime and fertilizer applications; increased crop yields; and higher land values, exceeding by several times the normal terracing cost, are very generally considered to outweigh any disadvantages involved by a good margin. The best proof of this is the widespread use of terraces over a long period of years and their universal popularity with practically all progressive farmers who have granted them a fair trial. Today (1936), upwards of 17,000,000 acres of cultivated land are "terrace farmed" in the United States and the practice is growing by leaps and bounds into areas not heretofore considered vulnerable to erosion. Terraces are least costly and most efficient when used as conservators of virgin soil when first it is put under the plow, and are at their worst when used in an attempt to restore to cultivation lands already stripped of topsoil and disfigured with gullies.

CORRELATION OF METHODS

From the discussion in this and the foregoing chapters it is evident that the task of appraising a given set of conditions from a conservation standpoint and of prescribing the best control practices, giving due consideration to climate, soil, topography, markets, crops, and human relations, is one requiring the combined ingenuity of botanists, agronomists, foresters, soil specialists, engineers, economists, and sociologists. While no one book can hope adequately to cover the entire subject, an attempt will be made in a later chapter to bring together some of the factors involved, to group lands into broad classifications, and to lay the foundation for general recommendations to be applied to specific cases by specialists in the various fields.

CHAPTER IV

RAINFALL AND RUNOFF

The source of all runoff is, of course, precipitation, as either rain, sleet, or snow. Although it is known that evaporation and precipitation are equal, considering the entire earth's surface as a unit, meteorological laws governing the characteristics and distribution of precipitation are as yet but imperfectly understood. Nevertheless it is possible to gain much information of practical value from studies of precipitation records widely distributed in location and extending over long periods of time. While melting snow and ice are responsible for severe erosion and flooding in many localities, it is generally recognized that, in all but very special cases, works designed to carry runoff from critical rains will have sufficient capacity to handle the lesser volume from thaws. It is therefore common practice to direct precipitation studies largely toward a determination of rainfall characteristics.

In general, the records indicate that the following aspects of rainfall are approximately true.

Intense storms usually cover only small areas and are of short duration.

Storms lasting several days cover large areas and fall at low intensity.

The magnitude and intensity of any storm bear a direct relation to its average frequency of recurrence.

There does not appear to be any close relationship between the total annual rainfall at a given locality and the number or magnitude of intense storms likely to occur in a given time period.

The total or mean annual rainfall does give a good indication of the total volume of runoff, most of which occurs at less than critical rates.

By "critical rate" of runoff is meant that rate which will produce the maximum volume per unit of time which is economically feasible to provide for in control channels.

Annual precipitation.—Figure 50 is a map of the United States showing the amount and distribution of mean annual precipitation as determined from all reliable records to date. The irregular lines

Fig. 50.—Map of the United States showing mean annual precipitation.

superimposed on the map join points of equal annual precipitation in amounts as shown by the numerals in the lines, which represent yearly totals in inches. These numerals are average or mean values for the entire period of record and the total for any single year may vary widely therefrom; in a period of 100 years a single year's record may vary as much as 50 per cent above or below the mean. The data are of value chiefly as differentiating humid, semiarid, and arid regions, and as indicators of the normal volume of runoff in any locality, most of which occurs at less than critical rates. There is nothing in these data to indicate how the total annual precipitation is distributed throughout the year by months or by seasons. Such data are available from publications of the U. S. Weather Bureau when needed for special studies. From the standpoint of erosion, suffice it to say that the most damaging or critical rains are those which occur just before and after and during the growing season.

Factors Affecting Runoff.—Some of the factors affecting runoff have already been mentioned in Chap. II. It is evident that these may be grouped into (1) rainfall characteristics and (2) watershed characteristics.

In erosion studies the rainfall characteristic producing the largest percentage and rate of runoff will invariably be storms of high intensity and short duration because of the rolling or hilly nature and small size of the areas involved.

Watershed characteristics governing the amount and rate of runoff are: type, erosive condition, and physical nature of the soil; degree and length of slope; distribution and kind of vegetal cover; size and shape of drainage area; and upon whether or not channels exist to hasten the time required for water to concentrate at the point of exit.

The "time of concentration" is all-important because it determines the duration of the rain that will produce maximum runoff. It is measured by following the route taken by a given particle of water in traveling from the most remote part of the watershed to the point of exit and estimating the velocity of travel along various parts of the route. Maximum discharge occurs at the instant when water from all parts of the watershed first reaches the exit, and this means that the "critical rain" for any particular watershed is one which continues for a length of time equal to the time of concentration. Since the time of concentration varies with all the factors enumerated above, it will seldom be the same on any two watersheds, and hence the critical rain will vary to the same extent. It is a well-known meteorological fact that the more intense the rate of rainfall the shorter the time it lasts, so that, for a watershed of a given size and shape, the more the time of concentration can be prolonged the lower the rate of rainfall which must be dealt with.

NOTE: The terms "watershed," "drainage area," and "catchment area" are commonly used interchangeably.

Runoff Formula.—To design erosion structures with the proper capacity to meet the needs of their respective conditions it is necessary to make a quantitative determination of the critical runoff. This can be done by use of the following rational equation:

$$Q = CIA$$

where Q = critical rate of runoff in cubic feet per second.

C = runoff coefficient, (partially a coefficient of imperviousness) representing the ratio of the rate of runoff to the rate of rainfall.

I = rainfall intensity in cubic feet per second per acre, which unit happens to be approximately identical with the rate of rainfall in inches per hour.

A = watershed area in acres.

This equation was proposed by C. E. Ramser[1] as a result of measurements of rates of runoff and rainfall from small agricultural areas. The degree of accuracy with which critical runoff can be computed from the rational formula is of course no greater than that of the least accurate element, but even so it is far superior to empirical formulas which are quite inflexible and make no adequate provision for the many variables involved.

In the present state of our knowledge the elements most difficult to evaluate are proper values for the coefficient, C, and the time of concentration which determines the rainfall rate to be selected for a particular locality. The watershed area can be taken from a map or measured in the field.

RAMSER, C. E., *Jour. of Agr. Research*, Vol. 34, No. 9, May 1, 1927.

Ramser suggests control values for C as follows:[1]

Kind of watershed	Values of C
Cultivated rolling, 5 to 10% slopes	0.60
Cultivated hilly, 10 to 30% slopes	0.72
Pasture rolling, 5 to 10% slopes	0.36
Pasture hilly, 10 to 30% slopes	0.42
Timber rolling, 5 to 10% slopes	0.18
Timber hilly, 10 to 30% slopes	0.21

These values are a composite measure of all the variable factors affecting runoff. They should be considered as somewhere near the upper average limit and as applying to relatively impervious soils. To be on the safe side they are recommended for use unless a particular soil is definitely known to be exceptionally absorptive. The tables and charts presented in the two preceding chapters should be helpful in deciding when a reduction is warranted and how much of a reduction to make.

Accuracy of the time of concentration is dependent upon the accuracy with which the route of travel and velocity of flow can be judged.

This is not such a difficult task as it may first appear, since the line of travel is usually in a more or less well-defined channel or channels wherein distance of travel is the chief variable as between watersheds subject to erosion. This being true, and if the shape is not abnormal, times of concentration become almost direct functions of watershed sizes. At least the values given in the table shown on page 88 may be used as a basis for estimates.

As will be noted, the figures given represent minimum times of concentration for channel grades approximating 5 feet fall per 100 feet. Since soil and cover variables, and to some extent

---

[1] These figures are applicable only to small areas not exceeding 1000 acres. For larger areas combined values of C would probably vary somewhat as follows:

Square Miles	Values of C
2 to 5	0.2 to 0.3
6 to 50	0.1 to 0.2
50 to 200	0.05 to 0.1

prevailing watershed slopes, are taken care of in the values assigned to the runoff coefficient, C, the interval representing the time of concentration is useful chiefly in selecting the proper rainfall rate for a particular set of conditions. Any increase that can be induced in the time of concentration will, of course, not only allow greater opportunity for absorption but will automatically reduce the rate of rainfall which results in critical runoff and hence will also reduce the rate of runoff.

Size of watershed, acres	Time of minimum concentration, minutes	Size of watershed, acres	Time of minimum concentration, minutes
1	1.4	300	29
3	3.0	400	35
5	3.5	500	41
10	4.0	600	47
20	4.8	700	53
30	8.0	800	60
50	12.0	900	67
100	17.0	1000	75
200	23.0		

RAINFALL INTENSITIES

The critical rate of rainfall is that rain which will continue at average intensity in inches per hour for a duration period equal to the time of concentration. Critical rains for the same duration or time of concentration will vary with the locality being considered and with the frequency period chosen.

Choice of the proper frequency period will be determined by a consideration of the cost increments for various degrees of protection weighed against the probable damage resulting from lack of the same degrees of protection. In other words, since it is seldom practicable to make provision for the highest rainfall intensities ever recorded, it becomes necessary to decide how often it is permissible for the improvement to be overtaxed; whether once each year or only once in 5, 10, 25, 50 or 100 years. For most erosion structures, a frequency of 5 or 10 years is about all that is warranted, it being less expensive to repair the damage done than it is to provide extra capacity that is utilized only once in the time periods indicated. For large earth dams where failure of the entire structure would result from overtopping, a frequency exceeding 10 years, and up to 50 years or more in important cases, would probably be warranted. No decision should be made without careful weighing of costs and a consideration of all interests involved.

When the location and topography of a particular watershed are known together with its time of concentration and justifiable frequency period, there remains only to determine the proper

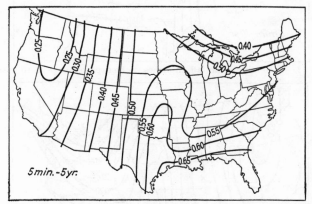

FIG. 51.—Five-minute rainfall, in inches, to be expected once in 5 years.

rate of rainfall to make possible a complete solution of the equation, $Q = CIA$. Heretofore this has involved a long and tedious search of records in and near the particular locality in question; but since the release of *U. S. Department of Agriculture Publication* 204, in August, 1935,[1] such search is no longer necessary to the same extent as formerly.

Figures 51 to 68, inclusive, are intensity-frequency charts taken from this bulletin.[2] These maps were prepared from data compiled by a large staff of statisticians from Weather Bureau

[1] YARNELL, DAVID L., "Rainfall Intensity—Frequency Data," Division of Drainage, U. S. Bur. Agr. Eng., *Misc. Pub.* 204, 1935.

[2] In interpreting these charts, especially from the standpoint of frequency, it should be recognized that variations in the degree of soil saturation at the beginning of a rain will upset direct correspondence between runoff intensity-frequency and rainfall intensity-frequency for conditions of watershed otherwise identical. The importance of this fact, however, is minimized in the case of unprotected, erosive slopes because the runoff is usually too rapid to permit much infiltration regardless of the original degree of wetness.

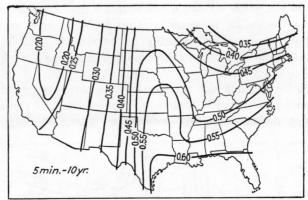

Fig. 52.—Five-minute rainfall, in inches, to be expected once in 10 years.

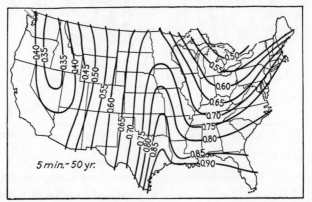

Fig. 53.—Five-minute rainfall, in inches, to be expected once in 50 years.

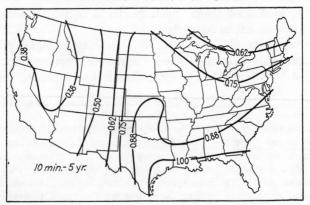

Fig. 54.—Ten-minute rainfall, in inches, to be expected once in 5 years.

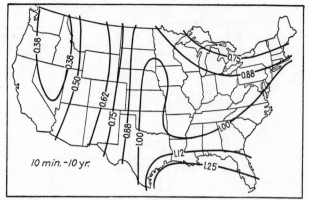

Fig. 55.—Ten-minute rainfall, in inches, to be expected once in 10 years.

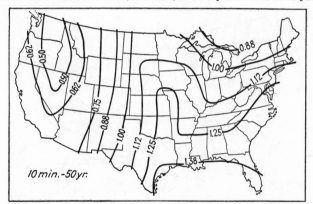

Fig. 56.—Ten-minute rainfall, in inches, to be expected once in 50 years.

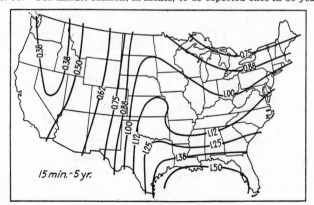

Fig. 57.—Fifteen-minute rainfall, in inches, to be expected once in 5 years.

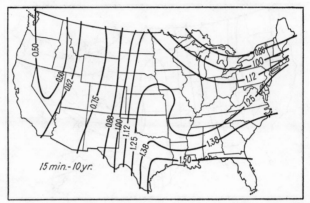

Fig. 58.—Fifteen-minute rainfall, in inches, to be expected once in 10 years.

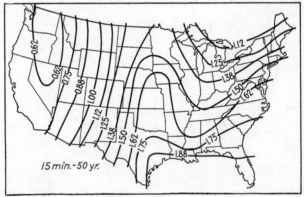

Fig. 59.—Fifteen-minute rainfall, in inches, to be expected once in 50 years.

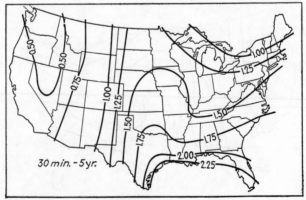

Fig. 60.—Thirty-minute rainfall, in inches, to be expected once in 5 years.

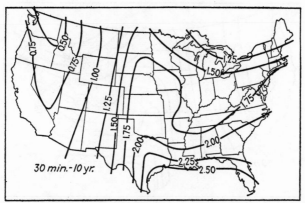

FIG. 61.—Thirty-minute rainfall, in inches, to be expected once in 10 years.

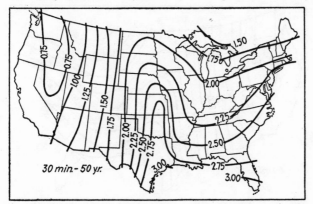

FIG. 62.—Thirty-minute rainfall, in inches, to be expected once in 50 years.

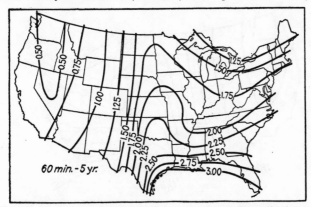

FIG. 63.—One-hour rainfall, in inches, to be expected once in 5 years.

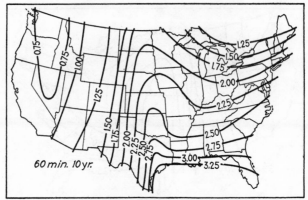

Fig. 64.—One-hour rainfall, in inches, to be expected once in 10 years.

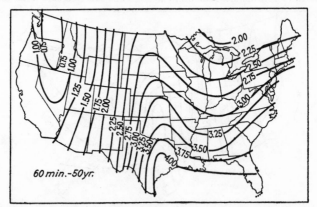

Fig. 65.—One-hour rainfall, in inches, to be expected once in 50 years.

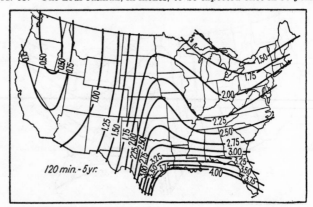

Fig. 66.—Two-hour rainfall, in inches, to be expected once in 5 years.

records of intense precipitation extending back to 1888. Automatic recording rain gages are required to obtain accurate records of intense precipitation lasting for short periods and, at the

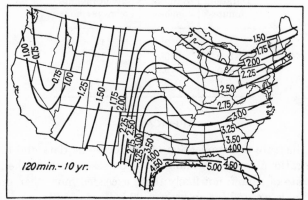

FIG. 67.—Two-hour rainfall, in inches, to be expected once in 10 years.

present time, the Weather Bureau maintains 211 such gages well distributed over the entire United States. There are also a number of other self-recording gages maintained for special purposes by various public agencies and private individuals.

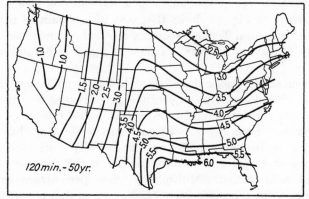

FIG. 68.—Two-hour rainfall, in inches, to be expected once in 50 years.

Intermediate values for both intensity and frequency between those shown on the maps may be obtained by interpolation. For duration periods less than 5 minutes (not included on the maps) and a frequency of once in 10 years, the following average intensities may be used:

Duration, minutes	Rainfall, inches	Rate of rainfall, inches per hour
1.4	0.26	11
3.0	0.50	10
3.5	0.52	9
4.0	0.53	8

APPLICATION

To illustrate the application of the foregoing data and the use of the rational runoff formula, let it be assumed that the maximum rate of runoff, not likely to be exceeded more than once in 10 years, is wanted for an area of 20.7 acres of hilly agricultural land near Jackson, Tenn. A fairly well defined channel leads from the upper reaches of the watershed to the point of exit, a distance by channel of 1200 feet, at an average rate of fall of 4.89 feet per 100 feet. The velocity of water flowing in the channel[1] is estimated at 245 feet per minute, which makes the time of concentration 5 minutes (practically the same as the value given in the foregoing tabulation for a watershed of 20 acres).

Reference to Fig. 52 shows that 0.55 inch of rainfall is to be expected in central Tennessee during a period of 5 minutes on an average of once in 10 years. This is at a rate of 6.6 inches per hour.

The soil on the tract is described as Lexington silt loam and is in a badly eroded state due to continuous cultivation in cotton for many years without special protection. The subsoil is quite impervious. From a reconnaissance survey the tract has been classified as 10 acres or 48 per cent of hilly cultivated land, 7.7 acres or 38 per cent of hilly pasture, and 3 acres or 14 per cent of hilly timber. Multiplying these percentages by the values of C for their respective conditions, as shown in the preceding tabulation, and adding gives 0.54 as the value of the runoff coefficient.

---

[1] More data on velocity, including use of a velocity formula, are found in Chap. V.

Substituting in $Q = CIA$, we have

$$Q = (0.54)(6.6)(20.7)$$

or

$$Q = 73.6 \text{ cubic feet per second}$$

which is the critical rate of runoff for the conditions assumed.

Runoff in Terrace Channels.—As another example of runoff computation, suppose it is desired to know the critical runoff at the end of each 300-foot section of a terrace 1200 feet long located in west central Texas on a slope averaging 6 feet fall per 100 feet. The soil is such that 0.60 would be about right for the runoff coefficient on unterraced land but with terraces and good soil and crop management the coefficient can safely be reduced to 0.36.* The slope distance to the next terrace above is about 60 feet, so that each 300-foot section serves an area of 0.41 acre between the two terraces (see Appendix for methods of making area computations).

Assuming a velocity of about 3 feet per second straight down the slope, and 1.5 feet per second in the terrace channel, the time of concentration in minutes at the ends of the 300-foot sections is respectively, 3.7, 7.0, 10.3, and 13.6. If it is deemed permissible to overtax the terrace capacity as often as once in 5 years the rainfall rates corresponding to the above times of concentration are (by interpolation between Figs. 51, 54, and 57 and supplementary data for intervals less than 5 minutes), respectively, 8.6,[1] 5.6, 5.2, and 4.6 inches per hour.

Substituting the above values in the formula $Q = CIA$, the following rates of runoff result:

First 300-foot section

$$Q = (0.36)(8.6)(0.41)$$
$$= 1.27 \text{ cu. ft. per sec.}$$

---

* For terraced watersheds the following reductions in the runoff coefficients previously given are warranted:

Watersheds of 1 acre, use 0.60 of previous coefficient.

Watersheds of 10 acres, use 0.70 of previous coefficient.

Watersheds of 30 acres, use 0.75 of previous coefficient.

Watersheds of 100 acres, use 0.90 of previous coefficient.

[1] Ten-year frequency for average intensity localities.

Second 300-foot section

$$Q = (0.36)(5.6)(0.82)$$
$$= 1.65 \text{ cu. ft. per sec.}$$

Third 300-foot section

$$Q = (0.36)(5.2)(1.23)$$
$$= 2.30 \text{ cu. ft. per sec.}$$

Fourth 300-foot section

$$Q = (0.36)(4.6)(1.64)$$
$$= 2.72 \text{ cu. ft. per sec.}$$

It should be remarked in this connection that these rates of runoff are about the minimum that good judgment would allow. In many cases a 10-year recurrence interval is the lowest that should be considered, and doubtless a runoff coefficient of 0.36 would sometimes be exceeded. The computation method, however, remains the same regardless of the numerical values involved and to illustrate this is the main purpose of the example quoted.

The above data and coefficients suggested are the best available information for design purposes at the present time. There is no doubt that the extensive investigations now being carried on by the various state and federal agencies will in time reveal more precise information on the values of constants which should be used under various conditions. However, until such information is available, it will be satisfactory for all practical purposes to use the data and constants presented herein.

It will be noted that the design data suggest using intensities for a ten-year frequency. It is believed, with the knowledge we now have, that this is the most logical frequency-interval to use. However, terraces are designed with capacities capable of taking care of the amount of water which will fall for a given frequency for the duration of time equivalent to the time of concentration of the area serving the terrace in question. This phase, from an academic standpoint, raises an interesting economical problem, *i.e.*, balancing the cost of building terraces of different sizes against their estimated length of service.

From the rainfall intensity maps contained in this book or from the maps in U.S.D.A. Bulletin 204, one can compile two sets of charts. On the first chart plot intensity as ordinate against duration as abscissa. A family of curves for various frequencies will be obtained. From this first chart, read the intensities for the various frequencies for the time of concentration of the area serving the terrace in question. Plot these values on another chart with intensity as ordinate and frequency as abscissa. Thus we have the different intensities for various frequencies for the time of concentration for the terrace we are studying. Using this curve and our assumed value of C, we can compute the required terrace capacity for different frequencies, and the size of terrace needed, and hence the cost. Thus we can compare the costs of a terrace with a ten-year-frequency-capacity against that with a five-year-frequency-capacity, or a fifteen-year-frequency-capacity with a ten-year-frequency-capacity. To put it another way, could a terrace with say a five or a ten-year-frequency-capacity enable the landowner to "get on his feet sufficiently from a money standpoint" to later rebuild his terraces so that they would have greater capacity? The commentator merely raises this question as one phase of the problem on which further study is desirable.[1]

[1] Comment by D. L. Yarnell submitted in response to a request by the author.

CHAPTER V

TERRACE DESIGN

Terracing as an art is as old as agriculture itself. As a science it dates from 1886 when P. H. Mangum, a farmer of Wake Forest, N. C., began to experiment with a "modified terrace" which would permit crossing with farm implements and allow the entire hillside to be cultivated. The following quotation from "The Progressive Farmer" of March, 1888, is of interest.

Mr. Mangum had perhaps the best system of hillside ditches in Wake County a few years since (1886) when he read of the level terrace system practiced to some extent in Georgia. He tried this system fairly on 25 acres and found that it would not do for his farm, which is a good representative tract of middle and Piedmont, North Carolina land. Finally Mr. Mangum worked out the scheme of the "modified terrace" which we saw and which I will briefly describe: He utilized his hillside ditches, plowing down the upper bank several times using hoes where necessary, allowing the lower embankment of the ditch to remain. In front of the embankment, where the ditch was, is a space of 10 feet on a dead level (crosswise) and about 12 inches below the embankment.

Terrace Types.—The terrace built by Mangum in 1886 is the progenitor of the modern broad-base ridge type terrace that is in practically universal use today. The narrow-base ridge type failed to establish itself in popularity because of numerous breaks in the bank and because it could not be cultivated or crossed. Also the narrow deep channel, above the ridge, is poorly proportioned hydraulically to carry maximum discharge at minimum velocity.

In the continental United States, terraces of the bench type are of little more than academic interest due to the large amount of earth moving involved and to the fact that they seriously impede if not prohibit the use of cultivating machinery. Nevertheless, if cultivated crops are to be grown in mountainous regions, bench terraces or their counterpart are essential. This

100

is attested to in many parts of the world today, notably in China and Japan, in the vineyards of Europe, and in the rice fields of the Philippine Islands. Figure 69 illustrates a view of what is described as the world's most extensive terraced rice fields located in the Philippine Islands. These terraces are the result of long centuries of toil by native tribes.

Fig. 69.—Bench terraces in the Philippine Islands. (*Courtesy U. S. Bureau of Agricultural Engineering.*)

Although bench terraces typify the true meaning of the word "terrace" more nearly than any other type, they are not practicable on the cultivated lands of continental United States on any extensive scale; and, since narrow-base ridge terraces are practically obsolete, whenever the word terrace is used hereafter it will refer to the broad-base, shallow-channel type.

DESIGN PRINCIPLES

In principle, terracing is essentially a process of constructing a series of drainage channels across the slope of hillsides whose function is to collect the runoff water before it attains harmful velocity and conduct it slowly to an erosion-proof outlet. The drainage channels, which intercept the runoff and prevent its rapid flow down the slope, are formed by throwing up low, broad embankments called terraces. The first terrace is located near enough to the crest of the slope to prevent the start of appreciable erosion, and the others are so spaced down the hillside as to serve the same purpose. Ordinarily the embankment is not constructed precisely on the contour but is given a slight fall longitudinally, so that the water that collects in the channel next to the embankment is conducted along the terrace to a suitable outlet usually located at a boundary of the field. Very often the outlet is a ditch on a steep grade that must itself be protected against wash.

The size and fall of the terrace channel must be adjusted to carry the maximum runoff without danger of appreciable scour or overtopping. Maximum or critical runoff is fixed by the formula $Q = CIA$, as has been pointed out in the previous chapter. The A in the formula is a function of the length of the terrace and the spacing between it and the adjacent terrace above—or to the top of the hillside (see Appendix for methods of computing).

TERRACE SPACING

Since the allowable spacing is governed mainly by the need for preventing appreciable erosion between the terraces, it will vary with the land slope for given soil and cultural conditions. For the sake of economy in construction and minimum interference with cultivation, it is desirable to space the terraces as widely as the soil and slope will permit without requiring too much maintenance at a time when the land is in the least resistant crop. Wide spacing calls for more capacity in the terrace channel to serve the larger watershed. Good cultural practices permit maximum spacing and, by increasing the time of concentration, reduce to a minimum the critical rate of rainfall and the runoff coefficient.

Trial spacings are usually expressed in feet of vertical drop from one terrace to the next as a function of the land slope, the simplest form being: add 3 to the per cent of slope and divide by 2. Thus, if the slope is 5 per cent, representing a fall of 5 feet per 100 feet, 3 plus 5 divided by 2 gives 4 feet as the proper vertical spacing. This rule of thumb is fairly accurate up to slopes of 6 per cent, but beyond that the spacings indicated are increasingly too large. Table 10 represents what is generally considered to be good average practice, though the exact figures are subject to variation in accord with local experience.

The spacings recommended for Alabama and Georgia are given in detail in Table 11, and Table 12 affords a comparison of the spacings recommended in recent federal and state publications for various parts of the country. Doubtless the difference of opinion noted arises in part from the probability that one specialist is thinking in terms of impoverished soil as it exists at the time of terrace construction, whereas another makes allowance for increased resistance to erosion after the soil has been

TABLE 10.—INTERVALS BETWEEN TERRACES AND LINEAL FEET PER ACRE

Slope of land, feet per 100 ft.	Vertical drop between terraces, feet		Distance between terraces in feet for wider spacing	Lineal feet of terrace per acre for wider spacing and uniform slopes
	Northern states	Southern states		
2	2.75	2.50	137.50	320
4	3.40	3.00	85.00	515
6	4.00	3.50	66.67	655
8	4.75	4.00	59.37	745
10	5.50	4.50	55.00	795
12	6.30	5.00	52.50	830
14	7.10	5.50	50.71	860

improved by the addition of fertilizer and humus and by good crop and cultural management. Unless there is positive assurance that the soil will be so treated following the construction work, the former viewpoint would seem to represent safer policy.

The major criterion in all cases is prevailing land slope, and this itself is subject to considerable variation in any given field so that, regardless of the spacing scale adopted, it can seldom be applied to the ground with absolute precision. It is common practice to measure the slope above the midpoint of a terrace and allow that to govern the spacing between it and the one next above. Appreciable reduction in land slope may so increase its length in comparison with the one next above as to require the use of an intermediate spur terrace to avoid abnormally large spacing (see Fig. 75, Chap. V).

TABLE 11.—TERRACE SPACINGS RECOMMENDED FOR ALABAMA AND GEORGIA CONDITIONS*

Slope of land, feet per 100 ft.	Vertical distance or drop between terraces, feet and inches		Horizontal distance between terraces, feet
1	2	6	180
2	2	9	140
3	3	0	100
4	3	3	80
5	3	6	75
6	3	9	63
7	4	0	57
8	4	3	53
9	4	6	50
10	4	9	48
12½	5	4	43
15	6	4	40

How to Use Table.—After the slope of a hill has been determined, select from Table 11 either the vertical or horizontal distance that will apply to the slope determined. By use of the level and rod, locate the terrace on the hill or pace down the hill the required horizontal distance. The latter method is the quickest and easiest to perform.

* From *Ala. Polytechnic Institute Ext. Circ.* 148. December, 1934.

Univ. Ga. Ext. Bull. 394, April, 1935. Georgia recommends 6.0 feet for 15 per cent slope.

TABLE 12.—RECOMMENDED TERRACE SPACINGS FROM VARIOUS FEDERAL AND STATE BULLETINS PUBLISHED IN 1932–1935 (FEET)

Slope, per cent	U. S. D. A. (southern states)	Ga.	Ala.	Kan.	Minn.	Iowa	
						(Eastern)	(Western)
2	2.5	....	2.75	2.5	2.75		
4	3.0	3.25	3.25	4.0	3.50	3.5	4.0
6	3.5	3.75	3.75	5.0	4.0	4.0	4.5
8	4.0	4.25	4.25	5.0	4.75	4.5	5.0
10	4.5	4.75	4.75	5.0	5.50	5.0	5.5
12	5.0	5.25	....	...	6.25	5.5	6.0
12.5	...	....	5.33				
14	5.5	....	....	...	7.00	6.0	6.5
15	...	6.0	6.33				

Note: The U. S. Department of Agriculture recommendations progress in increments of ½ foot for each 2 per cent increase in slope—a relationship easy to remember. The Minnesota recommendations coincide with those of the U. S. Department of Agriculture for northern states.

TERRACE GRADES

Successful terraces have been built with a variety of gradients (fall along the terrace water channel) as follows: level end to end; graded uniformly from one end to the other or from a point near the middle toward each end; with a grade varying from a minimum in the upper portion to a maximum at the lower end.

It is desirable, within practical limitations, to keep terrace grades as slight as possible and still impart sufficient velocity to the water to prevent overtopping or ponding.

That it is important to use the smallest permissible gradient is clearly evident from Table 13, which shows runoff and soil losses for terraces with different grades at several of the federal stations. This table shows losses for a 6-inch grade at Bethany nearly five times as much as for terraces with a level grade and about three times as much as a 2-inch grade, with substantially similar results at Guthrie. Since the main object of terracing is to retain as much soil as possible on the field, especially the rich silt lodging in terrace channels, these experiments indicate that a grade of 4 inches or 0.33 foot per 100 feet is about the maximum that should be used. Certainly a gradient of 0.4 per cent should not be exceeded except in very special circumstances.

Level Terraces.—Level terraces are satisfactory where the soil is sufficiently open to allow a rate of infiltration approximately equal to the rate of runoff or in regions of sparse rainfall where every drop of water counts. In the latter case it is frequently feasible to close both ends and force all surface water to soak in the ground. When terraces are built level, extreme care is needed to prevent low places developing in the bank with consequent outpouring of water from both directions along the terrace. This would not be so likely to happen with a graded terrace.

The spacing recommended in U. S. Department of Agriculture Bulletin 1669 for the level terraces on slopes of 10 per cent or less are:

Soil	Vertical Drop in Feet between Terraces
Sandy	4.5
Sandy loam	3.5
Clay loam	2.5
Clay	2.0

TABLE 13.—RUNOFF AND SOIL LOSSES FOR TERRACES WITH DIFFERENT GRADES AT SEVERAL OF THE SOIL EROSION STATIONS[1]

Terrace number	Land slope, per cent	Vertical spacing, feet	Length, feet	Grade, inches per 100 ft.	Soil losses, tons per acre	Runoff, per cent of rainfall	Rainfall, inches	Crops
					Average annual			
Guthrie Station (Three-year Period)								
3-C	4.3	3.5	1500	6	7.79	20.2	31.3	1931—Oats
4-C	4.4	3.5	1500	4	4.29	20.6	....	1932—Cotton
5-C	4.7	3.4	1500	2	3.53	20.6		1933—Corn
6-C	5.5	3.3	1500	0	2.05	16.6		
Bethany Station (Two-year Period)								
5-C	12 (approx.)	5 (approx.)	1200	8	3.92	13.2	29.4	1932—Corn
6-C	12 (approx.)	5 (approx.)	1200	6	1.87	12.0	....	1933—Oats followed by clover and timothy
7-C	12 (approx.)	5 (approx.)	1200	4	1.66	12.0		
8-C	12 (approx.)	5 (approx.)	1200	2	0.68	11.0		
9-C	12 (approx.)	5 (approx.)	1200	0	0.42	6.8		
Tyler Station (Three-Year Period)								
5-C	6.3	4	700	0 to 6	10.1	29.8	42.3	1931—Cotton} followed by rye and oats cover crop; 1932—Corn; 1933—Cotton
6-C	5.9	4	700	0 to 3	4.9	16.2	....	
LaCrosse Station (One Year)								
4-A	15 (approx.)	7	1400	0 to 6	7.1	....	26.8	1933—Barley followed by corn
5-A	15 (approx.)	7	1400	0 to 3	2.0			
6-A	15 (approx.)	7	1400	0 to 0	0.6			
Pullman Station (One year)								
15	24.0	17.0	685	24	13.67	29.3	28.8	Winter wheat stubble
16	26.7	13.5	780	18	11.40	23.2		1933—Fallow
17	23.5	14.2	780	12	9.05	13.6		Winter wheat
18	18.4	14.0	780	6	3.65	11.6		
19	15.2	13.8	780	0	1.28	15.1		

[1] See map, Chap. XIV; and tables, Chaps. II and III.

For steeper slopes these values may be increased one-half foot, and for terraces with open ends on permeable soils the same spacings as given in Table 10 will apply. Spacings one foot less than those given for the southern states are appropriate for regions of light rainfall where crops normally suffer severely from drought.

Graded Terraces.—The advantages of a terrace with uniform grade are, (1) ease with which it can be staked out, (2) less maintenance in removing silt from channels, and (3) less likelihood of ponding due to operation of field machinery in the channel.

While uniformly graded terraces have their stanch advocates, these advantages are not generally deemed sufficient to outweigh the savings in both soil and water obtainable from the use of a variable grade and other advantages to be pointed out later (see Table 19).

According to C. E. Ramser, Senior Drainage Engineer, U. S. Department of Agriculture:

A uniform graded terrace at Bethany having a grade of 4 inches per 100 feet gave a soil loss about 37 per cent greater and a water loss about 33 per cent greater than a variable graded terrace having a grade of 1 to 4 inches per 100 feet during a two-year period. Both terraces were 1,200 feet long, had vertical spacings of 5 feet, and were on the same land slope. Also, for the three largest storms that occurred during the year 1933, the average of the maximum rates of runoff during the storms for the uniform graded terrace were slightly over twice as great as for the variable grade terrace. Similar results were obtained on the Station at Tyler, Tex., where the soil loss was about 15 per cent greater and the water loss 27 per cent greater for a uniform than for a variable graded terrace. Also, the rate of runoff from one of the largest storms was about 40 per cent greater for the uniform graded terrace.

Again, the variable grade is more logical because the capacity increases with increased runoff, and this can be accomplished only by increasing the grade of terraces of constant cross section. It is always desirable to hold back the water as much as possible without ponding or undue hazard to the embankment, and this is assured more nearly by a variable grade, provided of course that the work of surveying and construction is accurately done.

It is common practice to divide a variable graded terrace into sections of 300 feet in length and increase the grade of each section progressively from the upper end toward the outlet approximately in accordance with the range of figures in Table 14. Where the length is not in excess of 300 feet a uniform grade of 0.15 to 0.30 per cent is satisfactory. Occasionally a very long terrace seems unavoidable, in which case the sections may be made about one-fifth of the total length with the maximum gradients for each section as shown in Table 14. The other and

TABLE 14.—GRADIENTS FOR VARIABLE GRADE TERRACES

Length of terrace, feet	Fall along terrace	
	Inches per 100 feet (minimum)	Feet per 100 feet (maximum)
0 to 300	Level	0.10
300 to 600	1	0.15
600 to 900	2	0.20
900 to 1200	3	0.30
1200 to 1500	4	0.40

less desirable alternative is to build up the bank at the lower end high enough to carry the additional discharge. For unusually impervious and scour-resistant soils, grades up to 0.50 per cent may sometimes become necessary but should be used as sparingly as possible.

Special Gradient Tables.—Where the infiltration rate of soils and other conditions are known with considerable accuracy, it is possible to compile gradient tables, applicable to limited areas, to fit the special situation. Tables 15 and 16 come under this category and have been prepared by the technical staff of the Soil Conservation Service for use in the territory contiguous to Bethany, Mo. The grades shown in these tables are considered necessary to prevent ponding resulting from the operation of field machinery in the terrace channel.

Special recommendations, applicable to Alabama, are found in Table 17.* They represent the best judgment of terracing specialists in that state as a result of long experience in building and maintaining terraces.

* *Ala. Polytechnic Inst., Agr. Ext. Circ. 148.*

TABLE 15.—TERRACE GRADE TABLE

Soils with Impervious Subsoils on Slopes Less than 12 Per Cent and with 50 Per Cent or More Topsoil Remaining

Soils with Open Subsoils Regardless of Slope or Degree of Erosion

1	2	3	4	5	6	7	8	9	10	11	12	13	14	15	16	Average grade	Total fall, feet
0.2	0.2	0.2	0.2													0.20	0.80
0.1	0.2	0.2	0.2	0.3												0.20	1.00
0.1	0.2	0.2	0.2	0.2	0.3											0.20	1.20
0.1	0.1	0.2	0.2	0.2	0.2	0.3	0.3									0.20	1.40
0.1	0.1	0.2	0.2	0.2	0.2	0.2	0.3	0.3								0.20	1.60
0.1	0.1	0.1	0.2	0.2	0.2	0.2	0.3	0.3	0.3							0.20	1.80
0.1	0.1	0.1	0.2	0.2	0.2	0.2	0.2	0.3	0.3	0.3						0.20	2.00
0.1	0.1	0.1	0.2	0.2	0.2	0.2	0.2	0.3	0.3	0.3						0.20	2.20
0.1	0.1	0.1	0.1	0.2	0.2	0.2	0.2	0.2	0.3	0.3	0.3	0.3				0.20	2.40
0.1	0.1	0.1	0.1	0.2	0.2	0.2	0.2	0.2	0.3	0.3	0.3	0.3	0.4			0.22	2.80
0.1	0.1	0.1	0.1	0.2	0.2	0.2	0.2	0.2	0.3	0.3	0.3	0.3	0.4	0.4		0.23	3.20
0.1	0.1	0.1	0.1	0.2	0.2	0.2	0.2	0.2	0.3	0.3	0.3	0.3	0.4	0.4	0.4	0.25	3.60
0.1	0.1	0.1	0.1	0.2	0.2	0.2	0.2	0.2	0.3	0.3	0.3	0.3	0.4	0.4	0.4	0.25	4.00

Length of terrace in units of 100 feet

TABLE 16.—TERRACE GRADE TABLE

Soils with Impervious Subsoils on Slopes of 12 Per Cent and Over and All Slopes with Less than 50 Per Cent of Top Soil Remaining

1	2	3	4	5	6	7	8	9	10	11	12	13	14	15	16	Average grade	Total fall, feet
0.3	0.3	0.3	0.3													0.30	1.2
0.2	0.3	0.3	0.3	0.4												0.30	1.5
0.2	0.3	0.3	0.3	0.3	0.4											0.30	1.8
0.2	0.2	0.3	0.3	0.3	0.4	0.4										0.30	2.1
0.2	0.2	0.3	0.3	0.3	0.3	0.4	0.4									0.30	2.4
0.2	0.2	0.2	0.3	0.3	0.3	0.4	0.4	0.4								0.30	2.7
0.2	0.2	0.2	0.3	0.3	0.3	0.3	0.4	0.4	0.4							0.30	3.0
0.2	0.2	0.2	0.2	0.3	0.3	0.3	0.4	0.4	0.4	0.4						0.30	3.3
0.2	0.2	0.2	0.2	0.3	0.3	0.3	0.3	0.4	0.4	0.4	0.4					0.30	3.6
0.2	0.2	0.2	0.2	0.3	0.3	0.3	0.3	0.4	0.4	0.4	0.4	0.5				0.32	4.1
0.2	0.2	0.2	0.2	0.3	0.3	0.3	0.3	0.4	0.4	0.4	0.4	0.5	0.5			0.33	4.6
0.2	0.2	0.2	0.2	0.3	0.3	0.3	0.3	0.4	0.4	0.4	0.4	0.5	0.5	0.5		0.34	5.1
0.2	0.2	0.2	0.2	0.3	0.3	0.3	0.3	0.4	0.4	0.4	0.4	0.5	0.5	0.5	0.5	0.35	5.6

Length of terrace in units of 100 feet

TABLE 17.—TERRACE LENGTHS AND GRADES AS RECOMMENDED FOR
ALABAMA

Terrace length, feet	Land slope		
	5 per cent	10 per cent	15 per cent
	Maximum inches fall per 100 ft. in terrace	Maximum inches fall per 100 ft. in terrace	Maximum inches fall per 100 ft. in terrace
Clay Subsoil			
0 to 100	0	0	0
100 to 400	1	1¼	1½
400 to 700	2	2½	2¾
700 to 1000	3	3½	4¼
1000 to 1300	4	4¾	5½
1300 to 1600	5	6	7
Sandy Subsoil			
0 to 100	0	0	0
100 to 400	¼	½	¾
400 to 700	¾	1¼	1½
700 to 1000	1¼	1¾	2½
1000 to 1300	1½	2½	3¼
1300 to 1600	2	3	4

LENGTH OF TERRACES

Experiments at the federal erosion stations indicate that long terraces produce more soil loss but less runoff than short ones. The maximum length of terrace, however, for a run in one direction should probably not exceed 2000 feet under any circumstances, and it is desirable to keep under 1200 feet if at all possible. Very long terraces require either impermissible grades or abnormally large cross sections or both to take care of the accumulated volume of water in their lower reaches. Large grades induce high velocities, which erode the channel; and large cross sections mean high banks, which impede the use of field machinery.

On the other hand, short terraces are somewhat more troublesome and expensive to build, owing to the extra time consumed in turning at the ends.

Sometimes, as an extreme measure, it becomes necessary to use natural depressions in the middle of fields as outlet ditches in order to keep the terrace lengths within limits. This entails special precautions to prevent washing in the outlet ditch and, by dividing the field, introduces waste land and added inconvenience in cultivation.

TERRACE CROSS SECTIONS

Theoretically it is possible to design terrace cross sections on the same basis that open ditches are designed for irrigation and

Fig. 70.—A practical and adequate terrace cross section.

land drainage, by adjusting the width and depth to provide sufficient waterway area to accommodate the critical runoff. Critical runoff is computed by the method explained in Chap. IV and, when this is known, the terrace channel is made to equal or exceed it in carrying capacity without resort to erosive velocities or to side slopes and bank heights that would cause undue interference with cultural practices. A practical terrace cross section is shown in Fig. 70.

Capacity Formula.—When the grade and dimensions of a channel are known, its carrying capacity may be computed from the formula,

$$Q = a\frac{1.486}{n}R^{\frac{2}{3}}S^{\frac{1}{2}}$$

where Q = carrying capacity or discharge in cubic feet per second.

a = cross-sectional area of channel in square feet.

n = a coefficient whose value depends on the degree of roughness or irregularity in the channel.

$R = a/p$ = the "hydraulic radius," which is the quotient of the cross-sectional area divided by the "wetted perimeter," p, or length of the cross line of contact between the water and the channel sides and bottom.

S = grade or rate of fall *expressed in feet per foot.*

When it is considered that the two-thirds power of R is simply the cube root of R squared and that the one-half power is the square root of S, it is seen that the formula is not so complex as it may first appear and yet is quite flexible and accurate. This formula is a combination of Manning's velocity formula

$$V = \frac{1.486}{n} R^{\frac{2}{3}} S^{\frac{1}{2}} *$$

where

V is the lineal velocity of flow in feet per second and

$$Q = aV$$

the discharge of a conduit of any shape being the product of the cross-sectional area times the lineal velocity.

For terrace channels that bear growing crops part of the time, a value of $n = 0.04$ is generally considered proper. At times when the growth is dense enough to greatly increase this value and cause overtopping, it is probable that little damage will be done. Values of n to fit a great variety of conditions have been carefully compiled from field observations by a number of investigators over a long period of years. Some of these values are shown in Table 18.

A complete solution of Manning's formula can be approximated from the diagram shown in Fig. 71 by following the directions on page 114.

Shape of Channel.—The effect of the channel shape on velocity is measured by the factor R in Manning's formula. A wide, shallow channel is not only better than a narrow, deep one of

* See tables in the Appendix giving two-thirds powers of R and square roots of S.

comparable capacity from the standpoint of machinery operation but also has the property of carrying approximately the same amount and rate of runoff at a lower velocity. This property is illustrated by the following example.

TABLE 18.—VALUES OF n FOR USE IN MANNING'S FORMULA

Surface	Perfect	Good	Fair	Bad
Canals and ditches:				
Earth, straight and uniform..............	0.017	0.020	0.0225[a]	0.025
Rock cuts, smooth and uniform..........	0.025	0.030	0.033[a]	0.035
Rock cuts, jagged and irregular..........	0.035	0.040	0.045	
Winding sluggish canals.................	0.0225	0.025[a]	0.0275	0.030
Dredged earth channels.................	0.025	0.0275[a]	0.030[a]	0.033
Canals with rough, stony beds, weeds on				
earth banks.........................	0.025	0.030	0.035[a]	0.040
Earth bottom, rubble sides..............	0.028	0.030[a]	0.033[a]	0.035
Natural stream channels:				
(1) Clean, straight bank, full stage, no				
rifts or deep pools..................	0.025	0.0275	0.030	0.033
(2) Same as (1), but some weeds and stones	0.030	0.033	0.035	0.040
(3) Winding, some pools and shoals, clean	0.033	0.035	0.040	0.045
(4) Same as (3), lower stages, more ineffective slopes and sections..............	0.040	0.045	0.050	0.055
(5) Same as (3), some weeds and stones..	0.035	0.040	0.045	0.050
(6) Same as (4), stony sections..........	0.045	0.050	0.055	0.060
(7) Sluggish river reaches, rather weedy or with very deep pools................	0.050	0.060	0.070	0.080
(8) Very weedy reaches.................	0.075	0.100	0.125	0.150

[a] Values commonly used in designing.

Assume two channels on a grade of 0.50 feet per 100 feet (0.005 feet per foot), one of which is 3 feet deep with a bottom width of 1 foot and a top width of 7 feet; and the other 1 foot deep, 12 feet wide at the bottom, and 26 feet wide on top. By Manning's formula the velocities and carrying capacities are as follows:

Narrow, deep channel

$$a = 12 \text{ sq. ft.}$$
$$p = 9.5 \text{ ft.}$$
$$R = \frac{a}{p} = \frac{12}{9.5} = 1.26$$

$$S = 0.005$$
$$n = 0.04$$
$$V = (37.15)(1.17)(0.0707)$$
$$= 3.07 \text{ ft. per sec.}$$
$$Q = aV = (12)(3.07)$$
$$= 36.84 \text{ cu. ft. per sec.}$$

Wide, shallow channel

$$a = 19 \text{ sq. ft.}$$
$$p = 26.1 \text{ ft.}$$
$$R = \frac{a}{p} = \frac{19}{26.1} = 0.73$$
$$S = 0.005$$
$$n = 0.04$$
$$V = (37.15)(0.811)(0.0707)$$
$$= 2.13 \text{ ft. per sec.}$$
$$Q = aV = (19)(2.13)$$
$$= 40.47 \text{ cu. ft. per sec.}$$

Although the deep channel has a cross-sectional area of only 12 square feet as compared with 19 square feet for the shallow

---

How to Use Diagram (Fig. 71)

1. Determine fall or slope of the channel in feet per foot (nearly always a decimal fraction).

2. Compute the hydraulic radius of the channel (divide cross-sectional area by the wetted perimeter).

3. On the chart at the right (or upper part) of the diagram find the point of intersection between the line representing slope and the line representing hydraulic radius (these lines will always intersect at an angle of 90 degrees).

4. From this point follow the nearest guide line across to its intersection with the line representing the assumed value of n (usually 0.040 for terrace channels) found on the chart at the left (or lower part).

5. Find the velocity as indicated by the velocity line nearest to the last intersection point.

By similar procedure the velocity of flow in a channel or conduit of any shape can be determined for any conditions within the limits of the diagram.

EXAMPLE—Adopting the same numerical values as those chosen for the narrow deep channel in the accompanying paragraph, *i.e.*, depth, 3 feet; bottom width, 1 foot; and top width, 7 feet. The procedure is as follows:

1. The slope is 0.005.

2. The hydraulic radius is 1.26.

3. The lines representing slope and hydraulic radius intersect very close to one of the guide lines (32d line from the beginning).

4. Following this guide line to the other chart, it is found to intersect the 0.040n line almost exactly on the velocity line representing a velocity of 3.0.

5. The velocity of flow in the assumed channel is therefore 3.0 feet per second. The exact velocity as determined by analytical computation is 3.07 feet per second. This computation is shown in the above paragraph.

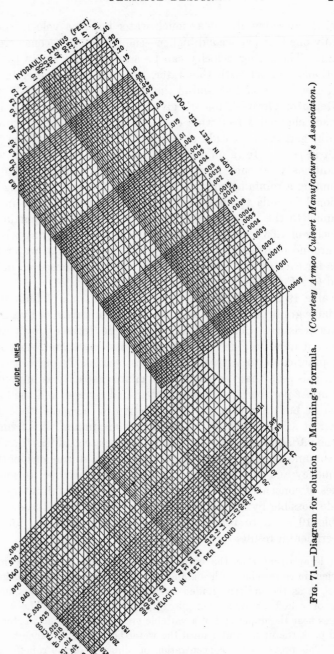

Fig. 71.—Diagram for solution of Manning's formula. (*Courtesy Armco Culvert Manufacturer's Association.*)

one, it can carry almost as much water but at a velocity practically one foot per second higher—enough to cause considerable scour. The higher velocity can be accounted for solely by less frictional contact with the water, the wetted perimeter in the first case being 9.5 feet and in the second, 26.1 feet.

Depth of Flow.—Table 19 gives the hydraulic elements in a terrace channel 3 feet wide on the bottom, 1.2 feet maximum depth, and 9.4 feet wide on top. This particular terrace was built in central Iowa on a uniform grade of 0.30 per cent. Soil conditions were such as to justify a runoff coefficient of 0.43. Adopting a rainfall frequency of once in 10 years, and using the rational formula to obtain critical runoff, water will rise in the channel to the depths indicated and flow away at a maximum velocity of 1.63 feet per second. Since this is an existing terrace on ground of irregular topography, the increments of watershed area for each section are not uniform but are as measured in the field (see Fig. 75).

Table 19 also shows data for the same channel if built on a variable grade and affords an interesting comparison of hydraulic characteristics. Since the variable grade terrace flows at a constant depth of one foot throughout its length and, since it is not practicable to vary a terrace cross section during construction, it is seen that considerable available capacity is unused in the upper portion of the uniformly graded terrace, and the bank must be built higher in the lower section to carry the "pile-up" water at a higher velocity. Again, the maximum rate of runoff in the variable channel is 2.39 cubic feet per second less than the maximum discharge in the uniform grade for storms of identical frequency and drainage area. This is due, of course, to longer times of concentration with consequent lower rainfall intensities made possible by the slower velocities. Altogether the data in Table 19 seem to provide full theoretical verification for the experimental results reported by Ramser:

It is apparent that the variable graded terrace is not only more efficient in conserving both soil and water but does not require as great a height as the uniform graded terrace due to the smaller maximum rate of runoff or maximum discharge during storms. The flatter grades near the upper end of a variable graded terrace tend to store or hold back the upper water until the water below has a chance to flow off. This prevents the concentration or piling up of the runoff water

TABLE 19.—HYDRAULIC ELEMENTS OF A TERRACE CHANNEL WITH BOTTOM WIDTH OF 3 FEET AND SIDE SLOPES OF 2.67 TO 1
(Angle with horizontal = 20° 32')

Distance from upper end, feet	Accumulated watershed area, acres	Time of concentration, minutes	Rainfall intensity, inches per hour	Runoff, cubic feet per second		Velocity for capacity discharge, feet per second	Depth of flow for capacity discharge, feet	Grade, feet per 100 ft.
				Computed maximum	Channel capacity			
Uniform grade								
400	1.10	6.1	6.50	3.07	3.20	1.16	0.6	0.3
800	2.70	10.7	5.71	6.65	7.05	1.45	0.9	0.3
1200	3.52	15.05	4.86	7.36	8.69	1.53	1.0	0.3
1600	5.24	19.2	4.26	9.62	10.49	1.61	1.1	0.3
2000	6.51	23.3	3.91	10.95	11.08	1 63	1.13	0.3
Variable grade								
400	1.10	13.7	5.00	2.36	2.83	0.50	1.0	0.032
800	2.70	21.3	4.05	4.70	5.00	0.88	1.0	0.10
1200	3.52	27.7	3.64	5.50	5.70	1.03	1.0	0.13
1600	5.24	32.5	3.34	7.51	7.90	1.39	1.0	0.25
2000	6.51	36.9	3.05	8.56	8.69	1.53	1.0	0.30

C in formula $Q = CIA = 0.43$.
n in Manning's formula = 0.04.
Total fall: uniform grade; 6.0 feet; variable grade, 3.25 feet.

near the lower or outlet end of the terrace so that a lower terrace embankment can be used for a variable graded terrace under the same field and rainfall conditions without the possibility of overtopping.

Another point in favor of the variable graded terrace is that the total fall from upper to lower ends is little more than half

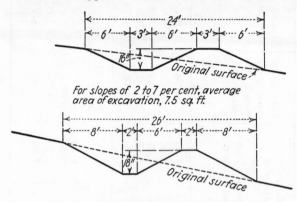

For slopes of 2 to 7 per cent, average area of excavation, 7.5 sq. ft.

For slopes of 8 per cent or more, average area of excavation, 9.5 sq. ft.

Fig. 72.—Dimensions of typical terrace cross sections.

the fall of a uniform grade, which allows closer conformity to the contour of the field and simplifies contour farming on terraced land.

Dimensions of Cross Section.—The ideal terrace cross section must have ample capacity to discharge maximum runoff; must be so shaped and laid out as to prevent undue ponding, silting, or scour in the channel; must have embankments low enough and

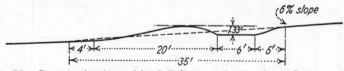

Fig. 73.—Cross section favored by Soil Conservation Service in Bethany, Mo. area. For use with Table 20.

with sufficiently flat side slopes not to impede easy manipulation of farm machinery; must be built so as to disturb as little topsoil as possible and expose the minimum amount of subsoil; and, finally, it must be practical to build with available equipment at reasonable cost and efficiency. The dimensions of such a cross section will necessarily not be the same on a steep as on a flat slope, and a cross section that fits a particular set of interlocking variables such as soil, spacing, grade, available equipment, etc., will not fit if an appreciable change is encountered in any one. Nevertheless, it is desirable to set up some sort of standard,

TABLE 20.—TERRACE SPACING AND SIZE FOR FORM OF CROSS SECTION SHOWN IN FIG. 73[1]

Slope (per cent)	Vertical interval, feet	Horizontal distance, feet	Ridge width, feet	Ridge height, feet	Channel width, feet	Disturbed width, feet	Disturbed (per cent)
2	2.50	125	20	1.25	8	37	30
3	3.00	100	20	1.25	8	37	37
4	3.50	88	20	1.25	7	36	41
5	4.00	80	20	1.25	7	36	45
6	4.40	73	20	1.33	6	35	48
7	4.80	69	18	1.33	6	33	48
8	5.20	65	18	1.33	5	32	49
9	5.50	61	16	1.33	5	31	51
10	5.70	57	16	1.50	4	30	53
11	5.90	54	14	1.50	4	29	54
12	6.00	50	13	1.50	4	28	56

[1] *Soil Conservation Service Handbook*, Bethany, Mo.

based on experience, to serve as a general guide, to be departed from when and to the extent that the circumstances of a particular situation may warrant.

Figure 72 is intended for this purpose, while Fig. 73 and Table 20 illustrate roughly the extent of departure that may often be justified.

CHAPTER VI

TERRACE LOCATION—PRINCIPLES AND PRACTICE

Planning the Layout.—From the foregoing discussion it can readily be seen that proper planning of a terrace layout is a task that calls for considerable ingenuity and resourcefulness. In matters of this kind there is no substitute for practical experience, but sound judgment is at least as dependent upon thorough theoretical understanding.

The first question to be decided is whether the land should be terraced at all. When gathering facts upon which to base a decision, the field should be examined by walking around the boundaries and exploring it from every angle. Outlet possibilities, prevailing degree and regularity of slopes, type and erosive condition of the soil, foreign land, if any, lying above the boundaries, approximate length of terraces required, and the intelligence and interest of the landowner or tenant, are all factors to be carefully weighed and considered.

Terraces are generally inadvisable on cultivated slopes above 15 per cent or on fields so cut up with gullies as to make the expense prohibitive. Thin soil, uniformly eroded, does not necessarily make terracing uneconomical, because terraces buttress and conserve applications of lime, fertilizer, and other soil-building practices that might otherwise be largely wasted. In all cases, however, the cost should be weighed against the probable increase in land value (generally estimated at a minimum of $8 per acre) before adjudging the project feasible. The difficulty and cost of procuring an erosion-proof outlet may also be a limiting factor in some situations. Unless the farmer understands the purpose of terraces, is sold on the idea and willing to take extra trouble to insure their proper functioning, it is usually unwise to try to force them upon him prematurely in spite of the fact that the alternative may be utter ruin within a few years.

120

If the reconnaissance survey results in a decision to go ahead, it is necessary to select the outlet or outlets to be used and envision a tentative arrangement of the terrace lines (sometimes, on very irregular ground, a topographic map may be necessary before this can be done). The next step is to measure the average slope above each tentative terrace and determine an appropriate spacing. With the spacing decided upon, the lines are ready to be staked out on the ground, beginning with the uppermost terrace and proceeding progressively down the slope. If some special feature exists part way down the hill, such as a sharp break in topography, a rocky point, the head of a large gully, a barn, or other obstacle, the position of a "key" terrace will arbitrarily be fixed and the other terraces must be adjusted to it. The key terrace should be the first one staked out, but, regardless of the order of staking, the uppermost terrace should be *built* first, followed by the others in next lower succession, to guard against the possibility of heavy rains overloading the lower terraces during construction.

Many times the layout could be greatly improved if several neighbors cooperated in a terracing program and thus enabled artificial property lines to be ignored and the best natural arrangement adopted. When this is not possible, and extraneous water is discharged upon the field to be terraced from higher land beyond its borders, such water must be intercepted and carried to an outlet by a different route through a diversion ditch located near the boundary. The grade and dimensions of the ditch can be determined by the methods already described.

Figures 74 to 77 illustrate the final position of terraces that have been carefully adjusted in every particular to fit the ground they serve.

Figure 74 shows a typical layout of terraces with variable grade on sandy loam soil. It is unfortunate that the outlet ditch on steep ground at the northeast corner could not have been avoided, but the length of the fourth terrace (from the summit) made it necessary. Only a relatively small amount of water is drained into it, however. It is always desirable and easier to drain *away* from steep slopes toward flat ones; but where this cannot be done the terrace grade is usually increased somewhat, as shown in the northeast portion of Terrace No. 3. Flow is divided in all terraces except the upper two, which drain away from the steep slope and discharge into dense timber. The northeast outlet ditch will need special protection from erosion in accordance with the principles discussed in Chap. IX. The south outlet ditch, being on flatter slopes, can probably be controlled by vegetation alone. Note that it is constructed inside the fence line to avoid overfalls into the highway side ditch. The water is carried parallel to the road until the velocity is sufficiently

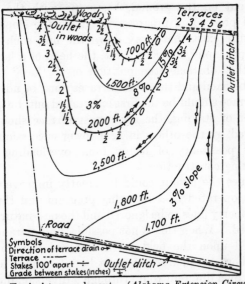

Fig. 74.—Typical terrace layout. (*Alabama Extension Circular* 148.)

reduced by flat land to allow it to be turned into the road ditch without possibility of damage from precipitous drops.

Figure 75 represents a portion of a terraced field in Iowa, with extremely irregular topography necessitating the use of spur terraces and unavoidable sharp bends in the terrace lines. While not exactly typical, such slopes as these are more or less common on glacial drift soils and have to be reckoned with. In the particular case cited, a topographic map of the field was a practical necessity before attempting to plan the layout. In doing this, as in all other cases, the field was protected in successive units beginning at the highest point with Terrace *A*. Spur Terrace *A-1* was necessary to break up the large area and excessive drop developed between the *A* and *B* terraces due to the discrepancy in their lengths; and the same thing was true of

Spur *B*-1 between Terraces *B* and *C*. The only practicable outlet for these upper terraces was along the property line fence on the east border, where ditches had to be constructed and protected from scour by special structures to be described later.

Figure 76 depicts one method of treating interior knolls not over 3 acres in extent with level terraces. Such knolls are a

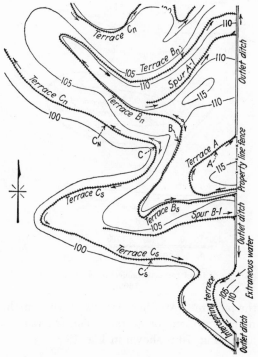

FIG. 75.—Example of a terrace layout on irregular topography. Only part of system is shown.

familiar problem in many sections of the country and are often quite baffling to handle. If the subsoil is too impervious to permit enclosed terraces, they will have to be graded so as to divide the water and drain from both directions toward an outlet ditch to be constructed where it will enter the woods with the shortest run and cause least inconvenience in farming. Sometimes a spiral layout, draining in one direction, only, will accomplish the same purpose better.

An air view of a system of terraces taken 10 years after construction is shown in Fig. 77. Note the old washes that have been stopped by diverting the upper water to outlets along the roads. Also note the crop growing in straight rows running parallel to the west boundary without regard to the terraces. The terraces in the freshly plowed field northwest of the farmstead discharge into timbered pasture land in the northeast

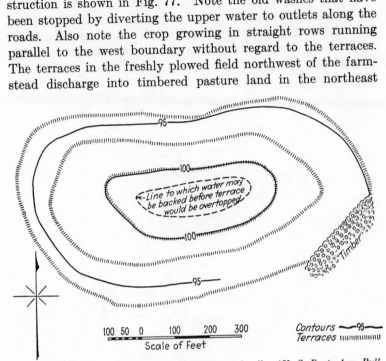

Line to which water may be backed before terrace would be overtopped

Timber

100 50 0   100   200   300
Scale of Feet

Contours ——95——
Terraces ıııııııııııı

FIG. 76.—Example of level terraces encircling a knoll. (*U. S. Dept. Agr. Bull.* 1669.)

corner of the picture. Another air view of what might be termed a more modern system of terraces constructed according to cross section in Fig. 70 is shown in Fig. 78.

SURVEYING PROCEDURE

For staking out the terrace lines some kind of a leveling instrument is necessary. The simplest device is a wooden *A*-frame built in the form of a capital *A* with the cross-bar horizontal when the legs are upright on a level surface and with a leg spread of 10 feet, 1 rod, or any other convenient unit. The fall to be given the terrace line is computed for a distance equal to the leg spread, and a block of wood is cut to this thickness and nailed to the end of one leg, increasing its length by that amount. To use the *A*-frame it is carried to the upper end of the first terrace

Fig. 77.—Air view of a well-planned system of terraces 10 years after construction.

Fig. 78.—Air view of layout with terraces constructed according to cross section shown in Fig. 70.

where the short leg is placed at the point of beginning. Holding the short leg stationary, the long leg is pivoted about it up or down the slope until the crossbar is horizontal as determined by a carpenter's level held or fastened against it. The long leg is now at a point on the terrace line. This point is marked on the ground and the short leg is moved to it, the process being repeated to establish the next point, and so on until the outlet is reached. This procedure is extremely awkward and tedious and requires great care to insure a fair degree of accuracy but may be tried if no better instruments are available.

FARM LEVELS

Turret Type.—Without any doubt the best results are secured in the least time from the use of a standard engineer's level and

FIG. 79.—Turret type of farm level. (*Courtesy Bostrom-Brady Manufacturing Company.*)

Philadelphia rod in the hands of trained surveyors, but it is equally true that satisfactory work can be done in a practical way by the use of an inexpensive farm level and rod. A popular type of farm level, illustrated in Fig. 79, may be had complete with rod for about $25. The rod is normally 5 feet long but can be extended to 9.5 feet, is equipped with a target, and is available with optional graduations in feet, inches, and quarter inches or in feet, tenths, and hundredths. The essential features of the level are a telescope containing a cross-hair reticule and lenses with magnifying power of 8 to 10 diameters, and a level bubble vial, both of which are mounted in a "turret" by means of adjustable upper and lower screws. The turret is perfectly round,[1] is of uniform height, and is held loosely against three flange screws which allow the turret to revolve freely about the faceplate. The faceplate is attached to the base plate or "spider" by a large center screw with compression spring and is movable with respect to the base plate by means of three leveling foot screws. The whole can be attached to a tripod, as shown in the illustration.

Adjustment of Turret Type Level.—The distinguishing characteristic of the turret type of farm level is the same as that of the engineer's wye level; namely, that its adjustments may be tested without the use of a rod and with a single set-up of the instrument. Briefly the procedure is as follows:

Set up the level on its tripod and, by manipulating the leveling screws and the eyepiece focusing sleeve, train the horizontal cross hair on some distant object such as the ridge roof line of a building or a window sill. Next, turn the flange screws a quarter turn or more until the turret can be removed from the faceplate and, after checking the cross-hair position, lift the entire turret with telescope and vial, turn it over, and replace in an inverted position on the faceplate bearings. If the level is in adjustment and the manipulating is carefully done, the horizontal cross hair will occupy the same position with respect to the distant object as it did before. If it does not, repeat the above operation several times and, if consistent results are secured, correct half the error by raising or lowering the object end of the telescope by means of the screws to which it is attached to the turret, alternately loosening one and tightening the other.

When the horizontal cross hair remains trained on the distant object in both direct and inverted positions, tighten the flange screws, and carefully level the instrument by swinging the bubble tube axis over two of the foot screws and turning the screws until the bubble shows level. Then swing over the remaining foot screw, again bring the bubble to the center, and repeat the process over each screw in turn until the level bubble remains in the center of its tube with the telescope in any position. If this is impossible after repeated trials, line up the bubble axis over two of the foot screws, bring it to the exact center of the tube, and swing around 180 degrees, pointing the telescope in the opposite direction. Note the new bubble position and repeat several

---

[1] As nearly so as good workmanship permits.

times to make sure that the bubble behaves consistently. If it does and is not in the center of its tube in the second position, bring it back *halfway* by raising or lowering either end of the tube by means of the two screws holding the tube in the turret. Now center the bubble with the foot screws and repeat the operation until the bubble remains in the center in any position.

Peg Test.—The accuracy of both adjustments may be checked, if desired, by running through the "peg test" as follows:

Set up the level on flat ground and suspend the plumb bob under the center of the instrument. Measure 100 feet on each side of the instrument in a straight line, preferably with a 100-foot steel tape, and drive a stake or "peg" firmly into the ground at both points, each 100 feet from the instrument. Have an assistant hold the rod on top of each stake in turn and slide the target up or down until it is bisected by the horizontal cross hair, while the bubble is in the exact center of its tube. Since both stakes are equidistant from the instrument, the difference in rod readings is the true difference in elevation of the stakes. Suppose, while held on Stake No. 1, the rod reading was 4.72, and on Stake No. 2 it was 3.60. This means that Stake No. 2 is 1.12 feet higher than Stake No. 1.

Now move the instrument to either stake, say No. 1, plant the tripod legs firmly in the ground so that either end of the telescope will come approximately over the stake when level. Level up with the foot screws and swing either end of the telescope in front of the rod held in a vertical position on top of the stake and read the height of the center of the telescope above the stake, using a pencil point against the rod to do this. Suppose it reads 5.10 feet. If the level is in perfect adjustment the reading on Stake No. 2 will be 3.98. If, instead, it is 4.00 or 3.96, the adjustment is sufficiently accurate for satisfactory work.

Dumpy Type Level.—Other farm levels, comparable to the engineer's dumpy level, are available at approximately the same price as the turret type and are equally satisfactory. As shown in the illustration, Fig. 80, the chief difference lies in the method of mounting the telescope and bubble tube on the faceplate and in the provision of four leveling foot screws instead of three. In leveling up the instrument the telescope is swung successively over each pair of foot screws, which must be turned simultaneously in opposite directions to move the bubble and maintain a firm bearing on the base plate. The trick of doing this is easy to acquire with a little practice.

Since neither the telescope nor the bubble tube is removable from its mounting or from the faceplate, the adjustment tests for cross hair and bubble must be made in reverse order. The bubble is adjusted *first* on the same principle as that just described, by lining the telescope over one pair of foot screws, swinging 180 degrees over the same pair (after having leveled as

Fig. 80.—Dumpy type of farm level. (*Courtesy Keuffel and Esser Company.*)

closely as possible over both pairs), and making the same corrections, if necessary, in the same manner as before. When the bubble is in adjustment, the instrument is made to read correctly in the peg test by moving the object end of the telescope, and hence the horizontal cross hair, up or down the full amount of the error. This is accomplished by manipulating the upper and lower set screws in the telescope mounting with a screw driver, loosening one and tightening the other until the desired correction is attained.

Utility of Farm Level.—Both the turret or wye type and the dumpy type of farm levels bear 360 single degree graduations on the faceplate for turning off angles and can be equipped with stadia wires for reading distances, at a small extra charge.

The farm jobs, aside from laying out terraces, that can be accomplished by the use of a level, rod, and 100-foot steel tape include: leveling the foundation and laying off right angles for a building; setting a septic tank at proper depth relative to basement; running grades for tile lines, small ditches, and sanitary sewers; determining possibilities of drainage outlets; running strip farming contours; and lining up and turning off angles for fences.

Use of Level.—Inasmuch as each farm level is shipped with a set of instructions on its care, adjustment, and use, prepared by the manufacturer, and the entire subject of leveling is covered in numerous textbooks on surveying, only such comment will be given here as seems helpful in applying its use to terracing and other farm jobs.

Before attempting to use the level the surveyor should read all instructions and examine the instrument thoroughly, noting its construction and particularly the provision made for adjusting the telescope tube and bubble vial. Adjusting screws should not be tampered with, however, until the user is thoroughly convinced, after repeated trials, that the instrument is, in fact, out of adjustment and is not merely made to appear so by careless manipulation. Although the telescope lens has a magnifying power of about 8 diameters, it is not advisable to take readings with the rod much farther than 250 feet from the instrument.

After reading the manufacturer's instructions and learning how to set up the instrument so that the bubble remains in the center of the vial with the telescope in any position, a practice circuit should be run to determine the degree of accuracy that can be attained. In doing this the level is set up about 100 or 200 feet from some point of fixed elevation, such as the corner of a building foundation or simply the top of a stake driven in the ground. The rod is held on this point called a "bench mark" (*B. M.*), in surveyor's parlance, by a helper; and with the instrument level and focused on the rod by pulling the eyepiece in or out, the helper slides the target up or down until its horizontal diameter coincides with the horizontal cross hair of the instrument. The target is then clamped and its position in feet, tenths and hundredths (or in feet and inches) is read and recorded as the vertical distance of the line of sight (height of instrument) above the initial point or bench mark. The rodman then proceeds to a point about the same horizontal distance from the instrument on the opposite side from the bench mark, drives a stake, holds the rod on the stake and goes through the same procedure as before to determine the new target position. The instrument is then moved beyond this "turning point" (*T. P.*), set up, leveled, focused on the rod; and the whole process, which might be described as playing leap frog, is repeated as many times as may be necessary to complete the circuit chosen and return to the point of beginning or bench mark. The difference between the original elevation as assumed for the bench mark and the elevation as determined from the final rod reading is the error of the circuit, and this should not be more than one-tenth foot for 8 or 9 setups of the instrument. A convenient form of notes to keep track of the rod readings and elevations is shown in Table 21, which, mathematically, is nothing more than simple addition and subtraction.

TABLE 21.—SAMPLE FORM OF NOTES FOR LEVELING

Station	Back sight rod reading (plus)	Height of instrument	Front sight rod reading (minus)	Elevation
B. M.	3.56	103.56		100.00 (assumed)
T. P. 1	5.01	104.29	4.28	99.28
T. P. 2	1.62	100.11	5.80	98.49
T. P. 3	3.36	98.74	4.73	95.38
T. P. 4	4.28	98.57	4.45	94.29
T. P. 5	3.97	100.25	2.29	96.28
T. P. 6	4.21	104.98	0.52	100.77
B. M.			4.90	100.08
Error = 0.08 ft.				

While only one front sight (minus sight) is given for each setup, the rod could have been held on any number of points within range of the instrument and their elevations secured by merely subtracting the rod readings from the appropriate "height of instrument" (*H. I.*). For each setup there is only one back sight but there may be any number of front sights.

Application to Terrace Layout.—Figure 81 illustrates the use of the level and rod in determining the prevailing slope of a field preparatory to selecting the proper spacing for the terraces. If the slope is quite steep the downhill sight for a distance of 100 feet may be clear over the top of the rod, in which case a reading may be taken at 50 feet and the difference multiplied by two.

With the terrace spacing decided upon, the location of the first terrace below the top of the hill can then be determined as shown in Fig. 82 or by measuring or pacing down the slope the

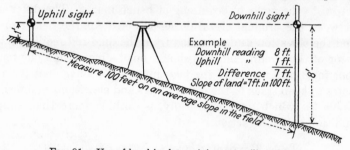

Example
Downhill reading   8 ft.
Uphill   "   1 ft.
Difference   7 ft.
Slope of land = 7ft. in 100 ft.

FIG. 81.—Use of level in determining prevailing slope.

distance equivalent to the vertical drop. So far as practicable, it is desirable to begin at the outlet to stake out the terrace line, the procedure for which is as follows:

Assuming the downhill rod in Fig. 82 to be at the outlet of the first terrace and that the grade for the lowest 300 feet is to be 4 inches per 100 feet, or 0.33 per cent, the rodman lowers the target 2 inches, or 0.165 feet, and proceeds 50 feet by measuring or pacing in the general direction of the terrace line and holds the rod for a trial reading. The instrumentman focuses on the

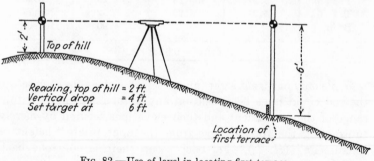

Reading, top of hill = 2 ft.
Vertical drop   = 4 ft.
Set target at   6 ft.

Location of
first terrace

FIG. 82.—Use of level in locating first terrace.

target, checks the level bubble, and signals the rodman to move up or down the hill until the horizontal cross hair bisects the target. The bottom of the rod at this point is on grade, and its position is marked by a stake. *Caution:* For all readings the rod should be held on "average ground," neither in a local low spot, nor on top of a row or clod; this is especially applicable when locating on plowed ground or after harvesting a crop grown in rows.

Having driven a stake on grade at the first 50-foot point, the rodman then lowers the target another 2 inches, or 0.165 feet, proceeds another 50 feet, and goes through the same process as before to locate the grade at this point, driving a stake to mark it. This procedure is repeated until the point is reached where the grade is to be reduced, after which the target setting is adjusted to the new grade and the work continued. When the rodman reaches a point about 250 feet from the instrument, he

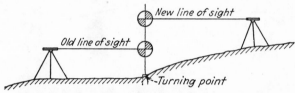

New line of sight

Old line of sight

Turning point

Fig. 83.—Illustrating change of position and determination of new height of instrument from turning point.

should drive a stake nearly flush with the ground and use it as a turning point for a new instrument position, as already explained and as illustrated in Fig. 83.

It is obvious that, in order to determine a trial grade line and the points where it should change, it is necessary to estimate the terrace length before knowing its exact position. This can be done on fairly uniform slopes closely enough for practical purposes, but, while staking out any terrace, one should be constantly on the lookout for opportunities to improve the location by altering the grade or by making slight shifts in the entire line. It sometimes happens that the upper portions of the line fit the ground so badly as to necessitate abandonment and a complete rerun on a new grade.

Unless the change in direction of the line being staked is gradual enough to permit accurate tracing with a plow or other implement, intermediate stakes should be set at 25-foot points or closer. This is most frequently necessary at gully crossings where the stakes should be set uphill a slight amount off grade, if this does not make the terrace too crooked, in order to provide extra earth for the embankment when cutting the channel to grade. It must be admitted, however, that this practice is seldom feasible, due to the sharp bend created in the terrace. Good practice in such cases is illustrated by a sketch in the following chapter (Fig. 85).

When the first terrace has been satisfactorily located, it is customary to return to the outlet, spot the second terrace, as indicated in Fig. 84, and proceed as before with the staking out. This is continued until all the terraces in the field have been located and marked out on the ground ready for construction.

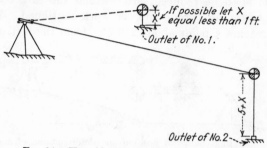

Fig. 84.—Use of level in locating second terrace.

It is convenient but not necessary to mark the station numbers on the stakes of each terrace indicating distance from the outlet. Thus, the outlet stake would be marked 0 + 00, and then in successive order, 0 + 50, 1 + 00, 1 + 50, 2 + 00, etc., each "station" or whole number representing 100 feet and the "pluses" fractional distances less than 100 feet. When some time will elapse before the terraces are constructed, it is very desirable to follow this practice, marking the terrace number or letter on each stake in addition to the station number.

CHAPTER VII

TERRACE CONSTRUCTION METHODS AND MACHINERY

Terraces have been built with a great variety of implement and power combinations ranging from a simple two-horse plow and homemade drag to pretentious elevating graders pulled by 50- to 75-horsepower tractors. For most conditions the first is too slow and tedious and wasteful of labor, and the second involves too great an overhead charge on the high initial investment considering the number of days per year the outfit can probably be kept busy. Extremely heavy grading equipment disturbs the soil over a wide area, builds terraces unnecessarily large, is awkward to turn at terrace ends, is difficult to negotiate over farm roads and bridges and through gates, and seems generally out of place amid ordinary farm surroundings. Conditions on large ranches bordering the Great Plains area of the Southwest may be an exception.

The combination ordinarily best suited for a particular situation will be determined very largely by the law of diminishing returns, which fixes the point where an increase in investment results in decreased returns per dollar. All cost factors must of course be taken into account when making comparisons, remembering, however, that the value of farm labor (and to a less extent farm power) varies somewhat with the seasons and with the demands of regular farming operations.

When to Terrace.—As a rule, the best time to build terraces is in late summer and early fall after crops have been harvested, although a shorter period is available in the spring between the time that frost leaves the ground and the latest date for planting. The speed with which terraces can be completed in such cases is an important factor. In the South, where frost is seldom encountered, terracing may be undertaken at any time that the land is free from crops and the soil is in tillable condition. When community equipment is available, it sometimes happens that farmers are willing to sacrifice a part of their growing crops rather than lose their turn at its use. If the soil is greatly impoverished prior to terracing, as it frequently is, loss of crops becomes of minor consequence.

CONSTRUCTION METHODS

After the terrace lines have been located by means of stakes or markers at normal intervals of 50 feet, it becomes necessary to trace out each line between the stakes, around peninsular points, and across gullies. This can best be done by having someone of experience and with a "trained eye" walk slowly ahead of the plow or other marking implement and indicate the direction of the line between stakes so as to smooth out minor

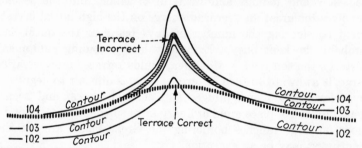

Fig. 85.—Sketch indicating practicable crossing of gullies in wide depressions.

irregularities and maintain the intended grade throughout. The driver of the power unit follows close behind and lays his course on the "pilot," being especially careful to swing wide in going around points and, if practicable, in crossing gullies. Should the gully center line lie in a depression of appreciable width, a mathematically correct grade forms an apex too sharp and narrow for construction machinery to follow, in which case the only practicable procedure is indicated in Fig. 85. Extra work will be required to build the embankment up to grade at such locations, and a temporary water pocket will appear in the terrace channel.

Making Pilot Cut.—The method of marking out terrace lines with a tractor and light two-wheeled grader is shown in Fig. 86. There is no reason why a deeper pilot cut could not be made at the same time in ordinary soil. Terracing practice differs as to the location of the pilot cut with respect to the staked line as well as to whether the first cut should be cast uphill or downhill.

These variations are caused by different conceptions of the proper position of the stakes in relation to the finished terrace, some specialists maintaining that they should be under the embankment center line, others that they should be in the terrace channel, while still others insist that unavoidable irregularities should be equalized between embankment and channel by having the stake line come at the point of transition from channel

Fig. 86.—Marking out terrace alignment with tractor and light two-wheel grader. Note the walking "pilot" out in front.

cut to embankment fill. Inasmuch as a certain amount of extra work in shaving high places in the channel and filling sags in the embankment is almost inevitable, the author can see no material advantage in either plan so long as the practice in any one field is consistently the same.

Direction Earth Should Be Moved.—Another point concerning which opinion differs is whether the embankment should be thrown up by moving earth from both sides or from the upper side only. Here again, on moderate slopes at least, there does not seem to be any great advantage one way or the other, provided no appreciable channel is left parallel to the downhill toe of the embankment. A great deal depends on the type of equipment used and its ease of reversibility. Since on steep slopes it becomes increasingly difficult and theoretically uneconomical to move earth uphill, it would seem that, if a fixed standard is to be set, the practice of building entirely from the uphill side and moving all earth downhill has the greater merit notwithstanding the greater distance of moving. Even so, with blade equipment, one passage at least to smooth the downhill face of the bank would seem desirable unless it is preferred to use a harrow to accomplish the same result.

In the experimental work at the federal erosion station near Bethany, Mo., it has been found advantageous, when using a small blade grader with wheel-type tractor, to move the earth about as follows:

Prevailing land slope, per cent	From upper side, per cent	From lower side, per cent
6 or less..............	60	40
6 to 10..............	75	25
Over 10..............	90	10

In deciding this question, consideration should also be given to the amount of topsoil disturbed and its distribution in the embankment, having in mind availability for crop use. Subsoil exposed in the terrace channel has its fertility quickly restored by slight inter-terrace erosion and by a few trips with a manure spreader, but this is not true at the downhill toe of the bank. Concentration of topsoil in the embankment results in growth markedly more luxuriant than in other parts of the field.

Preliminary Preparation.—If the field to be terraced is free from gullies and ineffective terraces of an obsolete type, and there are no subdividing fences to be moved, and erosion-proof natural outlets are available, it may be that no preliminary work will be required ahead of construction, or that it will be limited to removing coarse stubble that might interfere with inexpensive equipment. In many cases, however, gullies too deep and wide to cross will have to be filled by the use of a wing plow, slip scraper, regular terracing equipment, or by special equipment such as that shown in Fig. 87, before proceeding with construction of the terraces. Also if old ridge types of terraces exist in improper locations, they must be leveled as additional work of preparation. Figure 88 illustrates this work under way with

FIG. 87.—Large tractor equipped with "bull-dozer," filling gullies preparatory to terracing. (*Courtesy Cleveland Tractor Company.*)

FIG. 88.—Tractor and grader leveling old ridge type terraces in ineffective locations in preparation for the construction of modern terraces. (*Courtesy The Austin-Western Road Machinery Company.*)

the tractor and grader that is to be used later to build the modern terraces.

Construction Details.—There are almost as many ideas regarding precisely the best procedure in building terraces as there are people engaged in this work. While the controlling factors are: type and condition of soil and soil cover, prevailing land slope, and equipment used, there is ample opportunity for

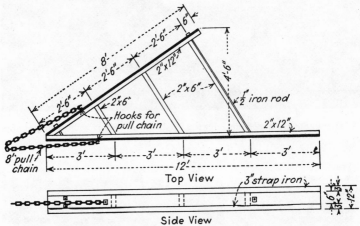

Fig. 89.—Homemade wooden V-drag for use in building terraces.

Bill of Materials

1—2″ × 12″ × 12′ − 0″ 2—½″ × 5″ bolts
1—2″ × 12″ × 8′ − 0″   4—⅜″ × 2½″ bolts
1—2″ × 6″ × 14′ − 0″   2 hooks
1—½″φ iron rod—5′ − 2″ 2 pieces 3″ strap iron 8′ − 0″ long
  (head at one end thread 2 pieces 3″ strap iron 12′ − 0″ long
  and nut at other)
(*From Ayres and Scoates, "Land Drainage and Reclamation."*)

considerable variation within these limits to accord with individual preferences. Inexperienced operators will soon form their own preferences after making a few trial runs with the most efficient equipment available.

It is possible to build terraces by making many trips with a common walking plow with or without a special moldboard attachment, by continually backfurrowing to the terrace bank. A slip scraper to pile the loosened earth into the embankment speeds up the process considerably and is popular in a few localities. If the cash outlay for purchase or rental of equipment must be kept to an absolute minimum, fairly efficient work can be done with a homemade V-drag built of wood according to the drawing shown in Fig. 89, or a reversible steel V-drag or ditcher can be bought at moderate cost. The dimensions of the drag can be varied to suit the number of horses or mules used and the kind of soil encountered, in accordance with Table 22.

TABLE 22.[1]—DIMENSIONS FOR HOMEMADE V-DRAG

	Number of horses or mules				
	2	3	4	6	8
Length of short wing, feet.	4½	5	6½	7	8
Length of long wing, feet..	8	9	11½	12½	14
Size of material for wings, inches................	2 by 8	2 by 10	2 by 12	2 by 12	2 by 12
Spread between wings for black land (33°)........	2½′	3′	3½′	4′	4′ 4″
Spread between wings for sandy land three-fifths of length of short wing (37°).................	2½′	3′	3′ 11″	4′ 6″	4′ 10″

[1] *A. & M. Coll. of Tex. Ext. Bull.* B 51.

Figure 90 shows the construction procedure in building terraces in Alabama with horse-drawn equipment. This method was devised by M. L. Nichols and has been used extensively with much success. Each step in the process is clearly shown by the drawing and accompanying notes.

One method of building terraces with a blade grader working from the upper side only is illustrated in Fig. 91. This method is featured by making the first cut so as to place the completed embankment over the line and grade stakes, and by the assumption that the field will be plowed and cultivated so as to leave a dead furrow in the terrace channel and gradually increase its capacity.

Figures 92 and 93 illustrate conventional methods of using blade graders where it is desired to make the first cut so that the stake line falls in the completed channel. The terrace in Fig. 92 is built from both sides and the one in Fig. 93 from the upper side only.

The angle the blade makes with the line of travel is adjustable on all graders and should be as flat as possible and still insure scouring of the soil against the blade.   Sharper angles are usually

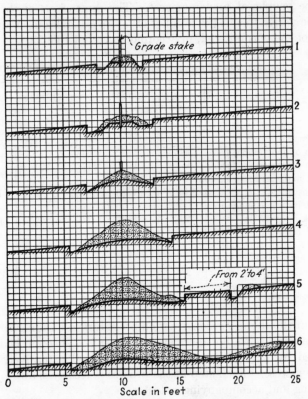

FIG. 90.—Constructing terrace from both sides with horse-drawn plow and V-drag.   Throw the first furrow up the hill on the stakes.   Four furrows should be thrown to the stakes before the drag is started.   Narrow plow cuts should be made and followed with the drag to insure a height of 18 to 20 inches before widening the terrace.   The plowing and dragging should be repeated until a width of 8 to 10 feet is obtained.   The next step in construction is the laying out a balk 2 to 4 feet wide on the upper side of the terrace.   In plowing out this balk above the terrace ridge, deep narrow plow cuts should be made on the upper side of the balk.   Plowing and dragging on both sides of the balk should continue until the entire balk is plowed and dragged out.   (*Alabama Extension Circular* 148.)

required for clay than for sandy loam, and for cut trips in any soil as compared with carry-over trips.

All graders are also provided with means of adjusting the depth of either end of the blade, and the depth of the cutting edge should be kept regulated so as to utilize the full capacity of the grader and power unit at all times. There should, of course, be a close relation between the sturdiness and weight of the grader and the capacity of the power unit with which it is used.

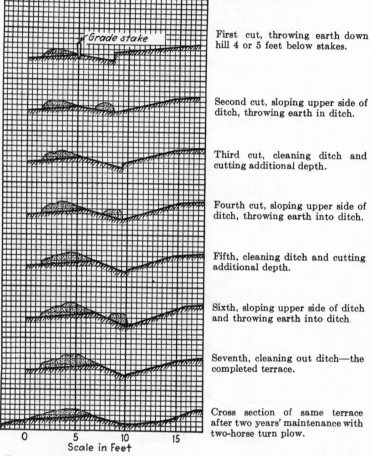

First cut, throwing earth down hill 4 or 5 feet below stakes.

Second cut, sloping upper side of ditch, throwing earth in ditch.

Third cut, cleaning ditch and cutting additional depth.

Fourth cut, sloping upper side of ditch, throwing earth into ditch.

Fifth, cleaning ditch and cutting additional depth.

Sixth, sloping upper side of ditch and throwing earth into ditch.

Seventh, cleaning out ditch—the completed terrace.

Cross section of same terrace after two years' maintenance with two-horse turn plow.

Fig. 91.—Constructing terrace from upper side only with blade grader. Note that grade stake is under embankment and channel is completed during maintenance.

A diagrammatic representation of the technique of building terraces with a Whirlwind rotary terracer is shown in Fig. 94. This machine, which embodies an entirely new principle of moving earth, is of very recent development but already has been used in such varied states as Iowa, Kansas, Missouri, Illinois, Mississippi, Georgia, the Carolinas, and Oklahoma. It will be described later.

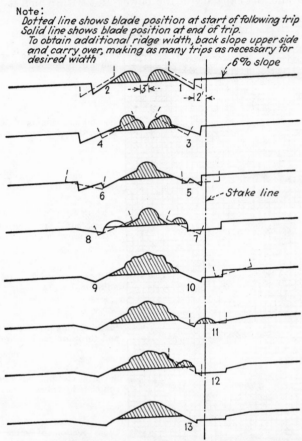

Note:
Dotted line shows blade position at start of following trip
Solid line shows blade position at end of trip.
To obtain additional ridge width, back slope upper side
and carry over, making as many trips as necessary for
desired width

FIG. 92.—Method of constructing terraces with 10-foot blade grader working from both sides. Land slope 6 per cent.

CONSTRUCTION EQUIPMENT

Aside from common farm implements and special homemade devices a great variety of equipment has been commercially developed to meet the terracing demands of various situations. Especially marked has been the activity in this field under the impetus of various federal emergency conservation programs, most of the effort until recently being directed toward the adaptation of machinery originally designed for use on highways,

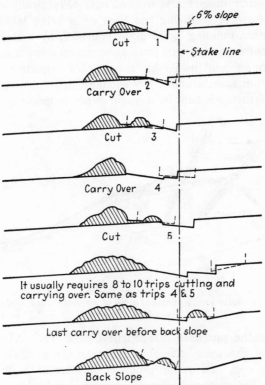

FIG. 93.—Method of constructing terraces with 10-foot blade grader working from upper side only. Land slope 6 per cent.

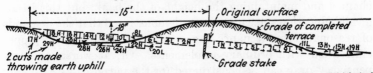

FIG. 94.—Diagram illustrating technique of building terraces with a Whirlwind rotary terracer. Numerals represent trips one way and the order in which furrows are made. Letters indicate rotor speed: *N*, neutral; *L*, low gear; *H*, high gear. No work is done on trips 21, 23, 25, and 27, which are made to get into position at a speed of 10 miles per hour, or maximum for the tractor used. Note that line level with top of bank extends uphill, well above disturbed ground.

principally blade graders. Inasmuch as terrace building is a specialized job of limited extent so far as any one farm is concerned, the cost of the most efficient equipment of this type ($4000 for tractor and grader) is prohibitive unless some means of community financing is worked out. Practically every conceivable form of financing has been or is being tried, whether it be custom building by straight contract, by rental from the manufacturer or dealer or from governmental units such as the county; or by joint ownership through the organization of local conservation associations. Occasionally title to enough land in need of terracing is held by a single owner or mortgage company

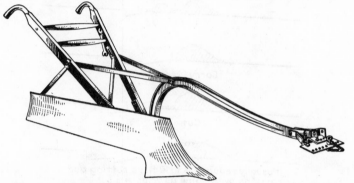

Fig. 95.—A popular and economical type of terracing plow. (*Courtesy G. A. Kelly Plow Company.*)

to justify the purchase of efficient machinery. Whatever the method of financing, the object is to make available the low operating cost and rapid progress of efficient equipment by spreading the overhead over a large number of jobs.

Terrace building by such methods has the disadvantage of leaving the farmer without means of cleaning out the terrace channel and maintaining the height of the bank, but this is not a valid objection since it has been demonstrated that the demands of reasonable maintenance can be met satisfactorily by proper cultivation with ordinary implements. Or, at worst, an inexpensive V-drag can be constructed for the purpose.

The following illustrations are arranged to give a good idea of the implement and power combinations that have been and are being used for terrace building.

Terracing Plows.—A popular type of plow that can be equipped for terrace building by attaching a special moldboard is illustrated in Fig. 95. The fact that this plow can be used for ordinary farm purposes when not needed for terracing, by a simple exchange of moldboards, makes it a very economical implement.

Fig. 96.—Terrace under construction with four horses and reversible steel V-drag.

Steel V-drags.—Figure 96 illustrates a terrace being built entirely from the upper side with four horses and a reversible steel V-drag (Martin ditcher). In soil of ordinary tilth advance plowing is not necessary with this implement, the wing angle of which is adjustable to suit variations in soil.

Fig. 97.—Terrace building with steel V-drag (Martin ditcher) and tractor. Note detachable arm to extend point of delivery to top of terrace bank.

Figure 97 depicts the same implement equipped with a detachable 2 by 6 extension arm being used with tractor power. The cost of this implement is less than $100.

Light Terracing Graders.—Two types of small graders especially designed for building terraces and which have been used

FIG. 98.—"Texas" terracer designed for use with either horse or tractor power.

extensively are shown in Figs. 98 and 99.   They may be used with either horse or tractor power.

Very recently another type of small grader has been put on the market.   It is illustrated in Fig. 100 where the construction

FIG. 99.—Corsicana terracer or ditcher.   (*Courtesy Corsicana Ditcher and Grader Company.*)

features are clearly shown.   This machine is made in two sizes: No. 1 with 6-foot blade and weight of 775 pounds; and No. 2

with 8-foot blade and weight of 825 pounds. In designing this terracer it was the aim of the manufacturers to produce a machine of sufficient strength to utilize all the power of farm tractors, whether crawler or wheel type, and also to keep the price within reach of individual buyers (about $160).

On all three implements the front wheel is intended to insure better control of the blade and make the cutting end less sensitive to surface irregularities than it would be if hitched directly to a

FIG. 100.—New type of light terracing grader. Note the platform upon which the operator stands. (*Courtesy The American Steel Scraper Company.*)

tractor, as is the case with the two-wheel graders to be described later. When so hitched it is difficult to manipulate the blade so as to cut lightly in depressions and deeply through ridges, which is desirable. What seems to be needed is a system of compensating levers to automatically raise the blade when the rear of the tractor is low and lower it when the tractor is high. So far as the author is aware no such device has ever been tried.

The use of a Corsicana terracer with animal power is illustrated in Fig. 101, and Fig. 102 shows a Texas terracer being pulled with a farm tractor. Incidentally, the terraces in Fig. 102 were laid out and constructed by local men with no previous experience after studying literature on the subject. The terraces functioned as intended and were inspected some time later by an extension engineer and found to be in good condition. This procedure must be considered exceptional, however, and is not to be recommended for general adoption.

Four-wheel Graders.—It often happens that four-wheel graders can be rented from county authorities during times

FIG. 101.—Use of Corsicana terracer with animal power.

when they are not needed for road work; and where land slopes are not too steep or irregular, good work can be expected. Figures 103 and 104 represent terraces under construction with

FIG. 102.—Use of Texas terracer with tractor power.

two four-wheel graders widely different in style, weight, and power requirements.

Special Terracing Graders.—The accelerated demand for terracing incident to various emergency conservation programs

Fig. 103.—Terrace constructed from upper side with light, four-wheel road grader and farm tractor.

Fig. 104.—Terrace under construction with "regular" road grader and 35-horsepower tractor. (*Courtesy The Austin-Western Road Machinery Company.*)

beginning in 1933 has been sufficient to attract the interest of machinery manufacturers who have developed efficient power machinery especially adapted for terrace building. A practical and efficient combination is a two-wheel, 4500-pound, 10-foot blade grader pulled by a 35- to 40-horsepower Diesel tractor. If the first cost, approximating $4000, can be raised, this outfit can build terraces at surprisingly low operating cost, the fuel consumption being only 1½ to 2 gallons of low-priced (6 cents per gallon) Diesel fuel per hour.

Fig. 105.—Two-wheel, 1400-pound, 8-foot blade grader with 22-horsepower tractor working in dry, hard yellow clay. (*Courtesy Caterpillar Tractor Company.*)

Figure 105 illustrates a less expensive combination consisting of a 22-horsepower tractor and two-wheel, 1400-pound, 8-foot blade grader. In the illustration the grader is apparently too light for the dry, hard, yellow clay in which it is working, as evidenced by the tendency to slip sidewise.

Figure 106 depicts a 40-horsepower Diesel tractor pulling a two-wheel, 4500-pound, 10-foot blade grader made by the same manufacturer which seems to be of a power and weight better suited to the job. The operators in this case are boys from a CCC camp in Illinois.

Figure 107 is an outfit of approximately the same weight and power building a terrace in sandy loam soil of the South. This soil is in ideal condition to be moved with a blade grader.

Fig. 106.—Two-wheel, 4500-pound, 10-foot blade grader with 40 horsepower Diesel tractor building terraces in Illinois. (*Courtesy Caterpillar Tractor Company.*)

Fig. 107.—Building a terrace from the upper side in sandy loam soil with a two-wheel, 4500-lb., 10-foot blade grader and 35–40-horsepower tractor. (*Courtesy Austin-Western Road Machinery Company.*)

Such equipment as that illustrated in Figs. 105, 106, and 107 has been designed especially for easy manipulation and mobility in building terraces under ordinary farm conditions.   The blade is easily reversible, and quick turns can be made in a limited space at the terrace ends.   Figures 106 and 107 illustrate types of equipment that are undoubtedly economical and practicable terracing outfits, subject only to limitations inherent in the blade method of moving earth and to the fact that special tractors are required that are not adapted to the needs of routine farm jobs.

Fig. 108.—Large elevating grader and 50-horsepower tractor building terrace core in Kansas.   (*Courtesy Caterpillar Tractor Company.*)

Heavy Elevating Graders.—On large farms of the Southwest with regular slopes of moderate declivity, the heavy equipment shown in Fig. 108 has been used with considerable economy and success.   Elevating graders of this class are operated with a separate power unit mounted on the grader and are equipped with a short carrier especially designed for terracing.   The best work is done with a 75-horsepower tractor to provide power for pulling and plowing.   After three to five round trips with the elevating grader the terrace is finished in two or more rounds with a 12-foot blade grader and 50-horsepower tractor.   This kind of construction has the advantage of placing a minimum amount of topsoil in the terrace core, and where a large amount of terracing is to be done under the special conditions mentioned the unit cost can be kept very low. The technique of using equipment of this kind is illustrated in Fig. 109. This is not included in the discussion of ordinary terrace-building technique because of its special nature.

After the main fill of 0.50 to 0.75 cubic yard per lineal foot of terrace has been completed with the elevating grader and the

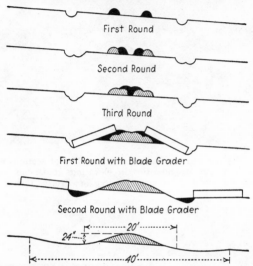

First Round

Second Round

Third Round

First Round with Blade Grader

Second Round with Blade Grader

Fig. 109.—Technique of building terraces. This drawing outlines the procedure used in building 40-foot terraces with a 50- or 75-horsepower Diesel tractor pulling the elevating grader, followed by a 50-horsepower Diesel tractor pulling a 12-foot blade. On a 156-mile check run at Mankato, Kansas, the total cost, including all items, for building the core and blading in the balance of the terrace with this Diesel power was only $16.04 per mile. The cost of these two operations, exclusive of fresno work and transportation, was only $.87 per acre, which is a real record for building terraces of this type.

12-foot blade grader has back-sloped the furrows and distributed topsoil over the terrace, it is customary to smooth out irregularities and prepare for seeding by the use of a 50-horsepower tractor pulling three heavy disk harrows. One round with this outfit of 30 feet of disks, which is illustrated in Fig. 110, is said to leave the field so no water will collect in low spots.

Where conditions are suitable for this class of equipment it may be remarked in passing that a modification of the familiar template or bucket excavator might very possibly complete a terrace in one trip with the greatest economy of all.

Light Elevating Grader.—The small elevating grader shown in Fig. 111 was designed by J. C. Wooley of Missouri especially

FIG. 110.—Fifty-horsepower tractor and three 10-foot sections of heavy disk harrows smoothing out irregularities in elevating grader-built terraces and preparing them for seeding. (*Courtesy Caterpillar Tractor Company.*)

FIG. 111.—Light elevating grader building terraces with general-purpose farm tractor. (*Courtesy Cleveland Tractor Company.*)

for terracing and allied work. As can be seen from the photograph it is equipped with a 26-inch disk plow to deliver the earth to a belt conveyor that is operated from the power take-off of the tractor. It is intended for use with general-purpose farm tractors and is popular in some localities. The usual construction technique consists in plowing along the line of stakes and moving the earth downhill, the return cut being made just below the soil deposited from the first cut. The two rows of soil thus deposited outline the lower and upper edges of the terrace embankment and the cuts in additional rounds are so made as to fill in the interspace two furrows deep. By skillful manipulation, including variable depths of end cuts, a uniformly shaped terrace results; but a channel of appreciable size is inevitable on the downhill side. Ten to twelve rounds or more are required for an embankment 20 feet wide and 18 inches high when soil conditions are just right. It is to be noted that the machine is designed for one-man operation, the entire mechanism being under control of the tractor driver.

Advantages claimed for this type of terracer are: (1) it will work in any soil in which a disk plow will operate, (2) it has the light draft and the rolling, slicing action found in a disk plow, and (3) it has greater capacity with less power (compared with blade graders) as it moves the earth horizontally on a free rolling belt. Another advantage lies in its ability to form an embankment approximating a uniform height when crossing low spots by reason of delayed delivery of a given plow cut occasioned by the time required for the earth to travel up the belt. This same feature, however, entails more finishing work at the terrace extremities. The cost of the elevator grader-terracer is about $950 in Kansas City, Mo.

Multiple-disk Plow.—As shown by the illustrations in Figs. 112 and 113, it is possible to construct terraces by the use of a multiple-disk plow and general-purpose farm tractor. However, so far as the author is aware, this implement has not, as yet, come into extensive use for building terraces. Terraces so constructed would have the advantage of being ready for seeding without additional preparation. The artist's sketch represented by Fig. 112 is included for its value in clearly showing the dimensions and proportions of a typical terrace and the relation of a terrace system to the general landscape.

Whirlwind Rotary Terracer.—One of the promising machines being developed for building terraces is the invention of E. V. Collins of Iowa, the idea for which came to him while experiment-

ing with a machine for killing white grubs.   This light and simple
but effective machine is shown by Fig. 114 to consist essentially

Fig. 112.—Artist's sketch showing terraces under construction with a multiple-disk plow and the relation of a terrace system to the general landscape.   (*Courtesy J. I. Case Company.*)

Fig. 113.—Photograph of a multiple-disk plow building a terrace.   (*Courtesy J. I. Case Company.*)

of an 18-inch plow with modified moldboard to deliver the earth
to a 14-inch spiral-bladed rotor, a transmission gear-box con-

trolling the rotor speed, power take-off connections to the tractor, and a sturdy frame supported on two pneumatic-tired wheels.

FIG. 114.—Side view of Whirlwind rotary terracer. (*Courtesy The Parsons Company.*)

FIG. 115.—Whirlwind rotary terracer in action. (*Courtesy The Parsons Company.*)

Figure 115 shows the earth being thrown or "sprayed" in a sidewise direction, the length and density of the fan being regulated by the pitch of the blades and the speed of the rotor.

The machine is characterized by extreme mobility and operates on the principle of placing a relatively small quantity of earth during each trip, making up in speed, both of transit and in turning at the ends, what it lacks in unit capacity. The operating technique in forming terraces has already been pointed out in Fig. 94. The finished terrace cross section shown in Fig. 70 was built with this machine as well as those shown in the air view of Fig. 78.

Fig. 116.—System of newly constructed terraces after a light rain showing amount of ponding to expect before clean-up work is complete.

Like the steel V-drags, light graders, and other equipment described, the rotary terracer can be used with an ordinary farm tractor and its cost (about $450) is not beyond the purchasing power of a neighborhood group of farmers. The author was privileged to direct a three months "proving ground" test of this machine in 1934, during which time 64 miles of terraces were built on 54 farms scattered over 18 counties in Iowa by a single terracer. Should experience prove the need, the machine could be made reversible by the use of a duplicate rotor and special reversible plowshare.

COMPLETION AND CHECKING OF TERRACE GRADES

Aside from the construction of terrace outlets where none exist naturally, which will be treated in Chap. IX, there is usually a considerable amount of unavoidable clean-up work in bringing the embankments to grade at gully crossings and other low areas, dressing up the terrace at its outlet junction, and smoothing out appreciable irregularities.   While it is seldom practicable

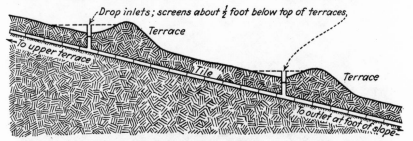

FIG. 117.—Method of removing water standing above terraces in a gully or draw. Also used as outlet for level terraces.

or necessary to dress the channel to its exact theoretical grade, it is desirable to run a line of check levels before the construction equipment leaves the field so that back cuts can be made where necessary to bring about reasonable drainage.   Figure 116 shows a system of newly constructed terraces after a light rain, which

FIG. 118.—Building up a low place in a terrace embankment with a team of mules, one man, and a slip scraper.

is quite typical of the amount of ponding to expect before the clean-up work is finished.

If the depth of the ponds formed at gully crossings is excessive or if the ponds are otherwise objectionable, they can be drained under the terraces through a line of tile laid down the slope, as indicated in Fig. 117.

A conventional method of building up low places in the bank with a team of mules or horses, one man, and a slip scraper is

Fig. 119.—Filling low spot in terrace embankment with tractor and Fresno rotary scraper.

shown in Fig. 118; and Fig. 119 shows the same kind of work under way with power equipment.

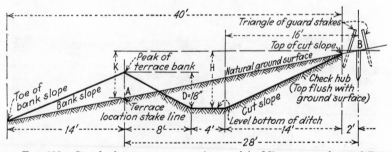

Fig. 120.—Standard terrace cross section used in Minnesota and especially adapted for quick and accurate checking. (*Special Bulletin* 171, *Agricultural Extension Division, University of Minnesota.*)

A rather elaborate system of checking the grade of a completed terrace has been proposed by H. B. Roe of Minnesota and is reproduced here to serve as a guide for whatever degree of precision may seem justified in any particular case.

TABLE 23.—DATA FOR USE IN CHECKING CONSTRUCTION OF TERRACES

Natural slope across terrace line, feet per 100 ft.	Vertical distance K between A and B in figure, feet	Vertical distance H, from bottom of ditch to B in figure, feet
2	0.56	1.07
3	0.84	1.29
4	1.12	1.51
5	1.40	1.73
6	1.68	1.95
8	2.24	2.39
10	2.80	2.83
12	3.36	3.27
14	3.92	3.71

With constant reference to Fig. 120 and Table 23 procedure in staking and checking should be as follows:

Locate the terrace lines as already outlined, bearing in mind that linear measurement by pacing along the terrace is sufficiently accurate, but that care in leveling is necessary, and that stakes must be set at frequent intervals on sharp curves.

As each line stake is set (Position A in figure) drive a hub stake with firm, square-sawed top solidly into and flush with the surface of the ground, 28 feet up hill from the line stake at right angles to the terrace line. (Position B in figure). This hub stake should be protected from disturbance during construction by a tripod of stakes driven around it as shown in the figure.

Take a level reading on the top of this hub stake. The difference between this reading and that on the ground at the line stake should be recorded in the notes opposite the proper station number. This difference is the value of K in the figure and in Column 2 in the table.

In Column 3 of the table, opposite the value of K just determined, will be found the vertical distance, H, from the top of the hub to the bottom of the finished ditch. When the grading is ready for testing, place one end of a 16-foot straightedge, equipped with a small level, on top of the hub stake, the other end extending out over the bottom of the ditch. Hold the straightedge level, measure the distance from its *under edge to the bottom of the ditch.* If this value is less than the value of H just found, the ditch is still too high by the amount of the difference. If it is more, the ditch is already too deep by the amount of the difference.

Check the top of the ridge by leveling in a similar manner from the point just tested in the bottom of the *finished* ditch up to the straightedge held level on the top of the ridge opposite. If this value is less than 18 inches, the ridge is low by that amount; if greater, the ridge is high by the difference.

ILLUSTRATIVE EXAMPLE

At a given station assume that the level reading on the rod at the line stake is 6.44 and that the reading on the corresponding hub stake is 4.20. Then $K = 6.44 - 4.20$ or 2.24. The corresponding value of H is 2.39. Next suppose the distance from the straightedge to the bottom of the ditch, *as dug*, is 2.19. The ditch is then still high by an amount of $2.39 - 2.19$ or 0.20.

At the same time and point, if the straightedge held on top of the ridge is 1.05 above the point in the ditch just tested, the ridge is low by an amount $1.50 - 0.20 - 1.05$ or 0.25.

If the value of K found lies between two tabular values, the corresponding value of H may be found by proportion. Thus, if K as found is 2.20, H is 2.36.

In the manner described every point of the grading where a stake was originally set may be quickly tested and brought to correct grade.

A good pine board 1 by 4 by 16 feet makes a very serviceable straightedge when trued up with a jointer plane from time to time. *Always measure from the bottom edge of the straightedge.*[1]

It is possible to check roughly the height of a terrace embankment by simply using two measuring sticks (lath are satisfactory

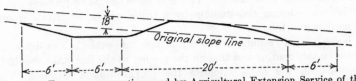

Fig. 121.—Terrace cross section used by Agricultural Extension Service of the University of Missouri. Designed for quick checking of bank height.

for the purpose) and sighting over the top when the sticks are held one above and one below the terrace on undisturbed ground. For example, in Fig. 121 if the lath are cut 18 inches long and used as indicated the bank height of a cross section such as that illustrated can quickly be checked.

[1] *Univ. Minn. Agr. Ext. Ser., Special Bull.* 171.

CHAPTER VIII

TERRACE CONSTRUCTION COSTS AND MAINTENANCE

From the foregoing chapters it is evident that the cost of terracing is necessarily quite .variable and is dependent upon numerous factors, chief among which are:

Texture and condition of soil, and kind of cover.
Prevailing degree and regularity of slopes.
Extent of erosion at time work is done.
Availability of erosion-proof natural outlets.
Kind of implements used.
Kind of power used to operate implements.
Dimensions of terrace channel and embankment.
Length of terraces, which determines time consumed in turning at ends.
Experience and skill of operators, and technique of building.
Manner in which work is financed.

No true and complete comparison of cost data is possible unless each of these factors is fully known and evaluated but, since no two have precisely the same weight and some are much more influential than others, comparisons close enough for practical purposes may be had when approximate conditions are given.

A rough idea of the relative weight to be ascribed to some of the more important factors can be gained from a study of cost records of terracing on 72 Iowa farms during the conservation program heretofore referred to. The predominant soil types in the areas concerned were various phases of Shelby, Clinton, Grundy, and Marshall silt loams with a sprinkling of Tama, Lindley, and Putnam. The usual soil condition was very dry to dry and hard, although a surprising number of terraces were built in soil described as moist to wet and very wet. The prevailing cover was stubble, but all possible types were represented including plowed, sod, clover, oats, and bare fallow ground.

The effect of soil variables on the cost of terracing is indicated in the following comparisons:

On the Scott farm in Taylor County the soil was dry Shelby with sod cover. The prevailing slope was 12 per cent and a terrace 1000 feet long was built with a steel V-drag and tractor

at a rate of 52 machine-hours per mile. On the Kinion farm in
Davis County, soil moist Shelby, sod cover, slope 11 per cent, a
terrace 1250 feet long was built with similar equipment at a rate
of 29.6 machine-hours per mile. Thus, unfavorable moisture
content brought about a 75 per cent increase in the time required
for construction.

The influence of texture on costs can be illustrated by com-
paring the Larson farm in Montgomery County with the Wilson
farm in Van Buren County. Terraces on both farms were built
by the Whirlwind rotary terracer on 10 per cent slopes, and the
only essential difference was soil type. Dry Marshall in the
first case required 6.8 machine-hours per mile of terrace and dry
Clinton in the second, 11 machine-hours.

The effect of variations in topography is threefold. In the
first place terraces on cultivated fields are practical only within a
definite slope range, and they are much less costly on flat slopes
than on steep, partly because the terrace cross section is easier to
form but principally because wider spacing permits a given
length of terrace to protect a larger acreage. On the third
count, non-uniform and irregular slopes require crooked and
irregular terraces, which greatly increases the difficulty and cost
of construction and necessitates more careful plowing and cultivation and larger expense for maintenance.

If the field being terraced is disfigured by small gullies, none of
which are too large to cross, the increased cost is reflected in the
amount of extra work required to bring the terrace bank up to
grade at the points of crossing.

Some idea of the combined influence of irregularity of topography and degree of erosion is given by a summation of the
extra work required to complete the terraces on the 72 farms for
which records were obtained. This is shown in the following
tabulation.

EXTRA WORK ON TERRACES

	Min. per farm	Av. per farm	Max. per farm	Av. per mile of terrace	Av. per acre protected
Man-hours.........	0	97.8	822	71.6	3.0
Team-hours........	0	39.5	369	28.9	1.2

The work required to provide erosion-proof outlets for terraces where none existed naturally is shown below:

WORK REQUIRED ON OUTLET CONSTRUCTION

	Min. per farm	Av. per farm	Max. per farm	Av. per mile of terrace	Av. per acre protected
Man-hours.........	0	69.0	651	50.5	2.1
Team-hours........	0	6.8	103	5.0	0.2

In interpreting these figures it should be remembered that the chief purpose of the project was to create employment for hand labor.

Effect of Variation in Implements and Power.—Variation in equipment used in building terraces, as in other forms of construction, usually constitutes the major factor in influencing cost. An analysis of available data from this point of view is summarized as shown in the tables on pages 168 and 169.

It will be noted that the major cost item when terracing with teams and V-drag, or with plows and slip scrapers, is for labor. Rightly or wrongly, farmers do not ordinarily include this at full value as a part of their cost, especially if the work is done during slack seasons when their time is not required for regular farm duties.

Whirlwind Rotary Terracer.—It is recognized that the low cost of terracing with the Whirlwind terracer is probably somewhat abnormal due to the services of skilled operators and other special circumstances. Nevertheless, this is the record established within a period of three months, using experimental equipment and dealing successfully with every condition encountered. Later trials in other states were equally successful except when working on land covered with stumps or stones, which would cause difficulty with any equipment.

On a short run near Meridian, Miss., using an 18-28 Hart Parr tractor, it is reported that 2150 feet of terrace of conventional width and 18 inches high was built in 26 rounds with a gasoline consumption of 3 gallons per hour for 7 hours. The tractor was operated in high gear with the Whirlwind terracer in second gear until the last 3 rounds when it was put in high. Such demon-

DAVIS COUNTY—WM. L. CREE FARM
(Exclusive of extra work)

Equipment: teams, slip scrapers, plow
Soil: Lindley loam, light weight, moist, stubble cover

Number of terraces...............	7			
Total length.....................	3360	feet.....or	0.635	mile
Total hours to build...............	21	.........or 33.2		per mile
Man-hours labor....................	161.5.........or 254			per mile
Horse-hours power..................	120	.........or 189		per mile
Acres protected....................	15	.........or 23.6		per mile
Cost of labor per mile....................at 30¢ per hr.......				$ 76.20
Cost of power per mile....................at 14¢ per hr.......				26.40
Cost of equipment per mile...............at 15¢ per hr.......				4.98
Total cost per mile...				$107.58
Cost per acre protected....................................				$ 4.56

DAVIS COUNTY—JOHN McGOWN FARM
(Exclusive of extra work)

Equipment: teams and V-drag
Soil: Shelby loam, medium weight, moist, sod cover

Number of terraces.................	4			
Total length.......................	3350 feet......or	0.63	mile
Total hours to build.................	23..........or 36.5		per mile
Man-hours labor.....................	175..........or 278		per mile
Horse-hours power...................	146..........or 232		per mile
Acres protected.....................	18..........or 28.6		per mile
Cost of labor per mile....................at 30¢ per hr.......			$ 83.40
Cost of power per mile....................at 14¢ per hr.......			32.48
Cost of equipment per mile...............at 10¢ per hr.......			3.65
Total cost per mile...			$119.53
Cost per acre protected....................................			$ 4.18

ADAIR COUNTY—A. S. HAMILTON FARM
(Exclusive of extra work)

Equipment: 15–27 tractor and light grader
Soil: Tama silt loam, both phases, medium weight, very dry, stubble, and
    sod cover

Number of terraces.................	6			
Total length.......................	8400	feet......or 1.59	miles
Total hours to build.................	41.5..........or 26.1		per mile
Man-hours labor.....................	72	..........or 45	per mile
Tractor-hours power.................	41.5..........or 26.1		per mile
Acres protected.....................	30	..........or 19	per mile
Cost of labor per mile....................at 30¢ per hr.......			$13.50
Cost of power per mile....................at 52¢ per hr.......			13.57
.Cost of equipment per mile...............at 15¢ per hr.......			3.90
Total cost per mile...			$30.97
Cost per acre protected....................................			$ 1.63

MADISON COUNTY—J. O. McCLEARY FARM
(Exclusive of extra work)

Equipment: General-purpose tractor and Texas grader
Soil: Sandy loam and clay, light weight, moist, bare and stubble cover

Number of terraces.................	11		
Total length......................	9300	feet......	1.76 miles
Total hours to built.................	32	..........or 18.2	per mile
Man-hours labor....................	120	..........or 68.2	per mile
Tractor-hours power................	32	..........or 18.2	per mile
Acres protected....................	31.5	.........or 18.0	per mile
Cost of labor per mile..................at 30¢ per hr.......			$20.46
Cost of power per mile...................at 52¢ per hr.......			9.46
Cost of equipment per mile................at 15¢ per hr.......			2.73

Total cost per mile... $32.65
Cost per acre protected...................................... $ 1.79

18 SOUTHERN IOWA COUNTIES—54 FARMS
(Including data kept by operators)
(Exclusive of extra work)

Equipment: Model U Allis-Chalmers tractor and Whirlwind rotary terracer

Total length of terraces...........	337,791	feet.....or 64	miles
Total hours to build..............	482.2	.........or 7.53	per mile
Man-hours labor.................	482.2	.........or 7.53	per mile
Tractor-hours power.............	482.2	.........or 7.53	per mile
Average horsepower..............	18.28		
Acres protected.................	1,216	............or 19	per mile
Cost of labor per mile (skilled)............at $1.50 per hr.......			$11.25
Cost of power per mile...................at 52¢ per hr.........			3.91
Cost of implement per mile..............at 20¢ per hr.........			1.50

Total cost per mile... $16.66
Cost per acre protected...................................... $ 0.88

strations as this must be considered as minimum performance because improvements in technique and other adaptations come quickly with experience in a strange environment.

The most adverse records are those collected in a test of various types of equipment conducted in Missouri in the spring of 1935. These are shown in Table 24.

This record for the Whirlwind terracer was made at a speed of only 335 lineal feet of terrace per hour. After making certain adjustments in the position of the rotor the rate was increased to 750 feet per hour, but performance at this rate is not included in Table 24.

TABLE 24.—TEST COMPARISON OF FOUR TYPES OF EQUIPMENT IN BUILDING TERRACES

Item	Light elevator-grader terracer	Whirl-wind rotary terracer	4-wheel blade grader	2-wheel blade grader
Tractor-hours per mile of terrace..	12.8	15.77	9.36	10.14
Horsepower-hours per mile of terrace*.....................	279.5	347.2	371.7	402.4
Man-hours per mile of terrace.....	12.8	15.77	18.72	20.28
Total cost per mile of terrace......	15.11	18.445	15.927	17.886
Cubic yards per lineal foot of terrace......................	0.495	0.46	0.312	0.377
Cubic yards of earth moved per rated horsepower hour..........	11.024	8.054	3.378	3.764

* Rated HP.

Probably a fair performance record for the Whirlwind, working under average conditions, is that obtained on 20 farms by a local conservation association in southern Iowa, as follows:

Length of terraces constructed, feet............... 123,845
Number of acres protected....................... 769
Average cost per acre........................... $ 1.54
Average cost per mile........................... $21.19

Light Elevating Grader-terracer.—The following data were secured on the performance of the Wooley elevating grader and general-purpose, track-type tractor at a demonstration near Athens, Ga. in 1935. The soil is described as Cecil series, *A, B,* and in a few places *C* horizon; red clay, piedmont plateau.

A. Length of terrace, feet............................. 960
   Cubic yards per lineal foot.......................... 0.7*
   Cubic yards of earth moved......................... 672
   Time... 2 hr. 15 min.
   Rounds made....................................... 11½
   Feet per lineal foot built per minute................. 7.26
   Cubic yards moved per minute....................... 5
   Cost per lineal foot of terrace built................. $0.0035†
   Cost per cubic yard of earth moved................. $0.005†
B. Length of terrace built, feet........................ 740
   Cubic yards per lineal foot.......................... 0.55*

* Actual instrument cross section readings.
† On basis of $1.50 per hour operating costs.

Cubic yards of earth moved......................... 407
Rounds made....................................... 8
Time.. 1 hr. 15 min.
Feet per lineal foot built per minute.................. 9.73
Cubic yards moved per minute....................... 5.4
Cost per lineal foot of terrace built................... $0.0024†
Cost per cubic yard of earth moved.................. $0.0046†

C. Length of terrace built, feet......................... 780
Cubic yards per lineal foot........................... 0.35*
Cubic yards of earth moved......................... 273
Rounds made....................................... 6
Time.. 1 hr.
Feet per lineal foot built per minute.................. 13
Cubic yards moved per minute....................... 4.5
Cost per lineal foot................................. $0.0019†
Cost per cubic yard of earth moved................. $0.0054†
   Total hours operation............................ 4½
   Total yards cast................................. 1352*
   Cubic yards per hour............................. 300

* Actual instrument cross section readings.
† On basis of $1.50 per hour operating costs.

UNIT COSTS FOR ABOVE COMPILATION

Operator.............................. $ 0.50 per hr.
Fuel consumption—2 gal. per hour @ 15 cts.   0.30
Terracer cost per hr. (repair and mainten-
  ance, interest on investment)..........   0.15
Tractor depreciation, repairs, interest on
  investment, oil, grease, etc.............   0.50
Tractor price......................... $1175.00 f.o.b. Cleveland
Terracer price........................   950.00 f.o.b. Kansas City

For comparison with this performance the author's records show that at a demonstration in Missouri in 1934, and before important improvements were made, it required 1 hour and 10 minutes and 14 rounds to complete 635 feet of terrace similar to *C* above. This is more in line with the following data for the same equipment as before but working in more difficult soil:

A. Soil—Unusually dry alfalfa sod:
  Length of terrace................................... 2050 ft.
  Yards per lineal foot................................ 0.33
  Yards of earth moved............................... 683
  Time... 4½ hr.
  Rounds made....................................... 12
  Yards moved per hour............................... 152
  Feet of terrace built per hour....................... 455

Cost of operation per hour............................ $ 1.72
Cost per yard of earth............................... $ 0.0113
Cost per mile of terrace............................. $19.95

B. Soil—Wheat stubble grown up with weeds (very dry):

Length of terrace.................................... 1100 ft.
Yards per lineal foot................................ 0.66
Yards of earth moved................................ 733
Time.. 2 hours
Rounds made... 13
Yards moved per hour................................ 366
Feet of terrace built per hour...................... 550
Cost of operation per hour.......................... $ 1.72
Cost per yard of earth.............................. $ 0.0047
Cost per mile of terrace............................ $16.52

Unit Costs for Above Compilation

Operator per hour................................... $ 0.60
Fuel consumption—2¾ gal. per hour @ 16.9 cts........   0.47
Tractor depreciation, repairs, interest on investment, oil,
    grease, etc. per hour...........................   0.50
Terracer cost per hour, depreciation, interest on invest-
    ment, repairs...................................   0.15
                                                     ———————
    Total... $ 1.72

Two-wheel Blade Graders.—The best record that has come to the author's attention for this class of equipment was made in Missouri by a two-wheel 4500-pound, 10-foot blade grader pulled by a 40-hp Diesel Hillside Special tractor as shown below. The figures are for one mile of terrace, 38 feet overall width on a 5 per cent slope and containing 0.60 to 0.70 cubic yard per lineal foot in the embankment. Soil conditions were exceptionally favorable and the time required was 8 hours.

Cost of building one mile of terrace:

Fuel, 16 gals. at 6 cts............................. $ 0.96
Oil and grease (60-hr. crankcase change) at 60 cts. per gal.........   0.90
Labor, 2 men at 50 cts. per hr......................   8.00
Repairs, estimated $1,106 in 10,000 hrs.............   0.88
6% interest for 5 yrs. (total $800).................   0.64
Depreciation, $4,425 in 10,000 hrs..................   3.54
                                                     ———————
Total cost per mile................................. $14.92
Yardage, approximate................................ 3168
Cost per cubic yard approx.......................... $0.005

The following record applies to similar equipment working in extremely difficult soil conditions in the Mississippi valley:

No. of terraces built.....................................	18
Number of feet of terrace built..........................	12,650
Number of feet of outlets built.........................	950
Total number of feet completed..........................	13,600
Number of miles terrace completed......................	2.576
Number of working hours................................	55.5
Total fuel used, gallons.................................	88
Total oil used, quarts—track wheels and motor............	16
Total grease used, pounds...............................	1
Fuel used per hour, gallons..............................	1.585
Oil used per hour, quarts—track wheels and motor.........	0.288
Cost of fuel..	$ 8.64
Cost of labor, 122 man hours............................	$ 91.50
Total operating cost....................................	$100.14
Cost per mile...	$ 38.90
Cost per foot...	$ .0074

Probably a fair average record for Diesel 40 tractors and 4500-pound, 10-foot blade terracers is as follows. This work was done in northeastern Kansas in 1935 and is doubly interesting because of the large expense for outlet ditch construction.

Feet of terraces built...................................	17,060
Hours worked...	49½
Feet of terrace built per hour...........................	345
Acres terraced per hour (20 acres per mile)...............	1.3
Feet of outlet ditch constructed.........................	2,675
Hours worked...	9
Total hours worked.....................................	58½
Total fuel used—gallons #3 fuel oil......................	145

(Includes loading equipment on truck and traveling from buildings to field, etc. during two weeks' time, which is not counted in operating time of 58½ hr.).

Total lubricating oil used (crankcase and track frames).....	7 gal.

Unit Costs for Above Compilation

	58½ Hours	Per Hour
Fuel 145 gal. @ 5 cts...............................	$ 7.25	.124
Oil 7 gal. @ 60 cts................................	4.20	.072
Depreciation $4250—10,000 hr......................	24.86	.425
Repairs and maintenance (estimated).................	17.55	.30
Labor @ 50 cts.—2 men............................	58.50	1.00
Total..		$ 1.921

Cost per acre—terrace construction............................   1.48
Cost per mile—terrace construction............................ $22.64
Cost per acre—outlet construction............................ $11.92
Total cost per acre.. $13.40

Terrace dimensions: 40 ft. total width; 18 to 24 in. ridge height above bottom of channel; 80 per cent or more of the soil being moved from upper side; excavation below original slope line as shown on cross section of completed terrace—about 0.45 yd. per ft.

The following data refer to work in Texas where the same type of terracers were used with 55-horsepower gasoline, track-type tractors and 6-foot, 1¼-yard, rotary Fresno scrapers. The *A* data is about normal for the conditions described, and that shown in *B* indicates a typically large increase in cost where the land is badly gullied.

A. Soil condition: Mixed Texas black gumbo and light loam.
   General conditions: Fields have been under constant cultivation and are gently sloping. Fields scattered over an area of 4 sq. mi., necessitating long, unproductive trips.
   Cost per mile of blade work...................... $ 27.92
   Cost per mile of Fresno work......................   4.09
   Terrace cost, total per mile......................   32.01
   Gasoline, per gallon..............................   .08
   Oil per gallon....................................   0.58 and 0.57
   Labor, $1.02 per hour for tractor and
      blade crews...................   .535 per hr. for fresno work.
   Terrace dimensions: 22 ft. wide berm to berm, 30 ft. wide outside to outside of borrow pit.

B. Soil condition: Texas black gumbo with heavy growth of thickly matted Johnson grass.
   General conditions: Soil was moist most of the time and this with the Johnson grass and soil structure gave trouble with dirt not rolling on moldboard. Abandoned land, badly gullied and washed, necessitating a large amount of fresno work.
   Cost per mile for blade work...................... $46.50
   Cost per mile for fresno work....................   25.35
   Terrace cost, total per mile.....................   71.85
   Gasoline, per gallon.............................   0.095
   Oil, per gallon..................................   0.475
   Labor, $1.35 per hour for tractor and blade crews
   Labor, 60 cts. per hour for fresno work
   General: Fresno used for filling gullies, bringing terraces up to grade and for building 25 ft. to 30 ft. at ends adjacent to fences and outlets.
   Terrace dimensions: 22 ft. wide berm to berm, 30 ft. wide outside to outside of borrow pit. Cross section area 12 sq. ft. or 0.44 cu. yd. per running foot.

TABLE 25.—COST OF TERRACE CONSTRUCTION AT CLARINDA, IOWA

Terrace No.	Machine used	Length of terrace, feet	Size of terrace Height, feet	Width To crest	Width Over all	Slope of land per 100 ft.	Terrace data Vertical interval, feet	Drainage area, acres	Lin. ft. of terrace per acre	Work per 100 ft. Trac. hrs. (Terracing machine)	Man hrs.	Cost of scraping per 100 ft. of terrace	Cost of grading Per 100 ft.	Per acre	Per mile	Condition of soil	Surface cover	Method of construction
C-1	Cat. Fifteen with Cat. Grader.	2421	1.38	12.3	25.2	5.82	3.95	3.76	644	0.41	0.83	$0.07	$0.27	$1.71	$14.00	Dry, dusty	Oat stubble, foxtail	½ round—lower side 13½ rounds—upper side
C-2	Cat. Sixty Austin Road Grader.	2417	0.91	10.4	24.6	9.03	4.06	2.48	975	0.16	0.31	.....	0.25	2.45	13.25	Dry, hard	Oat stubble, foxtail	7 rounds—all upper side
C-3	Cat. Sixty Austin Road Grader.	2350	1.13	12.6	25.8	9.52	4.59	2.62	897	0.15	0.30	0.05	0.24	2.15	12.67	Dry, hard	Oat stubble, foxtail	7 rounds—all upper side
C-4a	G. P. John Deere Martin Ideal.	1550	1.54	12.9	27.3	9.78	6.01	3.26	706	0.58	1.16	0.04	0.42	2.99	22.33	Dry, hard	Oat stubble, foxtail	1½ rounds—lower side 25½ rounds—upper side
C-4b	Cat. Fifteen Cat. Grader.	750	1.62	12.3	21.0					0.33	0.67	.....	0.21	1.51	11.31	Mellow	Corn stubble	14 rounds—all upper side
C-5a	Mod. D John Deere Texas Terracer.	1450	1.39	11.9	21.6	9.27	5.34	2.96	743	0.45	0.90	0.14	0.39	2.89	20.50	Dry, hard	½ in plowing, ½ in oat stubble	21 rounds—all upper side
C-5b	Cat. Fifteen, Cat. Grader.	750	1.60	13.4	20.9					0.30	0.60	.....	0.19	1.43	10.17	Mellow	Corn stubble	13 rounds—all upper side
C-6a	G. P. John Deere Martin Ideal.	1250	1.44	14.6	26.0	8.76	5.07	2.78	719	0.80	1.60	0.21	0.58	4.19	30.78	Dry, hard	¾ in plowing, ¼ in oat stubble	½ round—lower side 31½ rounds—upper side
C-6b	Cat. Fifteen Cat. Grader.	750	1.45	12.6	21.9					0.27	0.53	0.11	0.17	1.23	9.03	Mellow	Corn stubble	13 rounds—all upper side
C-7	Mod. D John Deere Texas Terracer.	900	1.47	12.4	20.5	9.56	4.88	1.05	857	0.56	1.11	0.11	0.48	4.12	25.39	Dry, hard	All in plowing	All upper side Model D: 18 rounds, 3½ hrs. G.P.: 5 rounds, 1½ hrs.
C-8	G. P. John Deere Martin and Texas.	900	1.67	14.2	24.8	9.52	4.68	1.01	891	0.78	1.56	0.14	0.57	5.07	30.03	Dry, hard	All in plowing	All upper side Martin: 27 rounds, 6 hrs.
C-9	G. P. John Deere Texas Terracer.	900	1.41	11.6	20.9	9.20	5.58	1.25	720	0.72	1.44	0.29	0.52	3.78	27.72	Dry, hard	All in plowing	Texas: 4 rounds, 1 hr. 21 rounds—all upper side
C-10	Cat. Fifteen Cat. Grader.	950	1.53	12.6	22.3	9.16	5.12	1.18	805	0.32	0.63	.....	0.20	1.63	10.72	Mellow	Corn stubble	14 rounds—all upper side
C-11	Cat. Fifteen Cat. Grader.	650	1.75	12.8	21.4	7.58	4.45	0.90	719	0.35	0.69	.....	0.22	1.60	11.73	Mellow	Corn stubble	12½ rounds—all up-per side

Heavy Equipment.—Cost records kept in Kansas on the 20,000-pound elevating graders, 10,000-pound, 12-foot blade graders, 6-foot rotary Fresno scrapers and 50- to 75-horsepower Diesel tractors clearly showed the following averages for a run of 156 miles.

Type of Work	Cost per Mile
Elevating grader placing core	$11.52
12-ft. blade grader to finish	$ 4.52
Fresno work raising low places and finishing terrace ends	$ 5.48

Considering the number of miles included and the large terrace cross section adopted for this work (see Fig. 109) the cost of $16.04 per mile for core building and blading is quite low.

Near Albion, Neb., where the Soil Conservation Service is building level terraces by similar methods, the cost for 5 rounds with an elevating grader followed by 6 rounds with a blade grader is reported as $28 per mile.

Miscellaneous Equipment.—Cost data on the construction of some of the experimental terraces on the federal erosion farm near Clarinda, Ia., are given in Table 25, which is self-explanatory.

In *U. S. Department of Agriculture Bulletin* 1669, Ramser suggests minimum costs for light equipment working under favorable conditions as to soil, slope, and terrace length as indicated in Table 26. These costs are based on the use of steel ditchers or terracers of the V-shape or grader type, using local power. Where the labor and power are paid for in cash, substitution of a

TABLE 26.—APPROXIMATE COSTS OF CONSTRUCTING TERRACES 15 INCHES HIGH, 20 FEET WIDE, AND NOT LESS THAN 1000 FEET LONG, IN LIGHT SOILS ON MODERATE LAND SLOPES

Description of land	Cost per acre	Remarks
Clean-cultivated land, no gullies	$1.50 to $ 2.50	
Grass or virgin land, no gullies	2.00 to 3.00	
Clean-cultivated land, small shallow gullies	3.00 to 6.00	Depending upon the number of gullies
Clean-cultivated land, gullies 3 to 6 feet deep	7.00 to 15.00	Depending upon the number of gullies
Newly cleared land, no gullies, most stumps grubbed out	7.00 to 12.00	Depending upon the kind and number of roots and stumps

homemade wooden drag would increase the cost 25 to 40 per cent. All costs are of course affected adversely by inexperience, poor equipment, and wet or very dry soil. The figures shown may be converted to approximate costs per mile by multiplying by 20.

Form for Cost Data.—Inasmuch as most cost figures collected in the past are of only partial value because all of the factors affecting costs are not recorded, the form shown on page 178 has been proposed as a standard for general use with the intention of making future data more truly comparable and reliable. Of course nothing can evaluate the difference in skill with which experienced operators may use the same equipment under identical conditions. Extreme variations of as much as 50 per cent in the cost of the same terraces may be attributable to this cause.

TERRACE CULTIVATION AND MAINTENANCE

All terraces should be closely watched during the first year while the loose soil is settling, and after each rain of sufficient

Fig. 122.—A thoroughly settled terrace one year after construction. Note cover crop during first year.

magnitude to cause runoff, minor adjustments and repairs will probably be necessary. During the period of settling it is advisable to seed the entire field to some kind of cover crop and not subject the fresh terraces to the hazard of open cultivation. Figure 122 shows a well-settled terrace a year after construction.

PROPOSED STANDARD FORM FOR TERRACE CONSTRUCTION COST DATA

Terracer..

Tractor................ Rating................ Field number................ Date................

Slope of land................ Soil type................ Location of field................ Owner................

Cover on land................ Condition of soil: Wet................ Degree of erosion................ Medium................ Dry................

Terrace number................ Length, feet................ Discharge capacity*................ Vertical interval: Above................ Below................

Acres drained................ Horizontal distance: Above................ Below................

Cross section area of ridge:† Max................ Min................ Cross section area of channel:‡ Max................ Min................

Ridge: Average height................ Average base width................ Channel: Average depth................ Average top width................

Terrace grade: Maximum................ Minimum................ Total fall................

CONSTRUCTION

Speed of outfit: Miles per hour................ Length of terrace, miles................ Time to construct................

Did machine complete terrace................? Other equipment necessary to complete................

Number men required to operate outfit................ Total man-hours................ Number of rounds, upper side................ lower side................

Fuel................ Oil................ Grease................ Total horsepower hours................

COST PER MILE OF TERRACE

Man-hours per mile of terrace................ Tractor hours per mile of terrace................

Machine hours per mile of terrace................ Horsepower hours per mile of terrace................

.... Man hours: @................

.... Gal. fuel for tractor @................

.... Gal. oil for tractor @................

.... Grease for tractor and terracer @................

.... Repair on tractor and machinery @................

Depreciation on tractor................

Depreciation on terracer................

Total cost of grading per mile of terrace................

Cost of extra work per mile of terrace................

Cost of outlet construction per mile of terrace................

* After allowing for settlement.
† Above original surface.
‡ Below original surface.

Remarks................

The amount of subsequent maintenance will be dependent upon the skill with which the terraces were designed and constructed and upon the judgment used in planning the cropping and cultivation system. Each year the field is in open-tilled row crops, one or more rounds with a plow, V-drag, small grader, or Whirlwind terracer will probably be needed after harvest to reestablish the bank height and clean out the channel. With a

Fig. 123.—Sowing oats across terrace with a 16-foot grain drill. (*Courtesy U. S. Bureau of Agricultural Engineering.*)

Whirlwind terracer there is no objection to throwing a part of the channel accumulation up the slope. Some damage to the embankment is unavoidable with even the utmost care and is not due entirely to the furrows of row crops, as can be seen from Fig. 123. In the main, however, the amount of such maintenance will be determined by the direction in which the furrows are run during times when row crops are grown.

The channel should of course be kept free of obstructions of all kinds, especially culverts at farm road crossings. On all but the steepest slopes, farm roads may pass directly over the terraces, and where this cannot be done with convenience a small bridge is preferable to a culvert and fill. Exceptionally heavy rains may cause silt bars to form in the terrace channel, which may be removed with shovels or with a team and scraper.

Records of terrace maintenance costs have been kept for several years at the Bethany, Mo., station of the federal Department of Agriculture and have averaged $4.54 per mile or $0.60 per acre per year for all of the experimental terraces on the farm (see Chap. XIV for map of the farm). This figure includes all expense for labor, equipment, and power, whether paid for in cash or not. The total annual cost of the terraces may be computed by adding interest at the current rate on the original construction cost per acre to the yearly cost for maintenance. This sum, if desired, may be weighed against the increase in land

Fig. 124.—Plowing following terrace construction showing proper direction of furrows with respect to the contour of the land and the terraces.

value (not less than $8 per acre) to determine the economic benefit accruing from the terraces.

When terracing is done on worn or eroded land the construction should be followed by heavy liming (where needed) and manuring and the growth of a suitable cover crop to be plowed under. The terraces will insure maximum returns from such practices and the most rapid restoration of fertility. The best crops to use will be determined by experience in a particular locality. Rye and vetch are good winter crops for widespread adaptation, and soybeans and cowpeas are examples of crops suitable for summer.

Plowing Terraced Land.—All terraced land should be plowed on the contour as nearly as possible and still maintain approximate parallelism with the terraces. Plowing should never be done straight up and down hill, whether the land is terraced or not. The proper direction of plowing with respect to contours and the terraces is shown in Fig. 124. By backfurrowing always to the terrace bank the work of maintaining adequate height is minimized and the embankment base is broadened. It is desirable to shift the dead furrow position more or less each time the field is plowed to round out the embankment cross section and keep the inter-terrace slope uniform.

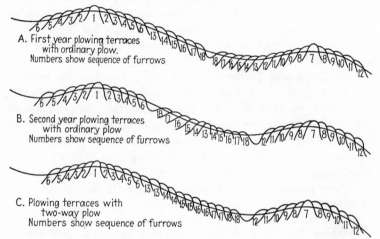

A. First year plowing terraces with ordinary plow. Numbers show sequence of furrows

B. Second year plowing terraces with ordinary plow Numbers show sequence of furrows

C. Plowing terraces with two-way plow Numbers show sequence of furrows

Fig. 125.—Method of plowing terraces with ordinary plow and with two-way plow.

A method of plowing advocated by the federal Soil Conservation Service is shown in Fig. 125. The first year backfurrows are placed on each bank, and then the area between is plowed out as indicated in Fig. 125, leaving a dead furrow about midway between the terraces. At the next plowing the embankments are backfurrowed as before until one furrow is in the channel bottom, after which backfurrows are placed on the old dead furrow and two new dead furrows are left as shown in the drawing. If a two-way plow is available, a single dead furrow can be placed permanently in the terrace channel and its position shifted only slightly from year to year. Also the inter-terrace furrows can all be turned uphill year after year, thus offsetting the natural tendency of the soil to move gradually down the slope.   Another advantage of two-way plowing is greater ease in handling lands of irregular width due to lack of parallelism in the terrace lines.

The Alabama practice of plowing for easy maintenance when cleanly cultivated crops are grown is to plow out the channel at least twice during the year by measuring from the embankment center line to the lowest part of the channel and using this distance as a guide in plowing.   For instance, if this distance is 7 feet, the first furrow is placed an equal distance up the slope, or 7 feet from the low point in the channel, and turned uphill. On the return trip a backfurrow is placed on the terrace bank and the plowing continued until a strip 14 feet wide has been opened. The remaining area between the terraces is then broken as a separate land.

Row Crops and Terraces.—It is recognized that the presence of terraces in cultivated fields introduces complications in laying out the rows that require considerable thought and study. Where the terraces are very crooked and irregular on steep slopes row crops may become impracticable, but in the great majority of cases a satisfactory solution can be applied without causing unreasonable inconvenience.   In the *Soil Conservation Service Handbook* previously referred to and quoted, the subject is treated as follows:

There are four main methods which may be used in planting row crops on a terraced field.   Each one has several variations.

Contour farming with the terraces, turning in the terrace channel on short rows.

Crop stripping with terraces, seeding down irregular areas between terraces, which has previously been discussed.

Selecting the key terrace in the field and running all rows above and below parallel to this key terrace, crossing the other terraces at whatever angle the rows may fall.

Straight, parallel rows on completely terraced fields under five per cent slope.

Contour Farming with Terraces.—The first method is used quite generally in the southern states where terracing is an old established practice, and it has proved to be a very effective measure in controlling erosion.   The second is an adaptation of the first, more fitted to the use of large machinery.   The third and fourth methods are not considered such effective farming practices in controlling erosion as the first two, and the terraces are more difficult to maintain. All terraced land should be contoured, although on fields completely terraced under five per cent slope crops may be planted in straight rows and corn checked. Maintenance, however, will be a larger item of expense. Fields of greater than four per cent when terraced always should be farmed for clean cultivated crops on the contour, or parallel with terraces.

When contour farming a terraced field by method one in cultivated or row crops, the area between any two adjacent terraces is farmed as

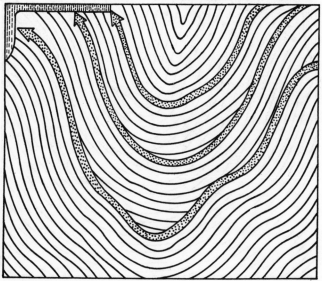

Fig. 126.—Contour farming terraced fields. Method suitable for slopes of 8 to 15 per cent.

a unit. Beginning on the ridge of the upper terrace, run all the rows parallel, as shown in Fig. 126. On the short rows, the terrace channel is used as the turn row. This method eliminates the necessity of ever crossing the terrace ridge. Each row acts as a small terrace and water concentrates only in the terrace channel, (thus) providing a very effective method of control. Pointing the short rows into the channel eliminates much of the trouble of the rows breaking over and resulting in "fanning" (silt bars) in the terrace channel. Farming in this manner is particularly adapted to single row equipment. (On slopes of 8 to 15 per cent, some authorities recommend changing the location of the point rows from year to year to prevent short washes forming near their ends.)

Crop Stripping with Terraces.—Crop stripping with terraces is to eliminate point rows. The irregular areas between terraces are seeded to an annual close-growing crop such as drilled soybeans, sudan, or small grain crop. This method provides regular width strips with no point rows for cultivated crops. Soybeans planted for hay make an ideal crop to be used in the irregular strips between terraces. Crop stripping with terraces is more adaptable to the use of large horse-drawn equipment and to tractor farming for cultivated crops than the

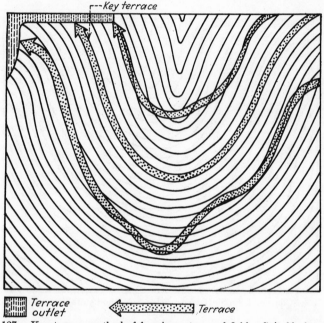

Fig. 127.—Key terrace method of farming a terraced field. Suitable for slopes up to 8 per cent.

other two suggested means of handling terraces and constitutes a very effective method of erosion control.

Key Terrace Farming.—The key terrace method of planting on terraces is shown in Fig. 127. In selecting the key terrace, consideration of the maximum number of rows that will follow the approximate contour of the field above and below the terrace is of prime importance. The longest terrace in the field will usually be the one to select. However, some other terrace may provide a better field layout, as is shown in Fig. 127. Run all rows parallel to the key terrace, both above and below the terrace. This method is particularly well adapted to fields where terraces are spaced uniformly apart but should be confined to the more gentle terraced slopes.

When furrow openers are used in planting across the terraces, it is very essential that the furrow openers be raised to prevent deep furrows crossing the terrace ridges. For the same reason cultivator shovels should also be raised when crossing the terrace ridge. The effective height of a terrace is no higher than its lowest point.

The chief advantage of using the key terrace as a guide for planting the field is to make possible larger fields of one crop and provide a fairly

FIG. 128.—A good example of row crops on terraced land.

simple method of laying off the field. However, the chief disadvantages are that extreme care must be exercised in crossing terraces with deep tillage machinery to prevent destruction of the terrace ridge, and more maintenance work will be required to prevent water breaking over at low spots. Point rows will be developed in finishing the field. Increased grades of the rows where they do not approximately follow the contour of the land will tend to cause increased soil movement between the terraces. As a result the terrace channel will fill with silt more quickly where the key terrace method of farming is used. Consequently, more frequent inspection of the terrace must be made and the terraces rebuilt when the terrace channel becomes too shallow.

Straight-row Farming.—On completely terraced fields of not over 4 per cent slope, corn may be checked and other row crops planted in straight rows. Care must be taken in crossing the terrace to prevent excessive lowering of the terrace ridge. Working across the terraces during a season will reduce the height of the terrace several inches, and this height must be restored to prevent destruction of the terraces. Plowing will not be sufficient to restore the terrace height, and some terracing equipment such as a grader, small terracer, or V-drag will be needed to obtain the desired height. However, on slopes under 5 per cent, it may be found economical to plant cultivated crops in straight rows and provide for the additional maintenance of the terraces caused by crossing them. In any case, do not cultivate across the terraces the first year or until the terrace ridges have fully settled.

The advantages of this method are that it is a simple way of laying out terraced fields for cultivated crops and that the terraces provide effective erosion control. The disadvantages are increased maintenance costs, closer inspection of terraces required, and increased soil movement between terraces.

Figure 128 is an illustration of well-planned row crops growing on terraced land.

CHAPTER IX

TERRACE OUTLETS

Nothing is more vital to the success of a system of terraces than good, dependable outlets and, strangely enough, nothing seems to have been more neglected. In extreme cases the expense of providing satisfactory outlets may nullify what otherwise would be a feasible undertaking. It goes without saying that, unless the runoff can be delivered to regular water courses at the foot of slopes without harmful erosion or gullying, the terraces themselves will give only temporary protection to the main body of the field. There is also the question of legal liability for damage to consider as laws of the humid states quite generally forbid the diversion of water from its natural direction of flow in such a way as to cause injury to adjoining property.

The selection, preparation, and maintenance of outlets in erosion-proof condition are indeed problems of prime importance; and no part of the terracing program is more subject to local variation. This is due not only to differences in environment for the legumes and grasses used in control but to variations in soil and runoff requirements and availability of natural outlets. For instance, in the transition zone between humid and arid conditions, such as the whole of North Dakota and parts of South Dakota, Nebraska, Kansas, Oklahoma, and Texas, no outlets are needed because terraces can be built level and all of the rainfall forced into the soil. The other extreme is found in regions of heavy rainfall and impervious soil, too badly depleted to grow grass, where the expense of permanent structures is often prohibitive. The vast majority of cases will, of course, fall somewhere between these two extremes.

Location.—The importance of outlet possibilities in planning terrace layouts has already been discussed, and this idea should now be carried one step further and considered in relation to possible rearrangement of fields to conform to future crop rotations. It is not always possible on land subject to erosion to

187

adhere to the conventional rectangular or square shapes, however desirable these may be for the most efficient operation of machinery.

A well-thought-out field arrangement from a conservation point of view is shown in Fig. 129, which also may be considered

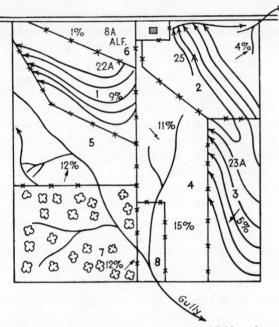

Fig. 129.—Farm map showing desirable arrangement of fields and terrace outlets on a farm of rolling topography.

Fields 1, 2, and 3 rotation
Fields 4, 5, and 7 pasture
Field 6 alfalfa, and 8 black locust
Field 1, terrace outlet into permanent pasture
Field 2, terrace outlet constructed along road; does not materially change rate of ,drainage through road culvert
Field 3, terrace outlet into permanent pasture

as a typical example of the work of the Soil Conservation Service in the Bethany, Mo., area. Note that the three terraced fields are approximately the same size and lend themselves readily to a three-year rotation of corn, oats, and clover. The three steeper fields, designated 4, 5, and 7, are to be left in permanent pasture and Field No. 8 is to be planted to black locust trees to help control erosion in the gullies. Symbols might have been shown in the gullies to represent control structures, the design and construction of which will be considered later.

Natural Outlets.—The ideal outlet is a dense growth of underbrush and timber on a moderate slope with a thick mulch of leaves and debris to spread out and partially absorb the water discharged from the terrace channels. Such an outlet is represented by Fig. 130, which pictures a scene in southern Georgia.

Fig. 130.—Ideal natural outlet for terraces. A thick stand of underbrush and timber on a moderate slope.

Next to woodland of the kind illustrated, a permanent pasture of tough sod that is not overgrazed is most satisfactory. In both cases it is good practice to extend each alternate terrace about 15 or 20 feet into the pasture or woods and stop the others at the grass edge in order to assist in thinning out the water and preventing its concentration. Figure 131 shows a terrace extended into the sod of a good pasture outlet.

Many terrace systems, especially in the south, have been discharging for years into natural outlets with entirely satisfactory results and with no extra cost whatever. Where thin grass or trees on steep slopes have been depended upon, however, enough cases of harmful erosion and gullying are on record to justify caution in making a choice and care in watching for evidences of failure. It is a mistake to place too much dependence on a natural outlet simply because it is natural.

CONSTRUCTED OUTLETS

A majority of the more difficult terracing jobs will require one or more specially constructed ditches to serve as terrace

Fig. 131.—Partially grazed pasture land serving as a terrace outlet.

outlets. These ditches are most commonly located along fence lines or parallel to public roads, and they are ordinarily excavated with the same equipment used to build the terraces. Sometimes a draw or watercourse is found in such a position that it can be utilized, in which case no excavation will be necessary. Almost without exception, outlet ditches are necessarily located on gradients steep enough to produce erosive velocities and hence require protection.

It is seldom advisable to empty terraces directly into road ditches, as the protection necessary both at the overfall and in the ditch itself usually throws the choice to some other alternative. Neglect of such protection in the past has been responsible for more terrace failures than any other single cause. If the road in question is part of a highly improved system, it is quite possible that highway officials will be glad to cooperate in providing for complete and safe disposition of the water. In any event, they should be consulted before using any road ditch for this purpose.

Channel Design.—A study of the Manning formula, which is repeated here for convenience,

$$V = \frac{1.486}{n} R^{\frac{2}{3}} S^{\frac{1}{2}}$$

and its companion formula,

$$Q = aV$$

shows that, for a given value of n and S, the velocity varies with the hydraulic radius. Since terrace outlets are usually located on steep slopes, it is desirable to reduce the velocity for a given discharge to as low a value as possible, and this can be done by designing the channel of such shape as to result in a minimum hydraulic radius. Remembering that the hydraulic radius is the quotient of the cross-sectional channel area divided by the wetted perimeter, it is seen that the larger the wetted perimeter, for a given area, the smaller will be the quotient. This is another way of saying that a given volume of water flowing down a given slope will be carried at a velocity that varies from a minimum for a wide shallow channel to a maximum for a narrow deep one. In wide shallow channels the bottom width may be assumed as the wetted perimeter with negligible error.

Vegetative Control.—Where permanent vegetation alone is relied upon for control the maximum velocity to be attained, on the average not oftener than once in 10 years, should be set at 5 feet per second. This is for best sod cover on ground containing not less than 50 per cent topsoil. For sod of poorer quality the 10-year maximum velocity should be reduced to 4 or even 3 feet per second depending upon the amount of topsoil present and the vigor of the stand. Assuming a maximum velocity of 5 feet per second and a roughness coefficient, n, of 0.04, channels of the widths shown on the curves of Fig. 132, flowing at a depth of one-twelfth the width, will have capacity to carry the amount of runoff shown as ordinates on the various slopes shown as abscissae. Twelve per cent is considered the maximum slope where vegetation alone can be depended upon for safe control.

The critical runoff for a 10-year frequency period is computed by use of the rational formula, $Q = CIA$, as described in Chap. IV, employing the reduced values of C recommended for terraced land. When this is known, the approximate width of channel for a given slope can be taken from Fig. 132.

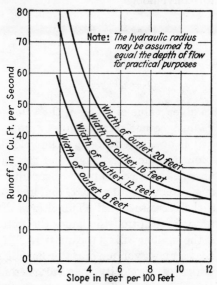

Fɪɢ. 132.—Limiting runoff for vegetatively controlled outlets for different slopes.
Manning's formula $V = 5.0$ ft. per sec.
$$n = 0.04$$
To determine runoff from terraced area by typical SCS method—
Frequency once in 12 years.

$$Q = CIA$$
Q = runoff in cu. ft. per sec.
C = .6 (slopes 5 to 10 per cent)
   = .5 (slopes 2 to 5 per cent)
   = .72 (slopes 10 to 15 per cent)
I = 6 cu. ft. per sec. per acre
  = 6 inches of rain per hour
A = Area in acres
Q = 3.0 A (2 to 5 per cent slope)
  = 3.6 A (5 to 10 per cent slope)
  = 4.3 A (10 to 15 per cent slope)

The minimum flow depth for any considerable period of time should be not less than 3 inches, and the outlet gradient should be 6 inches lower than the terrace gradient at the point of intersection. If this 6-inch drop is distributed over at least 10 feet of the terrace by hand work there is little danger of erosion.

Where this drop is more than 1 foot, an outlet structure will probably be necessary (see Figs. 143 and 144).

To provide a "freeboard" of 4 to 6 inches at the sides of the outlet channel above the computed depth of flow without deepening the gradient undesirably, it will be necessary in most cases to throw up banks of earth or levees at the sides in addition to the work of excavation. Since the discharge increases below the mouth of each terrace, the outlet width will need to be increased correspondingly when the critical discharge for the former width is exceeded. These width changes should be made gradually to avoid abrupt variations in cross section.

Suitable Vegetative Species.—The first principle to be observed in seeding outlet channels is to select perennial native grasses with tough fibrous root systems and of a species not susceptible to rank growth capable of materially reducing the discharge capacity. Trees, brush, vines, or cane should not be planted under any circumstances. Agricultural colleges in the various states should be consulted when selecting grasses suitable to a given locality.

In southern climates Bermuda grass is probably most satisfactory for general use, but centipede and carpet grass may be substituted except in semiarid sections of Texas and Oklahoma where buffalo or wire grass would probably be better. Johnson grass and lespedeza alone both grow too profusely and should not be planted unless the outlet ditch is part of a hay meadow where the grass will be cut regularly before it reaches a rank, woody stage.

Under Midwest conditions the Soil Conservation Service recommends the following mixtures:

For early spring seeding:

	Pounds
Timothy	6
Redtop	6
Lespedeza	7
Bluegrass	5
Orchard grass	4
Alsike clover	2

For late spring seeding:

	Pounds
Timothy	5
Redtop	5

	Pounds
Lespedeza	6
Sudan grass	6
Bluegrass	3
Orchard grass	3
Sweet clover	2

For fall seeding:

	Pounds
Timothy	10
Redtop	6
Bluegrass	4

All seeding should be done on well-prepared soil of reasonable fertility, either natural or artificial. Where necessary the Soil

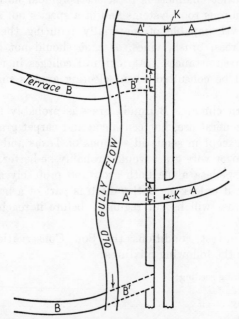

Fig. 133.—Use of temporary outlet in establishing vegetation.
After vegetation has become well established:
1. Sections B′ are added to B terraces to carry water across old gully.
2. Sections A′ are cut off of A terraces at points K and this material may be used to build levee Sections L.

Conservation Service suggests a 200-pound per acre application of lime, together with barnyard manure and a complete commercial fertilizer.

Establishing Vegetation.—Various expedients are used to protect the grass sprouts while they are becoming established. The surest and best way is to prepare and seed the outlet a year or two in advance of building the terraces. The next best procedure is to divert the terrace water into a temporary outlet of some kind until the regular channel is ready to receive it. One method of utilizing a temporary outlet is illustrated in Fig. 133.

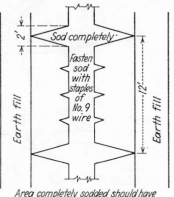

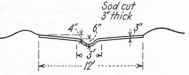

On moderate slopes where the volume of runoff is not too great the channel may be partially sodded, as indicated by Fig. 134, and the unsodded areas seeded. Ordinarily the seeded areas will be flooded so rarely and for such short intervals as to make failure unlikely.

Fig. 134.—Sodded low center outlet.

For larger discharges where the velocity, as determined by dividing the discharge by the cross-sectional area, exceeds 3 feet

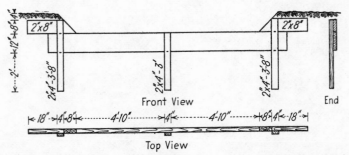

Fig. 135.—Terrace-outlet spreader of creosoted wood. Dimensions for 10-foot width.

per second it is probable that mechanical spreaders will be needed to assist the young grass in getting a start. Such a spreader, of

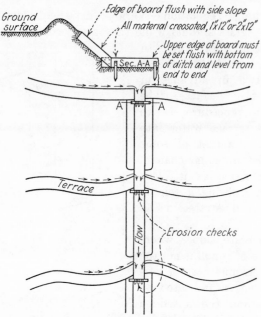

FIG. 136.—Sketch showing spreader checks installed.

FIG. 137.—Photograph illustrating use of spreader checks reinforced with sod, strips placed alongside.

creosoted wood, is illustrated in Fig. 135 and several suggested applications are indicated in Figs. 136, 137, and 138.

Experience in northern climates indicates that loosening of the spreader boards by the action of freezing and thawing causes leakage and rapid cutting unless the spreaders are supported by sod layers as shown in Fig. 137. If the sod fails to eliminate the trouble, the plank check dams to be described later may become necessary. Burlap has proved quite effective in protecting fresh seedings and is used as indicated in Fig. 138. It should be removed when the grass is about 2 inches high.

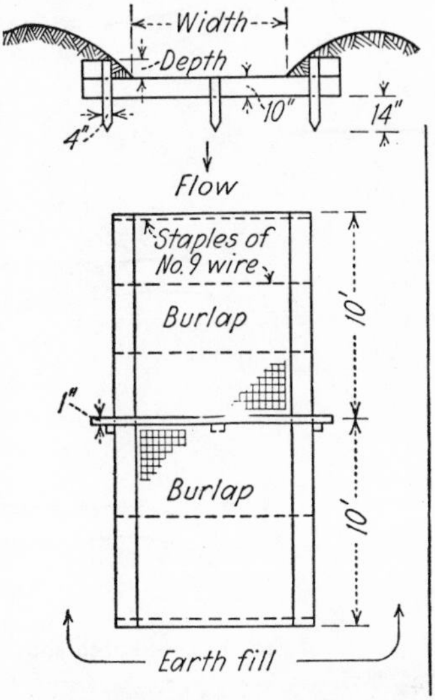

Other variations of the practices indicated have been tried, such as complete sodding, crosswise sod strips at intervals of 3 or 4 feet, and the use of burlap bags containing top soil and seed as sketched in Fig. 139.

A view of a typical outlet channel with established vegetation is shown in Fig. 140.

FIG. 138.—Use of spreader check with burlap cover for plantings. When outlet is sodded do not use burlap.

When once established, vegetated channels should be protected from damage by livestock and of course should not be used as a lane for transportation of farm machinery.

Outlet Structures.—On account of the expense, elaborate outlet structures should be avoided if at all possible. Situations apparently beyond the limit of safe control by vegetation can sometimes be altered to bring them within such limits by shifting the outlet location to slopes less steep or by dividing the water and using two or more outlets. This may be done by draining each alternate terrace in opposite directions or by dividing the flow in each individual terrace, depending on which method best fits the ground.

There will doubtless be occasional situations, however, which defy all efforts to bring the volume and velocity of the discharge

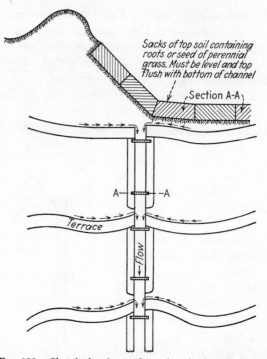

Sacks of top soil containing roots or seed of perennial grass. Must be level and top flush with bottom of channel

Section A-A

A———A

Terrace

Flow

Fig. 139.—Sketch showing sack erosion checks installed.

Fig. 140.—View of typical terrace-outlet channel with established vegetative protection. If livestock has access to the field it is desirable to fence both sides.

Fig. 141.—Terrace-outlet head flume of loose rock held together by woven wire. Tie wires are spaced at one-foot intervals in each direction.

Fig. 142.—Outlet similar to Fig. 141, but with extra protection of sodded border. (*Courtesy Caterpillar Tractor Company.*)

within the bounds of vegetative control. Although vegetation will still be effective in the upper portion of all outlets, a series of

Fig. 143.—Dams of limestone and mortar at entrance of terrace into road ditch. Upper dam protects the terrace and lower dam protects the ditch.

Fig. 144.—Type of outlet structure popular in Alabama.

structures must be used to "step down" the slope in lower reaches and reduce the velocity sufficiently to permit vegetal growth. Outlets of tile or second-grade bell-and-spigot sewer pipe have been used in a manner similar to that illustrated in Fig. 117 for gully pockets behind terraces; and continuous flumes of creosoted wood, galvanized metal, or thin concrete should also be considered.

The use of permanent structures for erosion prevention in outlet channels is essentially the same as their use for gully control, which subject will be treated in subsequent chapters.

Typical structures, of an inexpensive nature, to obviate the danger of excessive drops between terrace channels and outlet ditches are shown in Figs. 141, 142, 143, and 144. In frigid climates, asphalt mixtures to prevent frost damage have considerable merit.

All of the flumes designed to protect gully head overfalls, to be described later, are equally applicable to the conditions illustrated in these four figures.

CHAPTER X

CONTROL OF GULLIES

Theoretically, if a farm contains land in varying stages of erosion, it is logical to protect the best land from further loss first, but usually it is more practical to begin with the gullies if they are not too far gone. Numerous attempts have been made to group gullies into classes and prescribe treatment accordingly, but too many variables must be considered to enable this to work out well in practice. The best treatment of a given gully depends upon the gully location and dimensions; side and longitudinal channel slopes; size, shape, prevailing slope, cover, and drainage conditions of watershed; type of soil; and upon whether the gully is to be filled and restored to crop use, partially filled and used as a drainage channel, or merely protected against further enlargement.

In the final analysis, it is the volume and rate of runoff that is most influential in determining possible methods of control. Runoff, in turn, is a measure of the net effect of various combinations of the above-named factors.

Terminology.—The terminology on page 203 is suggested. It is similar to that used by the Soil Conservation Service and is quoted to show the variation range to be expected and to fix the meaning of terms that will be used later.

In addition, when describing a gully, notations should be made of the rate of erosion evident, whether active, partially active, or inactive, as well as the presence or absence of branch or side gullies.

Treatment of Small Gullies.—For checking small gullies, structures of the type to be described later are seldom necessary. Oftentimes finger gullies appear in a field that is later terraced. Diverting the water by terracing, and cultivation, eliminates the trouble.

If the gullies approach the upper limit in size for the "small" classification, a series of checks made of bags full of sod, or some

202

one of several patented devices, may ,be used. These latter
include sections of heavy wire bent into prongs and crimped into

Size of drainage area or watershed	Large, 25 acres or more Medium, 5 to 25 acres Small, 0 to 5 acres
Average slope of watershed	Hilly or steep, 10 per cent or more Rolling or medium, 5 to 10 per cent Slight, 0 to 5 per cent
Crops on watershed units	Cultivated Grass Brush Timber
Value of land on watershed	Good Medium Poor
Size of gully	Large, 10 by 10 feet or more Medium, 3 by 3 feet to 10 by 10 feet Small, 0 to 3 feet
Shape of gully	V-shaped Appreciable bottom width, steep side slopes ($\frac{1}{2}$ to 1 or steeper) Appreciable bottom width, flat side slopes (flatter than $\frac{1}{2}$ to 1)
Length of gully	Long, 800 feet or more Medium, 400 to 800 feet Short, 0 to 400 feet
Longitudinal slope or gradient	Steep, 4 per cent or more Medium, 1 to 4 per cent Slight, 0 to 1 per cent
Plant growth in gully	Bare Grass Trees Brush

light channel beams, and corrugated metal checks made complete
in one unit. The prong check sections are 3 feet long and $1\frac{1}{2}$ feet

high, are light enough to be easily handled, and can be moved from one part of the field to another as the fills become made. The corrugated metal check is double reverse-curved in plan and is particularly well adapted to side ditches along highways.

Should the cause of the gully be accidental or adventitious, such as having started from a wagon rut or cattle path, it may safely be filled with straw or brush and the sides plowed in.

Fig. 145.—Original condition of small gully in a field to be terraced.

This is a practice, however, that seldom works in other types of gullies, unless anchorage for the brush is provided or the water diverted. Successive stages in the restoration of a gully treated in this way are illustrated in Figs. 145 and 146. To prevent the formation of gullies in cultivated fields, it is commonly recommended that longitudinal sod strips be left undisturbed along the thalweg or flow line of swales and depressions. If the sod strips are not too. narrow, this practice is usually effective but only at the price of considerable inconvenience in plowing and cultivating, and it sometimes involves the sacrifice of appreciable areas of land from crop production. Uncontrolled weeds also become a menace.

Small gullies are sometimes reclaimed by the use of drain tile laid throughout their length and the sides plowed in. This is a very effective method but is relatively expensive.

Fig. 146.—Gully shown in Fig. 145 after being filled with brush, plowed in, and terraced. Field is ready for crops.

PRINCIPLES GOVERNING THE USE OF CHECK DAMS

The control of gullies by mechanical means is essentially a problem in applied hydraulics. Erosive velocities are reduced by constructing a series of checks which, in time, transform the longitudinal gradient of the gully from a uniform, steep slope to a succession of "steps" with low risers and long flat treads. These checks are usually of temporary character and serve to hold the fill and prevent washing while vegetation for permanent control is becoming established. If the intention is to fill the gully completely, additional checks are later built midway between the original structures, and this process is repeated as many times as may be necessary.

When the fill is complete future drainage must be diverted by terraces or else the fill must be left under a cover of undisturbed sod to prevent a recurrence of scour. Substantial checks of creosoted planks, masonry, or concrete are built where it is necessary to rely upon these alone for permanent or semipermanent control. Earth dams with drop inlet culverts are generally resorted to when both the gully to be reclaimed and its watershed are large.

Notch Capacity Required.—A very common cause of failure of checks, both temporary and permanent, to perform the function intended is insufficient notch capacity. Unless the notch is large enough to discharge water from intense rains without flooding the banks, the check is almost sure to be washed out around the ends and become ineffective. Figure 147 illustrates such a condi-

Fig. 147.—A check dam of permanent construction washed out around the ends due to insufficient notch capacity.

tion. It is therefore of first importance that the notch area conform to the requirements of Table 27.

To use the table it is first necessary to determine the runoff to be allowed for in cubic feet per second. When the watershed characteristics for the area under consideration are known this can be taken from the curves in Fig. 148. These curves are based on average conditions obtaining in the belt designated as Group 3 on the map shown in Fig. 149. Results secured from their use should be modified to conform to local conditions in accordance with the method described in Chap. IV. As a rule, runoffs in Group 2 and Group 1 of Fig. 149 will be larger because of the greater number of intense storms occurring in those localities.

Example.—To illustrate, suppose the watershed lying above a given check dam consists of 30 acres of land with slopes between 5 and 10 per cent, which would be classed as "rolling." Suppose further that about one-third of the watershed is cultivated, one-third pasture, and one-third timber. On the scale at the left of Fig. 148 follow the horizontal line opposite "30" (which happens

TABLE 27.—DISCHARGE IN CUBIC FEET PER SECOND FOR WEIR NOTCHES IN EROSION CHECK DAMS

Computed by formula

$$Q = 3.39LH^{3/2}*$$

where Q = discharge in cubic feet per second.

L = length of weir notch in feet.

H = depth of weir notch in feet.

Note: The Wisconsin model tests indicate that for weir notch dams of special design and operating under a maximum head of 1.5 feet under ideal conditions, the coefficient in this formula may be increased to 3.60.

Depth of weir notch, feet	Length of weir notch, feet								Depth of weir notch, feet
	1	2	3	4	5	6	7	8	
0.5	1.2	2.4	3.6	4.8	6.0	7.2	8.4	9.6	0.5
1.0	3.4	6.8	10.2	13.6	17.0	20.3	23.7	27.1	1.0
1.5	6.2	12.5	18.7	24.9	31.1	37.4	43.6	49.8	1.5
2.0	9.6	19.2	28.8	38.3	47.9	57.5	67.1	76.7	2.0
2.5	13.4	26.8	40.2	53.6	67.0	80.4	93.8	107.2	2.5
3.0	17.6	35.2	52.8	70.5	88.1	105.7	123.3	140.9	3.0
3.5	22.2	44.4	66.6	88.8	111.0	133.2	155.4	177.6	3.5
4.0	27.1	54.2	81.4	108.5	135.6	162.7	189.8	217.0	4.0
4.5	32.4	64.7	97.1	129.4	161.8	194.2	226.5	258.9	4.5
5.0	37.9	75.8	113.7	151.6	189.5	227.4	265.3	303.2	5.0
	9	10	11	12	13	14	15	16	
0.5	10.8	12.0	13.2	14.4	15.6	16.8	18.0	19.2	0.5
1.0	30.5	33.9	37.3	40.7	44.1	47.5	50.9	54.3	1.0
1.5	56.0	62.3	68.5	74.7	81.0	87.2	93.4	99.6	1.5
2.0	86.3	95.9	105.5	115.0	124.6	134.2	143.8	153.4	2.0
2.5	120.6	134.0	147.4	160.8	174.2	187.6	201.0	214.4	2.5
3.0	158.5	176.1	193.8	211.4	229.0	246.6	264.2	281.8	3.0
3.5	199.8	222.0	244.2	266.4	288.6	310.8	333.0	355.2	3.5
4.0	244.1	271.2	298.3	325.4	352.6	379.7	406.8	433.9	4.0
4.5	291.2	323.6	356.0	388.3	420.7	453.1	485.4	517.8	4.5
5.0	341.1	379.0	416.9	454.8	492.7	530.6	568.5	606.4	5.0

* King's *Handbook of Hydraulics.*

to be at the top) to the right until it intersects the curve marked "rolling timber." Then follow down the vertical line to the point of intersection with the horizontal axis where the runoff for this condition is found to be 30.0 cubic feet per second. One-

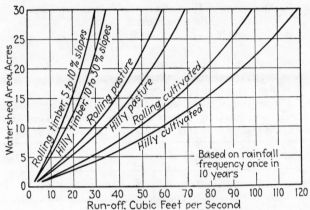

Fig. 148.—Ramser's curves showing runoff to be discharged through the notches of check dams.

third of 30.0 is 10.0 cubic feet per second. Go back to the 30-acre line and continue until the "rolling pasture" curve is intersected.

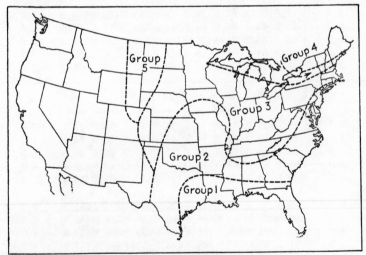

Fig. 149.—Boundaries of areas of similar rainfall intensities for short periods. (*Meyers'* "*Hydrology.*")

Following down the vertical line the runoff is seen to be 59.0 cubic feet per second, one-third of which is 19.7 cubic feet per second.

Repeat this process once again for the "rolling cultivated" curve where 99.0 cubic feet per second is found to be the runoff, and one-third of 99.0 is 33.0 cubic feet per second. The total runoff to be provided for then is

$$10.0 + 19.7 + 33.0 = 62.7 \text{ cu. ft. per sec.}$$

It is important to note that the proper figure is arrived at in this manner and *not* by adding the runoff from 10 acres of timber, pasture, and cultivated land. The reason for this is that the smaller the acreage, other factors remaining constant, the less time is required for water to concentrate at a common outlet, and the smaller the time of concentration the higher the rate of rainfall, and hence runoff, that must be provided for.

For the assumed problem, then, the required discharge capacity is 62.7 cubic feet per second. Suppose the gully is of such dimensions that a length of 7 feet is practicable for the notch. Entering Table 27 on the top line there is found under the numeral "7" and horizontally opposite the numeral "2.0" in the left-hand column, 67.1 cubic feet per second. This means that a notch 7 feet long and 2 feet deep would have a capacity slightly in excess of the required amount and is, therefore, the size that should be used. If only 5 feet of length had been available, the corresponding depth would need to be 2.5 feet.

This is easy to apply to checks of a type where rectangular notches are a part of the design. For other types, such as brush and wire checks, the center portion must be made low enough to allow, underneath a straight line joining the ends of the structure from bank to bank, the approximate notch area required.

This is made clear by reference to Fig. 150, which is a graphical representation of the effective notch area of all common types of check dams. A notch area of 14 square feet is required in all cases when *L* equals 7 feet.[1] Thus, if the top of the dam has the shape of Case *A*, the *H* in the figures would need to be 3 feet to give the necessary area, and not 2 feet as before. Similarly, the *H* in Case *B* must be 4 feet, but in Cases *C* and *D* it remains 2 feet, provided *L* is measured as indicated.

---

[1] This statement is not strictly correct since weir discharges are not directly proportional to the length times the average depth. It is sufficiently accurate, however, for the purpose intended.

Height of Check Dams.—Unless special precautions are taken the height of temporary check dams, from center of notch to bottom of gully, should not exceed 2.5 feet, and should preferably be less. For greater heights, the static pressure increases, tending to force leaks underneath the structure; and overfall scour is hard to control.

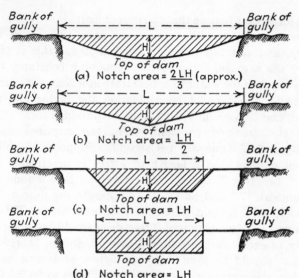

Fig. 150.—Graphical representation of effective notch areas of check dams.

Spacing of Check Dams.—For purposes of explanation it might be said that checks should be spaced so that the crest elevation of one will be the same as the bottom elevation of the adjacent check upstream. In other words, assuming the check to be watertight, a pool of water would be formed extending to the apron of the next dam above. In practice, however, this ideal is not often attained because too many structures would be required. Besides, even the most erosive soils will remain stable on some gradient steeper than dead level. For the types of soil usually encountered in gullied areas, the following grades are recommended:

For coarse sand with a considerable amount of small gravel—about 2 per cent.

For fine sand and silt loam—about 1 per cent.

For lighter silts and clays—about 0.5 per cent.

These figures do not conform to those usually found in published handbooks for stabilized gradients in the various soils. This difference may be accounted for in two ways: first, the handbooks usually assume the soil to be covered with vegetation, whereas in gully control the soil must be held stable while vegetation is growing; and second, if the soil is dense and tough

Fig. 151.—Series of wire checks illustrating usual spacing and height. Notch capacities, however, appear inadequate. The gully banks in this picture have been sloped and prepared for seeding.

enough to remain stable on steep grades, no gullies are likely to occur.

So far as spacing and height are concerned the wire checks illustrated in Fig. 151 represent good practice, but the notch capacities appear inadequate. The gully banks in this photograph have been sloped and prepared for seeding.

Other Design Factors.—In addition to the proper spacing and height and the allowance of ample notch capacity to take care of the runoff, check dams should be built far enough into the banks to be safe against water seeping around the ends and washing away the sides of the gully. This means that the dam must extend 1.5 to 2 feet into the *stabilized* side slopes, which are much flatter than those usually found in actively eroding gullies where the side slopes have not yet attained a permanent angle of repose.

Also, the checks should be trenched into the gully bottom a sufficient depth to resist undermining by static pressure, and the anchorage should be such as to withstand this pressure plus an allowance for impact of moving water and possibly ice. Loose brush and other debris thrown into a gully is generally ineffective, largely because of a tendency to float.

As an integral part of most check dams an apron or platform must be provided to catch the water falling over the top and conduct it away without scour. To accomplish this purpose the apron must be ample in both length and width. The need for this apron is less urgent and may become negligible where conditions permit a series of checks to be built so that the fill accumulated behind any one extends to the bottom of the next one above. In this case only the last or lowest check in the series requires such protection. This dam should preferably be built of permanent materials.

OVERFALL PROTECTION

The first point to receive attention in most gullies of appreciable size is at the upper end, where an abrupt drop or overhanging bank is generally found. When water falls over this head bank, it strikes the bottom and scours in all directions much as a waterspout or geyser would do if inverted. That part of the scour in the direction opposite to flow soon causes the bank to be undermined more and more until a section caves off and the process starts anew. Once started, gullies can advance into good land by this process a distance of 50 feet or more in one season, frequently where land slopes are flat enough to be otherwise stable.

Use of Brush.—The conventional method of protecting the head bank heretofore recommended has been to cut back under the bank and pack the cavity with straw and brush in the hope that further undermining will be prevented. Experience has conclusively demonstrated, however, that even though this purpose is accomplished, slow leaks inevitably develop through the brush and the runoff from intense rainfall leaps around the barrier and starts two new overfalls where only one existed before.

A better use of brush is to build one of the accepted designs, to be described later, and place it a short distance below the overhanging bank. When the intended fill occurs, the head bank will be eliminated and the overfall moved down to the dam, where it will be under control. Figure 152 illustrates the use of a

Fig. 152.—Use of double-post-row brush dam to bring under control several head banks with one structure.

double-post-row brush dam so placed as to bring under control several head banks with one structure.

Flumes.—A surer way of protecting overfalls is to cut back the head bank to a slope of about 30 degrees and install a flume of ordinary planks, creosoted planks, or galvanized iron. The lowest few feet of the flume should be bent to a flat grade and installed flush with the gully floor. The grade of the gully for at least 200 feet below the flume should not exceed 2 per cent for coarse sand and less for lighter soils. These grades should be obtained by excavation, if necessary, or insured by the construction of checks. The upper bank confluence wings should be sufficiently high and long enough to guide all the water into the flume without leakage. Frequently the wings are supplemented by earth or rock dikes.

A commercial flume of an approved type is shown in Fig. 153. The dimensions needed for a given installation may be deter-

Fig. 153.—Typical galvanized iron head flume.

mined approximately from Fig. 148 and Table 27, with an allowance for freeboard or extra depth to prevent splashing. Metal flumes should be anchored securely to avoid vibration under heavy flow.

Paved Channel.—In lieu of a flume, the head bank may be cut back as before, the sides smoothed, and the channel lined with tough sod, rubble masonry, or concrete reinforced with chicken wire. In the latter case the thickness need not be over 3 inches for low drops and small watersheds. The same precautions as before should be observed in regard to the wings and conditions at the outlet.

Fig. 154.—A concrete-lined head channel.

A concrete-lined head channel is shown in Fig. 154, which indicates a need for better protection at the outlet. In this case a load of rock would probably suffice, but for large watersheds and vertical drops exceeding 8 feet more elaborate precautions must be taken to dissipate the energy. Figure 155 represents a design developed at the hydraulic laboratory of the University of Wisconsin for this purpose. It is reproduced from *Research Bulletin* 122 of that institution.

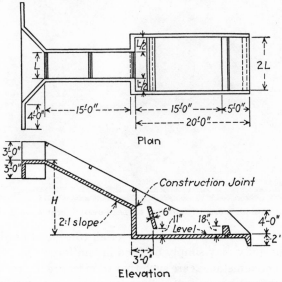

Plan

Elevation

Hydraulics of head flume or canal with steep slopes. $Q = 3.8LH^{3/2}$ c.f.s. At maximum head of 2.5′ feet, $Q = 15$ c.f.s. per foot of length (L), providing

$$L > 1\frac{1}{2}H.$$

Fig. 155.—Head channel developed at the University of Wisconsin to dissipate energy generated in drop. It should be used for large watersheds and vertical drops exceeding 8 feet.

Watertight Structures.—The best way to cure head overfalls, next to diverting the flow, is to build a permanent, watertight structure just below the head bank and count on this to hold the soil that is washed in above it. For a drop of 8 feet or less the rubble masonry dam shown in Fig. 156 will serve the purpose admirably if plenty of good rock is available.

For drops greater than 8 feet it will probably be more economical to use a full-sized earth dam with drop inlet culvert, the design and construction of which will be taken up later. However, from the standpoint of safety and good design, the rubble masonry dam is acceptable in gullies up to 12 feet deep. The design details of this dam are shown in Fig. 180.

Diversion Ditches.—The head banks of gullies in fields on which terraces are built lose their power to wreak further damage because the runoff is permanently diverted to other outlets.

Fɪɢ. 156.—Rubble masonry dam used for head overfall protection in Minnesota.

This is the most satisfactory way of all to control head erosion, since the gully may simply be filled in and forgotten.

If the circumstances are such that terraces are impracticable or are not otherwise needed, a diversion ditch above the heads of a series of gullies is frequently used to concentrate the flow in a single channel where it may more easily be dealt with.

CHAPTER XI

TEMPORARY AND SEMIPERMANENT CHECK DAMS

Check dams are conventionally distinguished from soil saving dams by reason of the fact that they are usually built of inexpensive and temporary materials in medium and small gullies where dependence for ultimate protection is placed on vegetation or some kind of plant cover. They do catch and hold small quantities of soil until the vegetation gains a foothold and to that extent are "soil savers." If cattle and hogs are allowed free access to the gully, however, or if for any other reason vegetation fails to start, all that has been gained by the check dams will be lost as soon as they disintegrate. It is important, therefore, to fence out all stock or build the dams of permanent materials unless the conservationist is willing to perform his work over again every few years.

BRUSH DAMS

Although brush dams are the least permanent of all types, are tedious to build, and are very difficult to render and keep even partially watertight, they are nevertheless recommended because of the nominal cash outlay required and because they can be made to function by giving almost constant attention to maintenance. It is believed that many farmers will prefer to build their dams of materials locally available and inspect them after every rain rather than spend money for materials of other types which are more permanent and do not require such continuous care.

Single-post Row: Longitudinal Brush.—The single-post row, longitudinal brush type of check consists of a single row of posts to which long branches laid lengthwise of the gully are anchored. As illustrated in Fig. 157 the longest branches are laid on the bottom, the length growing progressively less as the structure is built up, with the shortest on top and the butts placed upstream.

217

Every opportunity is utilized to hook forks in the brush around the anchor posts.

This type retard is adapted only to medium and small gullies. Its greatest advantage, as already stated, is the very small requirement for purchased materials. The chief weakness is the difficulty of preventing leaks and the constant attention required

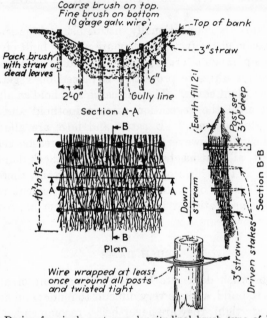

FIG. 157.—Design for single-post row, longitudinal brush type of brush dam.

to plug openings of appreciable size with straw as they develop. Unless this is done it is likely that a fill caught during one rain will be dissipated and washed away during the next.

The first step in construction, in this and all other check dams, is to cut the banks to a slope of 1:1 or flatter. Next, the gully bottom is excavated to a depth of 6 inches or more throughout the length of the dam and the earth is thrown upstream as illustrated in section *B-B* of Fig. 157. This excavation is carried up into the banks as far as necessary to provide the required notch area. The posts are then set and firmly tamped at intervals of 2 feet in holes dug 3 feet deep. Straw is packed into all the excavated portion, and the first branches, carefully selected for length and uniformity, are laid on the straw and firmly tramped into place. As the dam is built up, straw is used liberally to fill large interstices in the brush and finally No. 9 or 10 gage galvanized wire is threaded in and out around the anchor posts, securely stapled, and twisted tight.

As the leaves wither and the green brush dries out, it is almost impossible to keep the structure as firm as it needs to be for satisfactory performance. This difficulty led to the adoption of

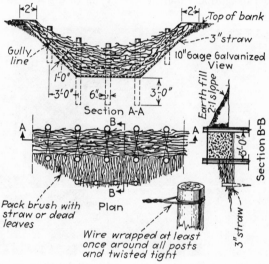

Fig. 158.—Design for double-post row, crosswise brush type of brush dam.

the additional rows of driven stakes and wire illustrated in Fig. 157. When the brush shrinks these stakes can be driven deeper to take up the slack.

The life of such dams is estimated at from 3 to 5 years under the most unfavorable conditions. This can be increased by the use of hedge or creosoted posts and slow-rotting brush.

The amount of wire and staples required for a dam of known dimensions is evident from the drawings. The cash outlay required is about two cents per lineal foot of dam, making no allowance for the wire and staples on the driven stakes. The labor required is three-fourths of one man-hour per lineal foot.

Double-post Row: Crosswise Brush.—The double-post row, crosswise brush type of check is adapted to medium gullies and also to large ones where the object is not to induce filling but merely to prevent further cutting. This proved to be a more popular type than the single-post row in spite of the greater number of posts required and the additional labor for trimming brush. These disadvantages are offset by greater ease in securing a more nearly watertight structure, less excavation, and superior stability due to the extra posts.

As indicated in Fig. 158, the first step in construction (after flattening the banks, when necessary) is to dig a trench the full

Fig. 159.—Double-post row dam showing fill caught after one intense rain.

length of the dam and about 3 feet wide and one foot deep across the gully and up into the banks. The posts are then set and tamped on 3-foot centers in both directions, and the trimmed brush or poles laid crosswise between the posts on a bed of straw. As the dam is built up the interstices between the branches are packed tightly with straw, dead leaves, or dried weeds.

Construction details are the same as those described for the single-post row dam and are apparent from the drawings.

Judging from field performance the double-post row dam is the most dependable by a good margin, although other types have their place. Figure 159 shows the fill caught after one intense rain of 4 inches, and Fig. 160 shows a view of a typical dam of this type.

Figure 161 is a diagram representing the time required for the construction of 305 typical cases of double-post row dams. For a height of two feet the labor requirement is from 1.0 to 1.5 man-

Fig. 160.—Double-post row dam 9 months after completion. View looking upstream. (*Courtesy U. S. Bureau of Agricultural Engineering.*)

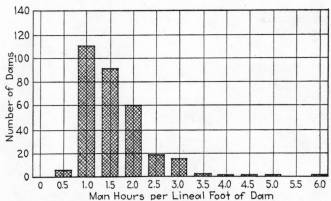

Fig. 161.—Graphical representation of labor required to build 305 typical dams of the double-post row type.

hours per lineal foot. The larger figures represent higher or very short dams or where some unusual condition is encountered such as thorny brush or hard bottomed gullies.

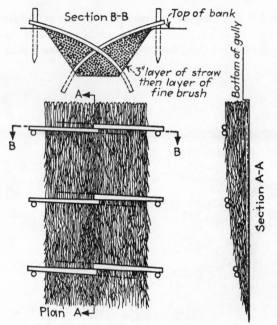

FIG. 162.—Design for pole-type brush dam.

FIG. 163.—View showing four pole-type brush dams on the experimental erosion farm at Guthrie, Okla. (*Courtesy U. S. Bureau of Agricultural Engineering.*)

The cost of wire and staples will seldom be over 2.5 cents per lineal foot.

Pole Type.—The pole-type brush dam, while not considered generally successful in Iowa, seems to work out satisfactorily when carefully constructed on small watersheds where the soil is predominantly sandy and the gully has a hard bottom. This type of dam is illustrated in Figs. 162 and 163.

WOVEN-WIRE DAMS

V-type.—The V-type check, shown in Fig. 164 is adapted only to gullies of V-shape or those with very narrow bottoms and small

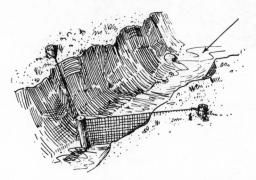

Perspective

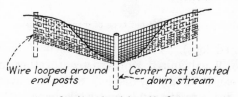

Wire looped around end posts   Center post slanted down stream

Section Looking Up Gully

Fig. 164.—V-type woven-wire check suitable for V-shaped gullies with small watersheds. Center post should not extend more than 18 inches above gully floor. Wire should be trenched into floor.

watersheds. The main construction features are the deep-set center post leaning downstream and bank trenches deep enough to bury all of the wire. Special precautions should be taken to leave the top of the center post low enough to allow the waterway area required by Table 27 between it and a level line joining the banks. Eighteen inches should be the maximum center height for this type of dam, which means that some of the woven wire will have to be trenched into the gully bottom.

Suspended-net Type.—The suspended-net dam is illustrated in Fig. 165, where the construction details are clearly shown. End posts are set at least 5 feet deep and placed well back from the edge of the banks. Additional resistance to the large stress to which they are subjected is secured by anchoring their tops to

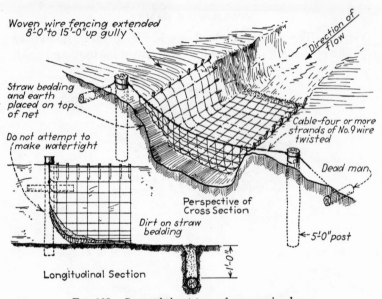

FIG. 165.—Suspended-net type of woven-wire dam.

deadmen (buried logs). The cable is formed of four or more strands of No. 9 galvanized wire twisted together, or a commercial cable can be used if available. Strips of woven wire are then wired endwise to the cable and while hanging loosely are bent and swung upstream 8 to 15 feet where they are anchored. Each strip is then secured by wire to its adjacent strips and the "basket" primed with straw and earth. Care should be taken to see that the wire extends clear up to the top of the banks, which have been sloped and smoothed to make a snug fit.

In action, this check seems to have the peculiar property of catching a fill both upstream and downstream, due probably to its ability to break up or "filter" the water into fine streams or sprays. It is flexible; and as the fill increases a load comes on the cable, which causes it to assume the form of a flat curve and leaves the filled gully wide and shallow with gently sloping

Fig. 166.—One of a series of suspended-net dams after about one year's service. Note the "basket" checks in the background which are being tried for overfall protection.

Fig. 167.—Corn growing on site of former gully after reclamation by suspended-net dams.

banks—a form easy to maintain. The same notch capacity should be provided as that allowed for any other type.

Suspended-net checks are adapted to medium-sized gullies and ordinarily require no apron if properly spaced. The dam farthest downstream in a series, however, should never be of this type since the gradient below is made steeper than before, causing the fill caught by one rain to be washed out by the next.

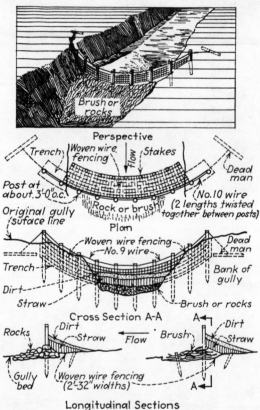

Fig. 168.—Fixed-basket type of woven-wire dam.

Typical examples of successful suspended-net dams are shown in Figs. 166 and 167.

Fixed-basket Type.—As shown in Fig. 168, posts are set 2½ to 3 feet apart across the gully and into trenches dug into the banks. Strips of woven wire are stapled to the posts; another strip is then wired crosswise to the bottom of the first and carried upstream the width of the strip where it is anchored by stakes into a cross trench below the gully floor. The basket thus formed is partially filled with straw and earth and, if necessary, an overfall apron is built of rocks or brush. A piece of No. 9 wire is threaded in and out and around the tops of the posts and anchored to deadmen in both banks, thus insuring that all the posts will act in unison even though one should become broken or washed out.

FIG. 169.—Typical view of a fixed-basket type wire dam shortly after completion.

The unit labor cost of building fixed-basket dams is shown in Fig. 170, which is a graphical representation of the labor required to build typical dams. From one-half to three-fourths man-hours per lineal foot is shown to cover a majority of cases.

Corncrib wire is adopted as standard for this and all other woven wire types. The wires are uniformly spaced 2 inches between vertical filler wires and 4 inches between the horizontal or line wires. The strips are 28 inches wide (or high) with No. 12½ gage galvanized wire at top and bottom and No. 14 wires as fillers.

Typical views of a fixed-basket dam shortly after construction and 16 months later are shown in Figs. 169 and 171. The need for fencing out livestock is evident.

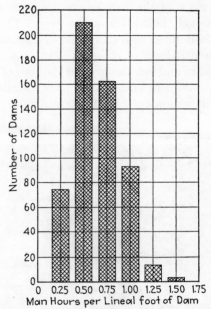

FIG. 170.—Graphical representation of labor required to build 555 woven-wire dams of the fixed-basket type.

FIG. 171.—The same dam 16 months later. The hog in the first view explains the absence of vegetation in the second.

COST COMPARISON

A summary of the cost in dollars per lineal foot for three popular types of check dams is given below. Labor cost is based on $3 per man-day of 6 hours actual work, or 50 cents per hour.

Single-post row brush:
Labor, providing brush and building, 1 hr...........	$0.500
Materials, wire and staples........................	0.015
½ post at 25 cts.................................	0.125
	———
Total cost per lineal foot........................	$0.640

Double-post row brush:
Labor, providing brush and building, 1.5 hrs........	$0.750
Materials, wire and staples........................	0.025
⅔ post at 25 cts.................................	0.170
	———
Total cost per lineal foot........................	$0.945

Fixed-basket type wire:
Labor, 0.6 hr....................................	$0.300
Materials, woven wire and staples.................	0.107
⅓ post at 25 cts.................................	0.083
	———
Total cost per lineal foot........................	$0.490

It is seen that, in each case, the large item of expense is for labor. This should make these designs attractive to the farmer who can frequently work at odd times, when his labor has little value for anything else, and thus construct a large number of check dams for very little cash outlay.

SEMIPERMANENT CHECK DAMS

The three recommended types of semipermanent check dams when properly constructed and maintained, have a reasonably long life and do not need supplementary vegetation for ultimate control to the same extent as the types heretofore described. On the other hand, they are more expensive to build and require a relatively extravagant use of materials that may not be available in many localities.

Loose-rock Dams.—Where stones or rocks of appreciable size and satisfactory quality are available, they may be used as barriers in medium-sized gullies if the drainage area is not too large—say 5 to 10 acres. The stones must be carefully fitted

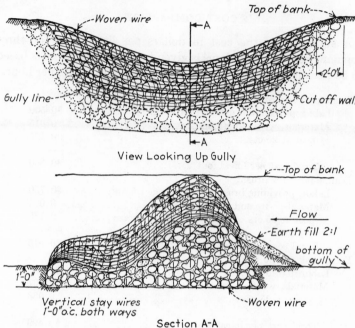

View Looking Up Gully

Section A-A

FIG. 172.—Loose-rock dam held in place by an envelope of woven wire.

FIG. 173.—Series of loose-rock dams in a farm gully.

together to make as dense a mass as possible and the structure trenched into the gully sides and bottom.

If the watershed is too large or the rocks too small, or if there is any other reason to doubt the holding power of the structure, the rocks should be set in cement mortar or enveloped in a cage of woven wire of the shape shown in Fig. 172. Vertical tie wires

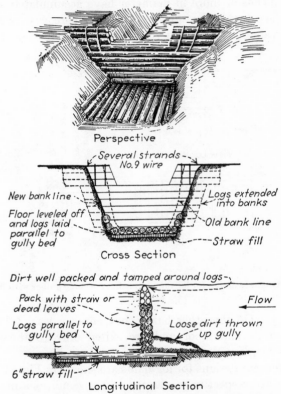

Perspective

Several strands No.9 wire

New bank line

Floor leveled off and logs laid parallel to gully bed

Logs extended into banks

Old bank line

Straw fill

Cross Section

Dirt well packed and tamped around logs

Pack with straw or dead leaves

Flow

Logs parallel to gully bed

Loose dirt thrown up gully

6"straw fill

Longitudinal Section

Fig. 174.—Design for log dam in medium or small gullies with stable bank slopes of 1 to 1 or steeper; watershed area not to exceed 30 acres.

to increase stability should extend through the structure at intervals of at least 2 feet, crosswise of the gully and at the points of inflection. If only very small rocks are available, the tie wires should be spaced 1 foot apart in both directions.

Loose-rock dams are quite popular among railroad and highway engineers for use in the precipitous gullies of hilly and mountainous regions where they have been effective even without mortar or restraining wire envelopes. The individual stones in such regions are usually large and flat and can be securely interlocked without resort to other means of binding. Ordinarily, however, loose-rock dams will be of the type shown in Fig. 173.

Log Dams.—Where timber is plentiful or where a large number of logs 4 inches or more in diameter have accumulated as remnants in the construction of brush dams, or where, as in parks, the aesthetic value of rustic structures is important, log dams fit in

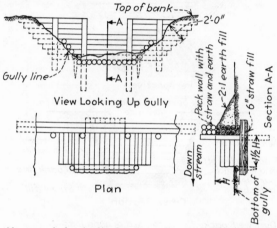

Fig. 175.—Alternate design for log dam in medium or large gullies with flat bank slopes.

very nicely. On the other hand, they entail a wasteful use of both materials and labor and are suited only to the special conditions mentioned.

Two alternate designs for log dams are shown in Figs. 174 and 175 which are respectively adapted to the conditions indicated in the legends. The height, from bottom of notch to bottom of gully, should never exceed 4 feet and should preferably be less than 3 feet. The notch area in every case should be carefully determined from Fig. 148 and Table 27. Care must be exercised to trim the logs so that they lie snugly together, and all cracks should be firmly caulked with straw or dead leaves before placing the earth backfill. The logs forming the apron or spill platform should be continued up the bank slopes to a point well beyond the extremities of the notch.

Fig. 176.—Typical small-log dam showing fill caught in one year; View looking downstream.

Fig. 177.—Upstream view of same dam showing gully definitely under control.

Figure 176 is a view looking downstream of a typical small log dam, showing a fill up to the notch level after one year.   Figure 177 is an upstream view of the same structure showing the gully definitely under control.

Plank Check Dams.—A brief mention of plank dams is included here because of their widespread use in the control of side ditches along highways and their popularity among highway engineers.

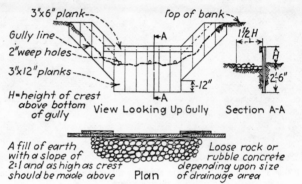

FIG. 178.—Conventional design for plain or creosoted-plank check dam.

Circumstances seldom warrant their use for gully control on agricultural land, but they are ideally adapted, in modified form, for terrace-outlet ditch protection.   A conventional design for a plank dam is shown in Fig. 178.   Either plain or creosoted planks may be used.

Discarded bridge planks may be salvaged and used for plank check dams with economy and satisfaction.   Notch areas are determined in the same manner as that previously described.

CHAPTER XII

PERMANENT OR SOIL-SAVING DAMS

The probable life of any structure is roughly proportional to its cost, and permanent dams are no exception to the general rule. The advantages of long life and self-sufficiency, however, frequently outweigh the disadvantage of costliness in many choice comparisons; but because of the expense, economic studies of the value of the soil saved and that of the surrounding land become increasingly important. A soil-saving dam, as the name implies, is expected to catch and hold considerable quantities of soil within its zone of influence and to prevent future losses without dependence on vegetation to aid. The presence of vegetation behind a permanent dam, therefore, represents double protection, and as such, is to be desired.

While soil saving dams may be, and frequently are, used as substitutes for temporary check dams in small- and medium-size gullies, their principal use is found in medium and large gullies draining watersheds of considerable size. Very often, a single dam at the lower end of a large gully system will flatten the gradient sufficiently to stop further cutting far above and beyond its anticipated zone of influence and thus enable vines, shrubs, and trees to get a start and develop protective cover throughout the length of the gully and its branches. In many cases vegetation would not have a chance to develop without the aid of the dam and, in fact, numerous instances could be cited of old established trees having the soil torn away from their roots by the force of water that was not checked mechanically.

Inasmuch as permanent dams frequently serve watersheds much larger than 30 acres, an extension of the runoff curves in Fig. 148 is necessary. These curves are shown in Fig. 179, and they are used in the same manner as that previously explained. It will be noted that Figs. 148 and 179 are based on a rainfall frequency of once in 10 years. This means that the discharge capacity of structures designed from these curves is expected to be exceeded, on the average, not oftener than once in 10 years. As pointed out in Chap. IV, it is assumed that the damage resulting from water in excess of the anticipated amount can be repaired once in 10 years for less than the cost of providing additional capacity. For dams with vertical drops of 15 feet or more, which usually serve very large watersheds, the probability of recurrence should be increased to longer periods, as will be shown.

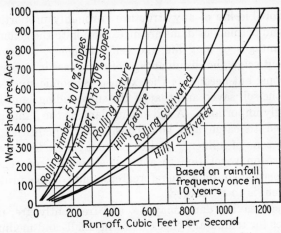

Fig. 179.—Ramser's curves showing runoff to be discharged over spillways or through culverts of permanent dams with vertical drops of 15 feet or less.

Like Fig. 148 the curves of Fig. 179 are based on rainfall intensities prevailing in Group 3 of the map shown in Fig. 149.

RUBBLE MASONRY DAMS

In areas where stone or rock of good quality abounds the rubble masonry dam shown in Fig. 180 is ideal for drops up to 10 feet. It is neat, durable, inexpensive, and effective and can be built with unskilled labor. The plans are simple and easy to follow and, as a rule, the only cash outlay is for Portland cement. Cement mortar should invariably be used in preference to lime mortar, as it has greater binding power and is more resistant to water and frost action. The stone or rock will probably need to be broken and shaped by hand to a reasonably uniform size.

Spillway crests in permanent dams are usually broader (thicker) than the notches of check dams, and this requires the use of a smaller coefficient in capacity formulas to allow for increased friction.   The values given in Table 28 are intended for spillways of this type, and they are applied as indicated in the example on page 240.   "Depth of weir notch" and "length of weir notch" in Table 27 correspond roughly to "head on crest" and "length of spillway" in Table 28.

After deciding upon the dimensions to be used for a given location from the data in Fig. 180, the gully floor is excavated to a depth of 1 foot throughout its width crosswise and for a sufficient

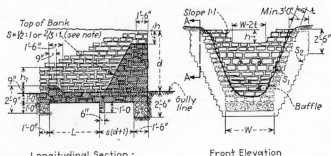

Longitudinal Section ·   Front Elevation

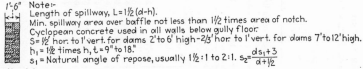

Note:-
Length of spillway, $L = 1\frac{1}{2}(d-h)$.
Min. spillway area over baffle not less than $1\frac{1}{2}$ times area of notch.
Cyclopean concrete used in all walls below gully floor.
$S = \frac{1}{2}$ hor. to 1' vert. for dams 2' to 6' high—$\frac{2}{3}$ hor. to 1' vert. for dams 7' to 12' high.
$h_1 = 1\frac{1}{2}$ times h, $t = 9"$ to 18."
$s_1 = $ Natural angle of repose, usually $1\frac{1}{2}:1$ to $2:1$. $s_2 = \frac{ds_1 + 3}{d + \frac{1}{2}}$

Section A-A

FIG. 180.—Standard design for rubble masonry dam for drops up to 10 feet.

distance lengthwise to include the longitudinal dam section, and the banks are cut back to a stable side slope.   A footing trench 1.5 feet wide and 1.5 feet deeper is dug across the gully and extended up both banks to the top, and the bottom part filled with cement mortar into which "hand size" rock are dropped to make "cyclopean" concrete.   The other footing trenches are then dug to the dimensions shown and filled in the same manner. Next, the main section of the dam is built, extending it into the banks, as shown, and leaving an irregular edge at the downstream toe to serve as a bond for the apron.   The apron is then laid and the side walls built up as indicated.

The baffle wall shown near the end of the apron is intended to help dissipate the energy of the water flowing past and prevent downstream erosion, but experience indicates that for flows less

TABLE 28.—DISCHARGE CAPACITY IN CUBIC FEET PER SECOND OF BROAD CRESTED SPILLWAYS FOR USE WITH MASONRY DAMS AND SIDE SPILLWAY EARTH DAMS

Computed by formula

$$Q = 3.2LH^{3/2}$$

where Q = discharge in cubic feet per second.
L = length of spillway in feet.
H = head of water on crest of spillway in feet.

Head on crest, feet	Length of spillway, feet													Head on crest, feet
	2	4	6	8	10	12	14	16	18	20	22	26	30	
0.5	2.3	4.5	6.8	9.1	11.3	13.6	15.8	18.1	20.4	22.6	24.9	29.4	33.9	0.5
1.0	6.4	12.8	19.2	25.6	32.0	38.4	44.8	51.2	57.6	64.0	70.4	83.2	96.0	1.0
1.5	11.8	23.5	35.2	47.0	58.8	70.5	82.3	94.1	105.8	117.6	129.3	152.8	176.4	1.5
2.0	18.1	36.2	54.3	72.4	90.5	108.6	126.7	144.8	162.9	181.0	199.1	235.3	271.5	2.0
2.5	25.3	50.6	75.9	101.2	126.5	151.8	177.1	202.4	227.7	253.0	278.3	328.9	379.5	2.5
3.0	33.3	66.5	99.8	133.0	166.3	199.5	232.8	266.0	299.3	332.5	365.8	432.3	498.8	3.0
3.5	41.9	83.8	125.7	167.6	209.5	251.4	293.4	335.3	377.2	419.1	461.0	544.8	628.6	3.5
4.0	51.2	102.4	153.6	204.8	256.0	307.2	358.4	409.6	460.8	512.0	563.2	665.6	768.0	4.0
4.5	61.1	122.2	183.3	244.4	305.5	366.6	427.7	488.8	549.8	610.9	672.0	794.2	916.4	4.5
5.0	71.6	143.1	214.7	286.2	357.8	429.3	500.9	572.4	644.0	715.5	787.1	930.2	1,073.3	5.0
5.5	82.6	165.1	247.7	330.2	412.8	495.4	577.9	660.5	743.0	825.6	908.2	1,073.3	1,238.4	5.5
6.0	94.1	188.2	282.2	376.3	470.4	564.5	658.6	752.6	846.7	940.8	1,034.9	1,223.0	1,411.2	6.0
6.5	106.0	212.1	318.1	424.2	530.2	636.3	742.3	848.4	954.4	1,060.5	1,166.5	1,378.6	1,590.7	6.5
7.0	118.5	237.1	355.6	474.1	592.6	711.2	829.7	948.2	1,066.8	1,185.3	1,303.8	1,540.9	1,777.9	7.0
7.5	131.5	262.9	394.4	525.8	657.3	788.7	920.2	1,051.6	1,183.1	1,314.6	1,446.0	1,708.9	1,971.8	7.5
8.0	144.8	289.7	434.5	579.3	724.2	869.0	1,013.8	1,158.7	1,303.5	1,448.3	1,593.2	1,882.8	2,172.5	8.0

than the peak, which are the most numerous, the wall has very little beneficial effect. Hence, its use may be considered optional.

Figure 181 illustrates a typical rubble masonry dam in Story County, Ia., just below the junction of two gullies, which it controls.

Fig. 181.—Typical rubble masonry dam at the junction of two gullies showing fill caught after one moderate rain.

CONCRETE DAMS

In localities where suitable stone or rock is not available there is no reason why mass concrete dams of the same dimensions and general design as shown in Fig. 180 should not be used, except high cost. It is usually better engineering, however, to specify thin sections of reinforced concrete in such situations, and this involves radical changes in design.

Sketch diagrams of two recent types of reinforced concrete weir notch dams are shown in Fig. 182. Type *A* is for use in gullies where the cross-sectional area is relatively small in comparison with the watershed area, and practically the entire gully width is needed for the notch or spillway length so as to produce maximum discharge capacity with a minimum depth of flow over the notch or spillway crest. Type *B* is suited for gullies that have enlarged out of proportion to the watershed drained, where it is possible to contract the cross-sectional area to a figure approximating its original size.   In this case a desirable flow depth over the crest can be secured with a relatively short notch.

Erosion control structures normally serve variable and unregulated flows that are usually less than the anticipated maximum. Hence, they may differ in general proportions and in design details from similar structures where the normal flow is the maximum and practically constant.

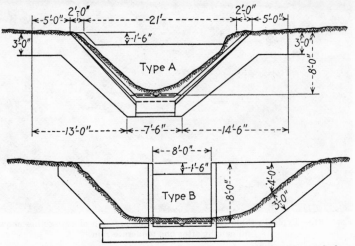

Fig. 182.—Sketch diagram of two types of reinforced concrete weir notch dams.

Detailed working drawings of Types *A* and *B* reinforced concrete dams are shown in Figs. 183 and 184.

To illustrate the use of these figures let it be assumed that one dam of each type is to be built in appropriate gullies.

Type A

Watershed area is 31 acres, rolling, cultivated.   Anticipated runoff from Fig. 179 (checked by Fig. 148) is 101.0 cubic feet per second.   Available weir notch length is 19 feet.   From Table 28, a weir depth of 1.5 feet (head on crest) will discharge 111.7 cubic feet per second.   Therefore, from proportions shown in Figs. 182 and 183,

$$N = 1.5 \text{ ft.} \qquad C = 22.0 \text{ ft.}$$

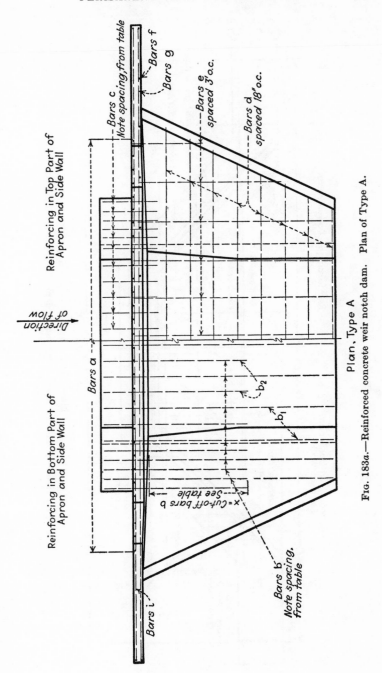

Plan. Type A

Fig. 183a.—Reinforced concrete weir notch dam. Plan of Type A.

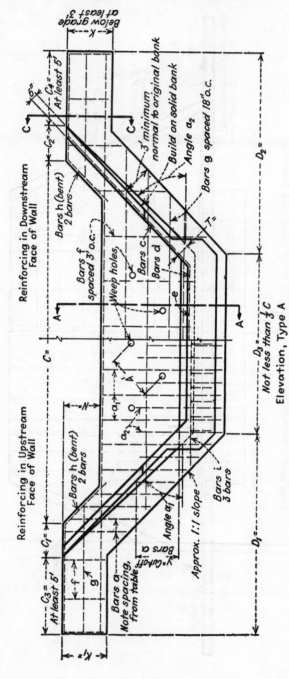

FIG. 183b.—Reinforced concrete weir notch dam. Elevation of Type A.

Also let it be assumed that the cross-sectional shape of the gully is such that the following dimensions are appropriate to make the structure fit the gully.

$D_1 = 13.0$ ft.	$C_1 = 2.0$ ft.	$K_1 = 3.0$ ft.
$D_2 = 14.5$ ft.	$C_2 = 2.0$ ft.	$K = 3.0$ ft.
$D_3 = 8.5$ ft.	$C_3 = 5.0$ ft.	
	$C_4 = 5.0$ ft.	

(D_1 and D_2 may have the same value if both gully banks are identical.)

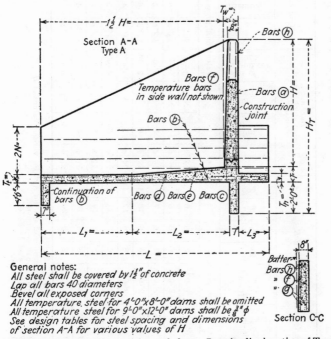

Fig. 183c.—Reinforced concrete weir notch dam. Longitudinal section of Type A.

Assuming H to be 9.0 feet, the following data may be taken from the design table on the following page.

$L = 16$ ft. 7 in.	$T_h = 6$ in.
$L_1 = 5$ ft. 6 in.	$T_t = 6$ in.
$L_2 = 8$ ft. 6 in.	$T = 14$ in.
$L_3 = 2$ ft. 0 in.	$T_w = 13$ in.

DESIGN TABLE FOR REINFORCED CONCRETE WEIR NOTCH DAMS. TYPE A

Working stress of concrete = 800 lbs. per sq. in.
Working stress of steel = 20,000 lbs. per sq. in.
H = Height to top of weir.
L = Total base length.

All concrete exposed to weather shall be proportioned for ultimate strength of 3000 lbs. per sq. in. in 28 days.

Weight of backfill 114 lbs. per cu.ft.   Equivalent fluid pressure 114 lbs. per sq. ft.

H (ft.)	L (ft.-in.)	L_1 (ft.-in.)	L_2 (ft.-in.)	Heel L_3 (ft.-in.)	T_h (in.)	T_t (in.)	T (in.)	T_w (in.)	Bars a. Tension steel in vert. cantilever — Size	Spacing (in.)	Portion cut-off	Point of cut-off (y) (ft.-in.)	Bars b. Tension steel in base — Size	Spacing (in.)	Portion cut-off	Point of cut-off (x) (ft.-in.)	Bars c. Tension steel in base — Size	Spacing (in.)	Length (ft.-in.)
4	7'-8"	0	6'-1"	1'-0"	6	6	6	8	$\frac{3}{8}''\phi$	9	None	—	$\frac{3}{8}''\phi$	9	None	—	$\frac{3}{8}''\phi$	12	2'-3"
5	10'-2"	0	7'-7"	2'-0"	6	6	6	8	$\frac{1}{2}''\phi$	8	None	—	$\frac{1}{2}''\phi$	6	$\frac{1}{2}$	3'-0"	$\frac{3}{8}''\phi$	12	3'-3"
6	11'-8"	8'-0"	1'-1"	2'-0"	7	6	7	8	$\frac{1}{2}''\phi$	5	$\frac{1}{2}$	3'-0"	$\frac{1}{2}''\phi$	5	$\frac{1}{2}$	4'-6"	$\frac{3}{8}''\phi$	9	3'-3"
7	13'-4"	6'-0"	4'-9"	2'-0"	6	6	10	10	$\frac{5}{8}''\phi$	6	$\frac{1}{2}$	3'-6"	$\frac{5}{8}''\phi$	6	$\frac{1}{2}$	5'-6"	$\frac{1}{2}''\phi$	12	3'-9"
8	14'-11"	6'-0"	6'-4"	2'-0"	6	6	12	11	$\frac{5}{8}''\phi$	5	$\frac{1}{2}$	4'-0"	$\frac{5}{8}''\phi$	4	$\frac{1}{2}$	6'-6"	$\frac{1}{2}''\phi$	10	3'-9"
9	16'-7"	5'-6"	8'-6"	2'-0"	6	6	14	13	$\frac{3}{4}''\phi$	6	$\frac{1}{2}$	4'-6"	$\frac{5}{8}''\phi$	5	$\frac{1}{2}$	7'-6"	$\frac{1}{2}''\phi$	9	3'-9"
10	19'-2"	6'-0"	9'-7"	3'-0"	8	6	14	14	$\frac{3}{4}''\phi$	5	$\frac{1}{2}$	5'-0"	$\frac{3}{4}''\phi$	5	$\frac{1}{2}$	7'-0"	$\frac{5}{8}''\phi$	10	5'-0"
11	20'-10"	5'-0"	12'-3"	3'-0"	8	8	16	16	$\frac{3}{4}''\phi$	4	$\frac{2}{3}$	6'-0"	$\frac{3}{4}''\phi$	4	$\frac{2}{3}$	10'-6"	$\frac{5}{8}''\phi$	8	5'-0"
12	22'-6"	6'-0"	12'-11"	3'-0"	8	8	20	18	$\frac{3}{4}''\phi$	$3\frac{1}{2}$	$\frac{2}{3}$	6'-6"	$\frac{3}{4}''\phi$	$3\frac{1}{2}$	$\frac{2}{3}$	12'-0"	$\frac{5}{8}''\phi$	7	5'-0"

General Notes:
See design tables for steel spacing and dimensions of section A–A for various values of H.
All temperature steel for 4'-0"–8'-0" dams shall be omitted.
All temperature steel for 9'-0"–12'-0" dams shall be $\frac{3}{8}''\phi$.
All steel shall be covered by $1\frac{1}{2}''$ of concrete.
Bevel all exposed corners.
Lap all bars 40 diameters.
All steel shall be covered with $1\frac{1}{2}''$ of concrete.

To accompany FIG. 183.

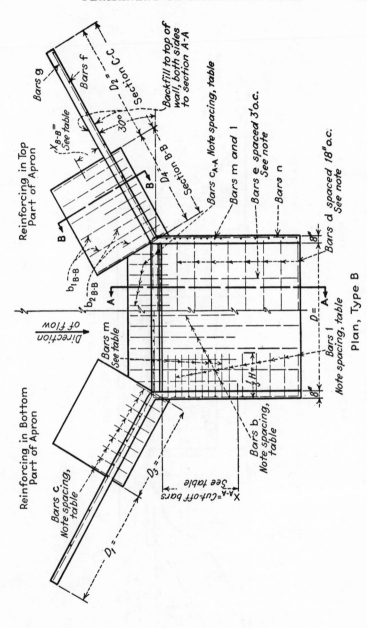

Reinforcing in Top Part of Apron

Bars g

Bars f

$D_2 = C$-C

Section C-C

30°

$X_{B-B} =$ See table

Backfill to top of wall, both sides to section A-A

Bars c_{A-A} Note spacing, table

Section B-B

$D_4 =$

Bars m and 1

Bars e spaced 3' o.c. See note

Bars n

$b_{1 B-B}$

$b_{2 B-B}$

Direction of Flow

Bars m See table

A

Bars d spaced 18" o.c. See note

8"

$D =$

Bars 1 Note spacing, table

$\frac{1}{3} H =$

8"

Plan, Type B

Reinforcing in Bottom Part of Apron

Bars c. Note spacing, table

$D_3 =$

$X_{A-A} =$ Cut-off bars See table

Bars b Note spacing, table

$D_1 =$

FIG. 184a.—Reinforced concrete weir notch dam. Plan of Type B.

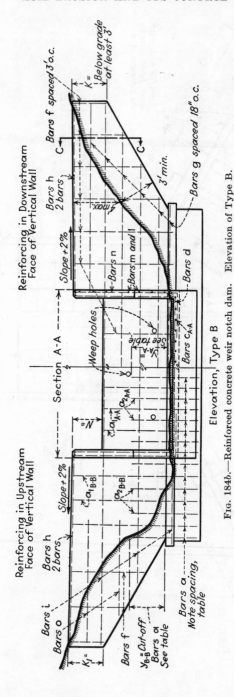

FIG. 184b.—Reinforced concrete weir notch dam. Elevation of Type B.

Reinforcing bars (*a*) are to be ¾-inch round at 6 inches on centers, and one-half of them are to be cut off 4 feet, 6 inches above the apron ($Y = 4.5$ feet).

Bars (*b*) are to be ¾-inch round at 5 inches on centers, and one-half of them are to be cut off 7.5 feet from front face of vertical wall ($X = 7.5$ feet).

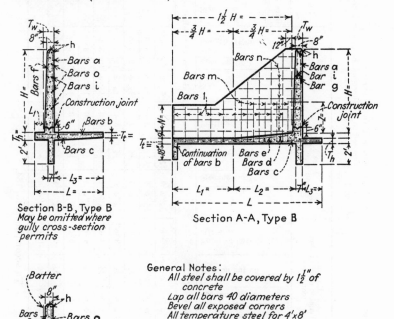

FIG. 184c.—Reinforced concrete weir notch dam. Various sections of Type B.

Bars (*c*) are to be ½-inch round at 9 inches on centers and are to be 3 feet, 9 inches long.

Temperature bars *d*, *e*, *f*, and *g* for a 9-foot dam as indicated in note are to be ⅜-inch round. For all dams, all vertical temperature steel in vertical wall, and all temperature steel running lengthwise of the apron shall be placed 3 feet on centers.

For all dams, all horizontal temperature steel in vertical wall and all transverse temperature steel in apron shall be placed 1.5 feet on centers.

DESIGN TABLE FOR REINFORCED CONCRETE WEIR NOTCH DAMS. TYPE B

All concrete exposed to weather shall be proportioned for ultimate strength of 3000 lbs. per sq. in. in 28 days.

Working stress of concrete = 800 lbs. per sq.in.
Working stress of steel = 20,000 lbs. per sq.in.
H = Height to top of weir L = Total base length.

Part A. Weight of backfill 114 lbs. per cu. ft.
Equivalent fluid pressure 114 lbs. per sq. ft.

Dimensions of dam for various heights of H.									Bars a. Tension steel in vert. cantilever.				Bars b. Tension steel in base.				Bars c. Tension steel in base.			Buttress reinforcement				
H (ft.)	L (ft.-in.)	L_1 (ft.-in.)	L_2 (ft.-in.)	Heel L_3 (ft.-in.)	T_h (in.)	T_t (in.)	T (in.)	T_u (in.)	Size	Spacing (in.)	Portion cut-off	Point of cut-off (y) (ft.-in.)	Size	Spacing (in.)	Portion cut-off	Portion cut-off (x) (ft.-in.)	Size	Spacing (in.)	Length (ft.-in.)	Bars l&m Size	Bars l&m Spacing (in.)	Z dist. bars m (ft.-in.)	Bars n Size	Bars n Spacing (in.)
4	7'-8"	0	6'-1"	1'-0"	6	6	8	8	$3/8''\phi$	9	None	—	$3/8''\phi$	9	None	—	$3/8''\phi$	12	2'-3"					
5	10'-2"	0	7'-7"	2'-0"	6	6	8	8	$1/2''\phi$	8	None	—	$1/2''\phi$	6	½	3'-0"	$3/8''\phi$	12	3'-3"					
6	11'-8"	8'-0"	1'-1"	2'-0"	7	6	8	10	$1/2''\phi$	5	½	3'-0"	$1/2''\phi$	5	½	4'-6"	$3/8''\phi$	9	3'-3"					
7	13'-4"	6'-0"	4'-9"	2'-0"	6	6	10	10	$5/8''\phi$	6	½	3'-6"	$5/8''\phi$	6	½	5'-6"	$1/2''\phi$	12	3'-9"					
8	14'-11"	6'-0"	6'-4"	2'-0"	6	6	11	11	$5/8''\phi$	5	½	4'-0"	$5/8''\phi$	4	½	6'-6"	$1/2''\phi$	10	3'-9"					
9	16'-7"	5'-6"	8'-6"	2'-0"	6	6	13	13	$3/4''\phi$	6	½	4'-6"	$3/4''\phi$	5	½	7'-6"	$1/2''\phi$	9	3'-9"					
10	19'-2"	6'-0"	9'-7"	3'-0"	8	6	14	14	$3/4''\phi$	5	½	5'-0"	$3/4''\phi$	5	½	7'-0"	$5/8''\phi$	10	5'-0"					
11	20'-10"	5'-0"	12'-3"	3'-0"	8	8	16	16	$3/4''\phi$	4	⅔	6'-0"	$3/4''\phi$	4	⅔	10'-6"	$5/8''\phi$	8	5'-0"					
12	22'-6"	6'-0"	12'-11"	3'-0"	8	8	18	18	$3/4''\phi$	3½	⅔	6'-6"	$3/4''\phi$	3½	⅔	12'-0"	$5/8''\phi$	7	5'-0"					

Section A-A.

To accompany Fig. 184.

DESIGN TABLE FOR REINFORCED CONCRETE WEIR NOTCH DAMS. TYPE B.—(Continued)

Section B-B. — Part B. Weight of backfill 114 lbs. per cu. ft. — Equivalent fluid pressure 80 lbs. per sq. ft.

	Dimensions of dam for various heights of H.								Bars a. Tension steel in vert. cantilever				Bars b. Tension steel in base.				Bars c. Tension steel in base			Buttress reinforcement				
H (ft.)	L (ft.-in.)	L_1 (ft.-in.)	L_2 (ft.-in.)	Heel L_3 (ft.-in.)	T_h (in.)	T_t (in.)	T (in.)	T_u (in.)	Size	Spacing (in.)	Portion cut-off	Point of cut-off (y) (ft.-in.)	Size	Spacing (in.)	Portion cut-off	Portion cut-off (x) (ft.-in.)	Size	Spacing (in.)	Length (ft.-in.)	Bars l&m Size	Bars l&m Spacing (in.)	Z dist. bars m (ft.-in.)	Bars n Size	Bars n Spacing (in.)
4	3'-6"	1'-0"		1'-10"	6	6	6	8	$\frac{3}{8}''\phi$	12	None	—	$\frac{3}{8}''\phi$	6	None	—	$\frac{3}{8}''\phi$	12	2'-0"	$\frac{3}{8}''\phi$	12	0	$\frac{1}{2}''\phi$	12
5	4'-0"	1'-0"		2'-4"	6	6	6	6	$\frac{1}{2}''\phi$	11	None	—	$\frac{1}{2}''\phi$	10	None	—	$\frac{3}{8}''\phi$	12	2'-0"	$\frac{3}{8}''\phi$	12	0	$\frac{1}{2}''\phi$	12
6	5'-0"	1'-0"		3'-4"	7	7	7	8	$\frac{1}{2}''\phi$	7	None	—	$\frac{1}{2}''\phi$	7	None	—	$\frac{3}{8}''\phi$	12	2'-0"	$\frac{3}{8}''\phi$	12	0	$\frac{1}{2}''\phi$	12
7	6'-0"	1'-0"		4'-2"	8	8	8	10	$\frac{5}{8}''\phi$	9	None	—	$\frac{5}{8}''\phi$	7	None	—	$\frac{3}{8}''\phi$	12	2'-0"	$\frac{3}{8}''\phi$	12	0	$\frac{1}{2}''\phi$	12
8	7'-0"	1'-0"		5'-1"	9	6	8	11	$\frac{5}{8}''\phi$	7	None	—	$\frac{5}{8}''\phi$	5½	None	—	$\frac{3}{8}''\phi$	12	2'-0"	$\frac{1}{2}''\phi$	16	3'-0"	$\frac{1}{2}''\phi$	12
9	8'-0"	1'-6"		5'-5"	11	6	9	13	$\frac{3}{4}''\phi$	8	None	—	$\frac{3}{4}''\phi$	8	None	—	$\frac{1}{2}''\phi$	12	3'-0"	$\frac{1}{2}''\phi$	14	3'-0"	$\frac{1}{2}''\phi$	12
10	9'-0"	1'-6"		6'-4"	12	6	11	14	$\frac{3}{4}''\phi$	7	½	8'-0"	$\frac{3}{4}''\phi$	5½	None	—	$\frac{1}{2}''\phi$	12	3'-0"	$\frac{1}{2}''\phi$	12	4'-0"	$\frac{5}{8}''\phi$	12
11	10'-0"	1'-6"		7'-2"	16	6	16	16	$\frac{3}{4}''\phi$	6	½	9'-0"	$\frac{3}{4}''\phi$	5½	½	4'-0"	$\frac{1}{2}''\phi$	12	3'-0"	$\frac{5}{8}''\phi$	14	4'-0"	$\frac{5}{8}''\phi$	12
12	11'-0"	1'-6"		8'-0"	16	6	18	18	$\frac{3}{4}''\phi$	5	½	10'-0"	$\frac{3}{4}''\phi$	4½	½	5'-0"	$\frac{1}{2}''\phi$	12	3'-0"	$\frac{5}{8}''\phi$	12	5'-0"	$\frac{5}{8}''\phi$	12

See design tables for steel spacing and dimensions of sections A-A & B-B for various values of H.

To accompany Fig. 184.

General Notes:
See design tables for steel spacing and dimensions of sections A-A & B-B for various values of H.
All temperature steel for 4'-0"–8'-0" dams shall be omitted.
All temperature steel for 9'-0"–12'-0" dams shall be $\frac{3}{8}''\phi$.
All steel shall be covered by 1½" of concrete.
Lap all bars 40 diameters.
Bevel all exposed corners.

The same arrangement of temperature steel that is in the apron and vertical wall under the weir notch, on the top and downstream sides of the respective slabs, shall be placed on both sides of the vertical wall and extended into the banks on each side of the weir notch.

TYPE B

Watershed area is 9.5 acres, rolling, cultivated. Anticipated runoff from Fig. 148 is 46.0 cubic feet per second. From Table 28 a 1.5 by 8-foot weir will discharge 47.0 cubic feet per second. Therefore, from proportions shown in Figs. 182 and 184,

$$N = 1.5 \text{ feet} \qquad \text{and} \qquad D = 8.0 \text{ feet}$$

Also, let it be assumed that the cross-sectional shape of the gully is such that the following dimensions are appropriate to make the structure fit the gully.

$$D_1 = 7.0 \text{ ft.} \qquad D_3 = 7.0 \text{ ft.} \qquad K = 3.0 \text{ ft.}$$
$$D_2 = 9.0 \text{ ft.} \qquad D_4 = 7.0 \text{ ft.} \qquad K_1 = 3.0 \text{ ft.}$$

Assume H to be 9 feet, as before.

Then, from Part A of the table in Fig. 184, section AA,

$$L \ = 16 \text{ ft. 7 in.} \qquad T_h = 6 \text{ in.}$$
$$L_1 = 5 \text{ ft. 6 in.} \qquad T_t = 6 \text{ in.}$$
$$L_2 = 8 \text{ ft. 6 in.} \qquad T = 14 \text{ in.}$$
$$L_3 = 2 \text{ ft. 0 in.} \qquad T_w = 13 \text{ in.}$$

Select reinforcing data, a, b, and c rods from this table for Section AA, in .the same manner as for Type A dam.

From Part B of the table, the dimensions are as follows:

$$H = 9 \text{ ft.} \qquad T_h = 11 \text{ in.}$$
$$L = 8 \text{ ft.} \qquad T_t = 6 \text{ in.}$$
$$L_1 = 1 \text{ ft. 6 in.} \qquad T = 9 \text{ in.}$$
$$L_3 = 5 \text{ ft. 5 in.} \qquad T_w = 13 \text{ in.}$$

Bars (a) are to be ¾-inch round at 8 inches on centers. Bars (b) are to be ¾-inch round at 8 inches on centers. Bars (c) are to be ⅜-inch round at 12 inches on centers and are to be 3 feet in length. Bars (l) and (m) in buttress are to be ½-inch round at 14 inches on centers, and the vertical arm on the (m) bar is to be 3 feet in length. Bars (n) in buttress are ⅝-inch round at 12-inch centers. Temperature steel, as indicated in

FIG. 185.—Example of Type A reinforced concrete weir notch dam.

FIG. 186.—Example of Type B reinforced concrete weir notch dam.

note, is to be $\frac{3}{8}$-inch round, and this steel is to be on both sides of Sections D_1 and D_2, since no other reinforcing is provided.

Pictorial examples of both types of weir notch dams are shown in Figs. 185 and 186.

EARTH DAMS

Earth dams are of two types, those with overbank spillways and those with drop inlet culverts. Very often, however, the culverts are designed to care for only ordinary discharges, allowance for excess water being made in the overbank spillway. The values in Table 28 will give the approximate dimensions of spillway required after the runoff has been determined from the curves of Figs. 148 and 179.

Location.—Earth dams should be built where the terrain is such that the influence of the dam will extend over an appreciable area and for a considerable distance upstream, preferably far enough to submerge the overfall at the head of one or more gullies. In estimating the influence distance the stabilized gradients for the various soil conditions previously given (0.5 to 2 per cent) may be used.

The best site for the dam is at a narrow neck with high banks where foundation conditions are good and where the grade of the gully floor is within the limits prescribed for at least 300 feet below the dam. The earth fill should be taken from projecting "knobs" or peninsulas in the gully banks *above* the dam site. All vegetation, stumps, and other foreign material should be plowed up and removed from the foundation before the first fill is placed. As the fill gains height, the earth should be excavated from approximately the same elevation as the point where it is to be unloaded, if at all possible.

The culvert should never be placed on filled soil. It should rest on a stable foundation that is shaped to fit the culvert barrel. The alignment should conform to the centerline of the gully below the dam, regardless of where this puts the inlet.

Side-spillway Dams.—Dams depending entirely on side spillways to carry runoff should be limited to watersheds of 20 acres or less. Invariably the spillway channel must be lined with concrete, corrugated roofing, or some other material more resistant to erosion than vegetation. Figure 187 illustrates what may happen when this precaution is neglected.

FIG. 187.—Close-up view of the side spillway of an earth dam where vegetation alone was depended upon to prevent scour.

FIG. 188.—Typical side-spillway earth dam after 2.75-inch rain. Watershed, 19 acres, hilly, cultivated. Energy at foot of spillway is dissipated by an up-curving apron discharging into the air. (*Courtesy U. S. Bureau of Agricultural Engineering.*)

Figure 188 is a picture of such a dam serving 19 acres with an experimental lining of concrete only 1½ inches thick, reinforced with ordinary poultry fence wire. It is designated as Dam B-4 on the federal erosion farm near Bethany, Mo. (see map in Chap. XIV, also Fig. 201), and has the following dimensions: height, 13 feet; top width, 5 feet; bottom width, 40 feet; length, 60 feet. The spillway is 6 feet wide at the bottom, 9 feet at the top, and has sides 20 inches high. This dam was built in May, 1932, and has given satisfactory service to date. Energy at the foot of the

Fig. 189.—View, looking upstream, of an earth dam with two side spillways which were later lined with concrete. The two issuing streams of water oppose each other and thus dissipate the energy generated in flowing down the inclines.

spillway is dissipated by an up-curving apron discharging into the air.

Figure 189 is a view looking upstream of an earth dam in Monroe County, Ia., with spillways around both ends of the dam before they were lined with concrete. An interesting feature of this design is the provision for energy dissipation by releasing two streams of water simultaneously from opposite banks. Side-spillway dams have the characteristic of forming pools of water which, being difficult to drain, usually remain until the earth fill is complete. If a farm pond is needed this is, of course, to be desired. In some cases, however, it is a distinct disadvantage, since the pool may become stagnant and unsightly and a breeding place for mosquitoes.

Drop-inlet Dams.—Soil-saving dams of the drop-inlet type are structures seldom involving an expenditure of less than $200 for the culvert material alone. Oftentimes the head of water created will run up to 20 or 25 feet, which involves pressures and volumes capable of doing serious damage, or even causing loss of life, in case of failure. Consequently when a structure of this type is contemplated, it is recommended that an engineer experienced in this sort of work be called in to design the dam and supervise its construction. The material that follows is intended to acquaint the landowner with the problems involved and to be of assistance to engineers.

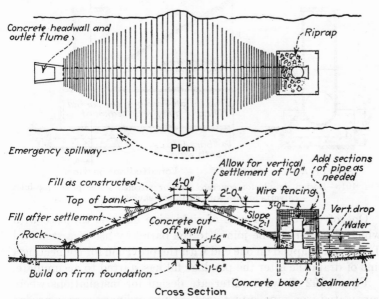

Fig. 190.—Plan and cross section of earth soil-saving dam with inlet drops of 5 to 15 feet. Concrete pipe or vitrified sewer pipe with cemented bell-and-spigot joints. Culvert gradient not less than 0.5 per cent.

Inlet Drop 5 to 15 Feet.—For dams with inlet drops of 5 to 15 feet, pipe culverts are usually less expensive than monolithic concrete and are fully as satisfactory when properly installed.

A general plan and cross section for dams of this type, using bell-and-spigot pipe made of concrete or vitrified clay, is shown in Fig. 190 which, together with Fig. 191, makes the main construction features evident. Attention is called particularly to the seepage ring or cutoff wall and to the necessity for laying on a firm bedding carefully rounded to fit the bottom quarter of the pipe. The earth fill should be carefully tamped under the haunches and up the sides of the pipe. Additional excavations for the bells should be made so that the pipe is evenly supported throughout its length. When the earth embankment exceeds about 10 feet in height over the top of the pipe, a special study should be made to determine the proper pipe strength to specify.[1] The joints should be caulked with oakum and wiped with cement to insure watertightness.

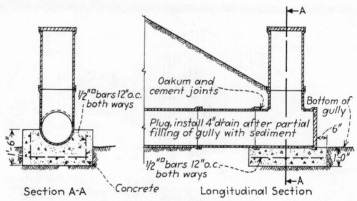

FIG. 191.—Design details for concrete pipe or vitrified sewer pipe drop-inlet culverts for use with earth soil-saving dams.

One of the best features of rigid pipe dams is the ease with which the riser can be joined to the barrel by use of a standard T-junction, capped on one end with the provision for connecting a line of drain tile after the pondage fill has started to accumulate.

Figure 192 shows an alternate design for installations where corrugated iron pipe is preferred. Only ordinary care is needed in preparing the foundation for this pipe, as it is flexible and will adapt itself readily to slight irregularities in load or in support. The important structural feature is to tamp the earth thoroughly under the haunches and up the sides of the pipe, so that when the load is transmitted to the side fill only a moderate deflection is permitted. Experience has indicated that no cutoff wall is needed with corrugated pipe, as the irregular line of contact formed by the corrugations with the surrounding earth does not permit seepage flow under the heads recommended. Reasonable watertightness is assured by following the directions in the note

[1] See various bulletins of the Ia. State Coll. Eng. Exp. Sta., particularly Nos. 93, 96, and 112.

in Fig. 192. The culvert barrel may be shop riveted in one piece or it may be obtained in sections of any length, forming multiples of 2 feet, which are securely joined in the field by the use of standard connecting bands and cinch bolts or by field riveting if the diameter exceeds 36 inches.

The junction between the barrel and riser should be formed by a 90-degree metal elbow with 2-foot sections of pipe riveted to each end. The barrel end is connected by a band to the culvert,

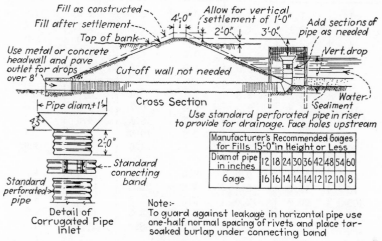

FIG. 192.—Alternate cross section, using corrugated iron pipe, for dam shown in Fig. 190.

and the riser end is banded to the funnel inlet shown in the drawing.[1] Whenever it is desired to increase the height of the riser, the funnel is removed and reconnected to an additional 2-foot section of pipe. To facilitate drainage of the pondage fill, standard perforated pipe should be used for the 2-foot section riveted to the riser end of the elbow (holes facing upstream), and each alternate section added thereafter should be perforated.

According to the best available information, the average life of plain, galvanized corrugated pipe is estimated at from 20 to 40 years, depending mainly upon the analysis of the base metal. Under special conditions and for individual culverts this life

[1] The Wisconsin model tests indicated the most efficient flare to be one whose maximum diameter is twice that of the pipe and whose depth is equal to the pipe diameter. For risers up to 18 inches in diameter this flare is preferable to the design shown in Fig. 192.

TABLE 29.—CROSS-SECTIONAL AREAS REQUIRED FOR DROP-INLET CULVERTS

Watershed area in acres	Cross-sectional area of culvert in square feet					
	Rolling land			Hilly land		
	Cultivated C = 1.0	Pasture 0.6	Woods 0.3	Cultivated 1.4	Pasture 0.8	Woods 0.4
1	1.9	1.1	0.6	2.7	1.5	0.8
2	2.1	1.3	0.6	2.9	1.7	0.8
4	2.5	1.5	0.8	3.5	2.0	1.0
6	2.9	1.7	0.9	4.1	2.3	1.2
8	3.4	2.0	1.0	4.8	2.7	1.4
10	3.8	2.3	1.1	5.3	3.0	1.5
15	4.8	2.9	1.4	6.7	3.8	1.9
20	5.8	3.5	1.7	8.1	4.6	2.3
30	7.8	4.7	2.3	10.9	6.2	3.1
40	9.7	5.8	2.9	13.6	7.8	3.9
50	11.5	6.9	3.5	16.1	9.2	4.6
75	15.9	9.5	4.8	22.3	12.7	6.4
100	20.0	12.0	6.0	28.0	16.0	8.0
125	23.8	14.3	7.1	33.3	19.0	9.5
150	27.3	16.4	8.2	38.2	21.9	10.9
200	33.7	20.2	10.1	47.2	27.0	13.5
250	39.4	23.6	11.8	55.2	31.5	15.8
300	44.4	26.6	13.3	62.2	35.5	17.8
350	48.9	29.3	14.7	68.5	39.1	19.6
400	53.0	31.8	15.9	74.2	42.4	21.2
500	60.0	36.0	18.0	84.0	48.0	24.0
600	65.8	39.5	19.7	92.1	52.6	26.3
700	70.8	42.5	21.2	99.1	56.6	28.3
800	75.0	45.0	22.5	105.0	60.0	30.0

Values computed by Ramser formula,

$$a = c\left(130 - \frac{77,000}{A + 600}\right)$$

where a = cross-sectional area of culvert in square feet.

A = watershed area in acres.

c = coefficient depending on nature and type of watershed.

Formula not recommended for areas larger than given in table.

Use above values for vertical drop through culvert up to 5 feet.

Multiply above values by 0.71 for drop through culvert = 10 feet.

Multiply above values by 0.58 for drop through culvert = 15 feet.

For fan or square shaped watersheds multiply above values by 1.25.

If side spillway of appreciable capacity is provided reduction of culvert area may be made accordingly.

may vary widely, up or down.   In particularly severe situations, corrugated pipe with a pavement of special analysis asphalt entirely filling the corrugations of the invert, and fully coated inside and out, is available at a higher price.

For culverts of the design shown in Figs. 190, 191, and 192, Table 29 may be used to determine the required cross-sectional area.   When this is known, Table 30 will give the proper diameter.   When required areas are intermediate, as they usually are

TABLE 30.—CROSS-SECTIONAL AREAS CORRESPONDING TO VARIOUS PIPE DIAMETERS

Diameter, inches	Area, square feet	Diameter, inches	Area, square feet
8	0.349	42	9.621
10	0.545	48	12.566
12	0.785	54	15.904
15	1.227	60	19.635
18	1.767	66	23.758
21	2.405	72	28.274
24	3.142	78	33.183
30	4.909	84	38.485
36	7.069	96	50.265

the next commercial size larger should be chosen.   It should be noted that the quantities shown in Table 29 are maximum values, which may be reduced under the conditions mentioned in the table unless the watershed is of unusual shape.   The values in Table 29 are based on an empirical formula developed by C. E. Ramser, Senior Drainage Engineer of the U. S. Department of Agriculture, after long experience in observing and measuring runoff from agricultural land in many parts of the United States under a wide variety of conditions.   No empirical formula ever devised, however, can be expected to fit perfectly any and all situations.   Readers who understand hydraulics should have no difficulty in finding the proper size pipe by their own calculations after having determined the required runoff by the methods of Chap. IV.

To illustrate the use of Tables 29 and 30, let it be assumed that a pipe culvert dam with an inlet drop of 12 feet (approximately 4 sections of sewer pipe riser, or 5 sections of corrugated pipe) is to serve an ordinary watershed of 25 acres of rolling cultivated land. Interpolating between 5.8 square feet for 20 acres and 7.8 square feet for 30 acres, 6.8 square feet is obtained. Interpolating likewise between a multiplying factor of 0.71 for a 10-foot drop and 0.58 for a 15-foot drop, 0.66 is found to be the factor corresponding to a 12-foot drop. Multiplying 0.66 by 6.8 gives 4.491 square feet as the proper cross-sectional area. The nearest commercial size from Table 30 is a 30-inch pipe with an area of 4.91 square feet. Therefore, a 30-inch culvert of either concrete, vitrified clay, or corrugated pipe should be used for the conditions assumed. Two lines of 30-inch pipe would accommodate a similar area of more than 50 acres or a single larger size could be used.

In case the watershed is made up partly of rolling and hilly land and is part pasture and woodland the same method as that previously described should be followed.

Corrugated pipe is considered to have equal capacity with smooth pipe of the same diameter because, under the most common and convenient structural arrangement, the increase in capacity due to the rounded junction and flared inlet will compensate for any reduction due to internal friction.[1]

Figure 193 illustrates an earth dam with a pipe culvert and emergency overbank spillway that was built in 1933.

The dam shown in Fig. 193 serves a watershed of 32 acres of slightly rolling cultivated and pasture land and is equipped with two lines of 21-inch vitrified sewer pipe. The risers are built on a concrete base, and an emergency spillway exists around one end. The materials used included:

> 72 ft. of 21-in. vitrified sewer pipe (2 lines)
> 200 ft. of 6-in. drain tile (for drainage of fill back of dam)
> 21 sacks of cement

[1] The author does not share the opinion held by some authorities that a discharge differential should apply to corrugated pipe as compared with clay or concrete under normal and practical installation conditions. The Iowa flow tests, reported in *Univ. Ia. Bull.* 1, constitute the chief evidence upon which such opinions are based and the authors of this bulletin have stated that, for short lengths of pipe with an unsubmerged outlet, internal friction has only a minor effect on discharge capacity as compared with the effect of flared inlets and outlets and of rounded junctions. Moreover, the measured difference for low heads comes well within the probable error with which runoff requirements can be estimated.

200 ft. of ⅝-in. reinforcing rods
6 cu. yds. of gravel
140 bd. ft. of lumber for forms

The dam is 90 feet long on top, 12 feet high, and has 2:1 side slopes.

Dam B-1 at the Bethany Station of the U. S. Department of Agriculture was built in 1930 at a total cost of $450, including the

Fig. 193.—Earth soil-saving dam with two lines of 21-inch vitrified sewer pipe and T-drop inlets.

culvert of 36-inch corrugated iron pipe. This dam drains 65 acres of combined rolling and hilly land, mostly cultivated, is 14 feet high, 11 feet top width, 40 feet bottom width, and 75 feet long (see map in Chap. IV).

Inlet Drops 10 to 25 Feet.—For dams developing heads from 10 to 25 feet, it is desirable to use monolithic concrete in a box type culvert and riser with an inlet of a special design based on recent model tests at the University of Wisconsin. These tests indicated that it would be permissible to place the specially designed inlet much closer to the crown of the dam than had hiterto been considered good practice. Also, by the use of special inlets, rounded junctions, flared outlets, and heads equal to 1.5

times the riser diameter over the inlet lip, a draft tube effect was developed in the culvert barrel that increased the discharge capacity far beyond that ordinarily expected. This fact, coupled with the shorter length of culvert, should result in real economy over the usual orthodox design. This advantage is offset, to a certain extent, by the necessity for precise adherence in construction to the prescribed design and by the possibility that flood debris may get into the riser stack and interfere with the draft tube action. Moreover, a large factor of safety is

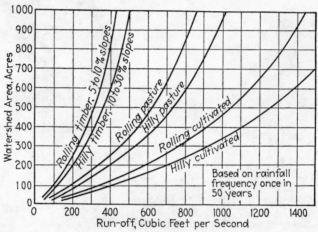

FIG. 194.—Runoff curves based on frequency of 50 years. For use with high head dams where the vertical drop is from 15 to 25 feet.

desirable because of the high heads created and the great damage that would follow failure.

These considerations make it desirable to base runoff requirements on greater rainfall recurrence intervals than those previously recommended. Varying conditions involved in the design of each individual structure of the type here considered demand the exercise of expert judgment in the choice of the proper frequency to apply in any given case. Probably the upper limit will not exceed 50 years, and this is the basis of the runoff curves shown in Fig. 194. Values intermediate between Fig. 194 and Fig. 179 can be interpolated with fair approximation when circumstances seem to warrant.

A general cross section of high head dams and pertinent details are shown in Fig. 195. A study of these drawings, which are based on the Wisconsin model tests and are substantially the same as modifications of the Wisconsin design found in a mimeo-

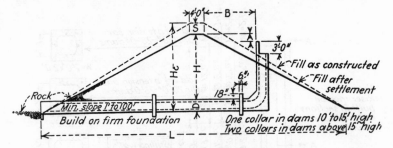

Table of Variables

H+D	Hc	S	A	B	L
10'-0"	11'-6"	1'-6"	1'-0"	9'-6"	44'-0"
15'-0"	17'-3"	2'-3"	1'-6"	12'-0"	64'-0"
20'-0"	23'-0"	3'-0"	2'-0"	14'-0"	84'-0"
25'-0"	29'-0"	4'-0"	2'-6"	16'-0"	104'-0"

FIG. 195a.—Special design, using reinforced concrete box culvert and riser, for high head soil-saving dams with vertical drops from 10 to 25 feet.

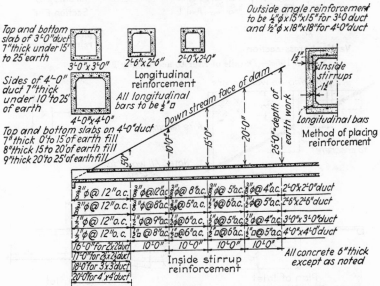

FIG. 195b.—Reinforcing details to accompany Fig. 195a.

graphed pamphlet of the U. S. Department of Agriculture entitled "Brief Instructions on Methods of Gully Control,"

together with the data in Table 31 will give all the information
needed for complete design of any given structure.

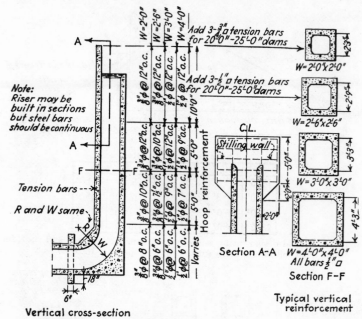

Fig. 195c.—Details of riser to accompany Fig. 195a.

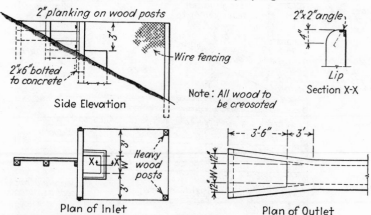

Fig. 195d.—Details of inlet and outlet to accompany Fig. 195a.

Having determined the proper runoff from Figs. 194 and 179,
the size of culvert to use for a given operating head can be taken

from Fig. 196. The operating head or total static head as here used is defined as the vertical distance from the surface of the water above the dam (one foot lower than the settled crown) to the inside of the culvert at the top of the outlet end.

TABLE 31.—BILL OF MATERIALS FOR MONOLITHIC CONCRETE CULVERTS OF HIGH HEAD DAMS

Factors		Concrete			Reinforcement—lin. ft.			
Height of dam $H + D$, ft.	Size of duct W, feet	Cement, bags	Sand, cu. yd.	Stone, cu. yd.	⅜ in. round	½ in. round	½ in. square	¾ in. square
10.0	2.0	60	5.0	10	640		450	
	2.5	66	5.5	11	830		460	
	3.0	78	6.5	13		1,000	660	
	4.0	112	9.5	19			1,730	
15.0	2.0	76	6.5	13	910		570	
	2.5	93	7.5	15	1,290		590	
	3.0	110	9.5	19		1,400	870	
	4.0	146	12.5	25			3,020	
20.0	2.0	93	8.0	16	1,400		700	
	2.5	117	10.0	20	1,400	320	750	3 pc. 14.0
	3.0	139	12.0	24		2,170	1,100	
	4.0	186	15.5	31			3,550	
25.0	2.0	111	9.5	19	2,000		820	
	2.5	141	12.0	24	1,960	710	880	3 pc. 14.0
	3.0	178	14.5	29		3,430	1,240	
	4.0	222	18.5	37			4,580	

For example, let it be desired to determine the size of culvert and riser to use in a soil-saving dam to operate under a head of 20 feet. The watershed is rolling and comprises 120 acres; 40 acres cultivated, 40 acres pasture, and 40 acres timber. A sodded depression exists around one end of the dam, which can be used as an auxiliary spillway. It is about 8 feet wide and will carry a flow of 1 foot average depth before water will begin to spill over the top of the dam. Reference to Table 28, will show the discharge capacity to be 25.6 cubic feet per second.

A rainfall frequency of once in 50 years is considered proper for this installation. From the curves of Fig. 194 the runoff

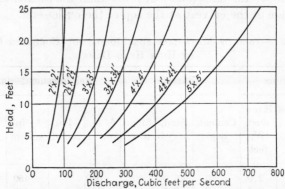

FIG. 196.—Dimension curves showing size of box culvert and riser for design in Fig. 195 when the operating head and required discharge capacity are known.

FIG. 197.—High head dam under construction showing forms in place for culvert barrel and plant set-up.

from 120 acres of rolling, cultivated, pasture, and timber land is, respectively, 385, 235, and 120 cubic feet per second. Dividing

Fig. 198.—Form work for riser of high head dam built to replace head flume shown at left.

Fig. 199.—Close-up view of a properly constructed inlet and stilling wall just after removal of forms.

each of these values by 3 and adding gives 246.6 cubic feet per second anticipated runoff. Deducting 25.6 for the overbank spillway, there remains 221 cubic feet per second to be discharged through the culvert.

Referring to Fig. 196, with a head of 20 feet and 221 cubic feet per second discharge capacity, it is found that a 3 by 3 foot culvert is the proper size to build.

Fig. 200.—High head dam under construction in California with provision for increasing the head as the fill accumulates. (*Courtesy U. S. Soil Conservation Service.*)

Figure 197 shows the forms in place and the plant set-up for a culvert barrel of the type being considered, Fig. 198, the form work for the riser, and Fig. 199, a close-up view of the inlet and stilling wall.

The bill of materials shown in Table 31 will be helpful in estimating quantities.

The high head dams shown in the foregoing illustrations were built in Buffalo County, Wis., in 1933. None of the dams illustrated make provision for building up the fill behind the dam in small increments as this was not considered necessary.

A novel arrangement for increasing the head as the fill accumulates is shown in Fig. 200, which illustrates a high head dam under construction in California. The concrete slabs at the top of the stack may be lowered as needed by sliding them between the steel guides.

PONDAGE FILL

It is surprising how rapidly fills accumulate behind soil-saving dams, where high heads are used and large areas impounded. An examination of Fig. 201, which is an accurate profile of the center line of two gullies drawn to scale, shows that a fill of more than a foot per year occurs in the long gully throughout its length. The high dam shown in the short gully is the side-spillway dam illustrated in Fig. 188, and the profile shows its pond to be filling at a rate of 2 feet per year. This pond has silted half full in $2\frac{1}{2}$ years.

On an inspection tour of Wisconsin in 1933, the author observed numerous fills behind earth dams that had accumulated at a still higher rate. In Buffalo County, Wis., a fill 17 feet deep had been deposited in less than 5 years. These fills are expedited by building diversion ditches or terraces on the high ground above the gully heads to conduct water to the "points" or peninsulas at the junction of lateral gullies and thus hasten the resumption of agricultural operations on "made land" at a lower level than that which originally existed.

Another method of speeding up reclamation is to lay a tile drain up the center line of the gully soon after the initial fill has been caught, cut back the banks to form flat side slopes with dynamite or earth-moving equipment, and till, fertilize, and seed the entire gully cross section to clover, alfalfa, or some similar crop.

STORAGE DAMS

It sometimes happens that gullies are working their way back into otherwise good permanent pasture land in locations where a supply of water for livestock is needed. If the watershed is not too large an earth dam with a relatively small tile line to serve as a "bleeder pipe" may be just the thing. The volume of storage required can be computed by taking the difference between the inflow from storms of maximum intensity for the duration periods shown on the charts in Chap. IV for the frequency period chosen, and the outflow for the same period as represented by the discharge of the tile when the water is midway

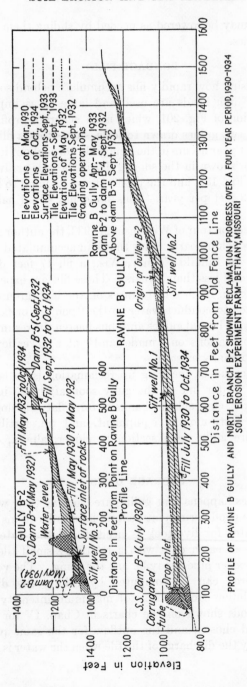

Fig. 201.

PROFILE OF RAVINE B GULLY AND NORTH BRANCH RECLAMATION PROGRESS OVER A FOUR YEAR PERIOD, 1930-1934
SOIL EROSION EXPERIMENT FARM–BETHANY, MISSOURI

between the elevation of the inlet lip and its maximum height. The effective gradient (S in Manning's formula) in this case is the slope of a line joining the water surfaces at the inlet and outlet ends of the tile. It is always desirable to provide sodded spillways to serve as a factor of safety against inaccuracy in necessary assumptions used in formulas and to take the excess discharge from very rare storms.

DROP INLETS ON EXISTING CULVERTS

One way of gaining great benefit at low cost is to erect drop inlets on existing highway culverts in situations where drop

Fig. 202.—Existing culvert under paved highway in Page County, Iowa, converted into a drop-inlet structure by enclosing the wings with a curtain wall. (*Courtesy U. S. Bureau Agr. Eng.*)

inlets are needed and can be built without subjecting the road embankment to undue hazard. The maximum estimated flow elevation should be kept at least 4 feet below the highway grade.

Many drop inlets have been built as a part of the original culvert design for improved highways, but a vastly greater number of opportunities exist for belated installations, especially along secondary roads.

A typical view of such an inlet is shown in Fig. 202. In designing the structure it may be considered a broad crested weir, the required crest length being taken from Table 28 when the anticipated runoff and permissible flow depth are known.[1]

[1] For a complete discussion of the hydraulics of head spillways with low drops, the reader is referred to Univ. Wis. *Research Bull.* 122.

CHAPTER XIII

SPECIAL USES OF VEGETATION

GULLY CONTROL

The ultimate purpose of building most check dams is to make possible the restoration of natural control through the growth of vegetation. In localities where sufficient topsoil remains and climatic and other conditions are favorable, vegetation will frequently reestablish itself without special effort on the part of man. Normally, however, devastation has advanced so far in gullied areas that unassisted natural revegetation will at best be sporadic and will require an inordinate length of time to become effective.

Four general types of vegetation are available: trees, shrubs, vines, and grasses. The following discussion follows closely the instructions[1] issued to emergency conservation technicians by officials of the U. S. Forest Service.

Trees in Gully Control

Trees will be the chief vegetation used on gullied areas. They produce heavy, deep, and broad-spreading root systems that help to hold soil particles together. In addition, they scatter over the ground a covering consisting of a mass of leaves, dead twigs, limbs, and often their own bodies. This litter absorbs large quantities of rainfall and enables a great amount of it to be stored and drained through the sponge-like cover without cutting the ground surface.

Trees also permit the growth of other vegetation such as weeds, grasses, shrubs, vines, and bushes in their midst. This supplementary growth makes the covering more effective in holding water and releasing it gradually into streams or other drainage channels.

[1] *U. S. Forest Ser. Mimeographed Handbook*, Region 9.

Trees grow and reproduce themselves, forming natural obstructions in the control of runoff. They are long-lived (sometimes growing for centuries) and can, therefore, be depended upon for extended service and for permanence as protective measures against erosion.

Trees can usually be established easier, cheaper, and more effectively on gullied areas than other vegetative coverings.

It should not be inferred from this, however, that groups of trees or forests can take care of an unlimited amount of rainfall. Ordinarily, they are effective if they cover the whole or the major portion of a slope, but their ground covering and root systems may be wholly powerless in preventing an accumulated flow from open fields above from cutting a channel through them. Heavy downpours may cause such a volume of water within the forest itself, but as a rule, runoff from the non-forested areas above is responsible for cutting through the forest floor below.

Advisability of Tree Planting.—There are certain eroded areas especially suited to reclamation by tree planting. These consist of slopes cut by gullies, usually to a depth of 3 feet or more, in which dams must be constructed in connection with the tree planting. Also, such areas are usually so depleted in soil fertility or otherwise unsuited to grasses, hay, or other farm crops, that it would be impractical to prolong them in that capacity.

There are other types of eroded land marked by gullies less in depth than those above mentioned, where reclamation can be achieved by tree planting alone.

In many instances it will be necessary to plant trees on the borders of the banks and at the heads of the gullies, extending them back as far as 50 feet or more, depending on the slope and character of the soil.

Tree planting is not advocated for erosion control where needed agricultural crops can be handled in such a way as to take care of erosion.

Occasionally areas are found where natural reforestation can be relied upon to control runoff. This can be judged by the proximity of seed trees, the prevailing winds when seeds ripen, character of soil, and the amount and rapidity of runoff. In some instances, other vegetative growths, such as vines, shrubs, and grasses will be found adequate and desirable, particularly in pasture lands.

Check Dams for Gully Planting.—The construction of gully control structures is discussed in detail in previous chapters, but since they are used extensively in gullies preparatory to setting trees, brief additional mention here will not be amiss.

It is essential that correct structures be made for successful tree planting. They usually should be of an inexpensive temporary type, but capable of holding the soil until the trees are established (a period of about five years). Their heights, generally from around 8 to 30 inches, should vary with the depth of the gully and the amount of soil to be caught for the trees. The ends of the dams should not be constructed so as to interfere with the necessary sloping of the banks for tree planting. Spaces between dams should contain sufficient earth for satisfactory settings.

If heavy drainage comes periodically through the gully to be planted, one or more permanent low structures may be necessary in order to stabilize the bottom for tree planting, since such runoff from areas above would otherwise continue to cut the channels deeper and cause the banks to fall in. The trees would thus have no chance to establish themselves. If the gully bottom is stabilized, trees will grow on it, even though there may be an occasional flow of water. In wind-blown and other loose soils, the cutting action of water is particularly noticeable, and gully bottoms of over 1 per cent gradient in these soils are rarely considered stabilized for tree planting. (See previous recommendations for maximum permissible gradients.)

Sometimes diversion ditches and dikes or terraces are necessary to conduct water away from the sides and heads of gullies preparatory to successful tree planting.

Sloping Gully Banks.—Working off the gully banks is desirable to secure cultivated ground in which to set the trees, and many times is necessary in order to flatten the side slopes sufficiently to permit satisfactory transplanting. A declivity of 1 to 1 (45°) for the side slopes is the usual rule but, under special conditions, trees have been planted successfully on somewhat steeper side slopes.

No set time can be fixed for doing this work, but it should be performed early enough in the fall and spring to permit sowing the banks to such grasses as will produce a satisfactory covering to protect against surface wash prior to setting the trees. Often it can and should be done at the time that the dams are built, as an initial deposit of earth will be provided and thus fulfil one of the objectives sought in plowing off the banks.

Sometimes the gully banks, particularly if composed of loose and sandy soil, can successfully be planted without sloping. It should be borne in mind that on perpendicular and other very steep banks a good portion of the soil worked off of them may wash away (when dams are not built), but in such instances, this is the price that must be paid for proper preparation.

Bank sloping can be accomplished by hand labor exclusively, but this is slow, difficult to do well and expensive. Where hand labor cannot be avoided, the use of grubbing hoes, mattocks, picks, spades, and shovels can be made effective. In all instances, however, where such tools are employed on bank sloping, the ground should be left rough instead of "shaved" as is often the case where spades are used for smoothing. When sloped by any method, banks should be left rough.

Teams with plows have proved to be of most value for this purpose, provided the plows are not too heavy and the gullies are not over 10 feet deep. Ordinary farm plows are too heavy to handle easily on gully banks, both for the men and the team. A plow weighing around 85 pounds is heavy enough for all practical purposes. The hillside plow is preferable to the one-way turning plow because its wing can be reversed. This enables it to be used both right- and left-handed, instead of having to drag it back one way. A long hitch and offset eveners are usually necessary to enable the team to gain good footing.

Tractors, when available, can be used advantageously in sloping banks because of the speed and depth of plowing that they make possible.

The matter of securing cultivated soil in which to set trees is not so important for conifers as for locusts, since conifers usually grow slowly and develop root systems slowly in either prepared or unprepared ground. If they are properly set on unworked areas, a high survival and normal growth may be expected. On the other hand, the locust, the chief tree used to date on raw gullied areas, is exceptionally responsive in height and diameter growth when set in prepared ground. This rapid growth is particularly desirable in erosion control because vigorous tops have corresponding heavy spreading roots and thus the chief object sought in tree planting for erosion control is attained. If planted without such preparation, the trees might live; but because of the hard ground in which the roots must grow, several years would be required before they became effective as a control measure.

When gully banks are steep, hard, and 10 feet or more high, dynamiting may be the best way to reduce them so that trees or other vegetation can successfully be set. As a general rule, the use of dynamite is not justified on banks less than 10 feet high. The exception is where soil is unusually hard or where other sloping methods are impracticable. Banks that can be worked off with little difficulty by plowing, or other methods, should not be blasted. Complete directions on the use of explosives for this purpose are available upon request to any of the large explosive manufacturers. The cost of bank "shooting" in Illinois in 1934 averaged about 10 cents per lineal foot of gully bank or $5\frac{1}{2}$ cents per cubic yard of soil loosened. These figures are based on a price of 10 cents per pound for explosives (4 cubic yards loosened per pound) and labor at $3 per man-day of 6 working hours.

Tree Planting.—Fall and spring are the two seasons for setting trees. Spring is the better of the two in frigid regions. Trees set then are not subject to heaving from freezes and thaws before the growing season, as are those set in the fall. An emergency may demand fall setting in order to complete a designated task in the spring, but such areas will in all probability need partial resetting in the spring.

The preferable spacing for trees on bank slopes and in the gully bottom is 3 or 4 feet apart, the trees being staggered; but on top of the banks and away from them they should not be more than $6\frac{1}{2}$ feet apart, preferably 6 feet. (For cottonwood and willow spacing, see "Tree Species.") Often, however, it is neither desirable nor practical to set every tree just so many feet apart. A hard narrow ridge or a hard knob on the side of the bank or a large rock might be the spot where the exact spacing falls. In such cases, good judgment must be the guide in choosing the place—a little more or a little less than the accepted distance for spacing.

Tools.—Grubbing hoes and mattocks are the best tools to use in setting trees on gullied areas. Holes of the desired width and depth (10 to 12 inches wide and 8 to 10 inches deep) can best be made with these tools, even on plowed ground, since such areas usually are not plowed deeply enough, and the holes must be made deeper than the ground is plowed.   If the ground is well plowed, however, the holes need not be so wide, since the desired loosening has already been done.   Shovels, spades, and straight blades can be used for making slits for planting where the ground is loose and needs no further cultivating—but this situation is rare.

Fig. 203.—Setting tree seedlings in St. Joe National Forest, Idaho.   (*Photo by U. S. Forest Service.*)

Setting Trees.—Trees should be set in holes as described above, with their roots down straight in deep holes and not doubled back or cramped as must be the case when set in shallow holes. They should be set at least to the top of the root collar, preferably a little over, but not exceeding 1 inch.   The ground should be packed firmly around the roots, either with the hands or with some tool made for that purpose, the feet being used for the final packing and mulching with a thin layer of soft soil raked by the foot over the packed ground as the finishing stroke.   Figure 203 illustrates a conventional method of organizing crews and setting out seedlings.

The "pocket" method is the best system to adopt in gully banks. A pocket ten inches or more wide with a flat bottom or shelf is made in the bank with a slight back slope. The tree should be set in a hole made near the center of the flat shelf. The pockets catch earth from above and hold moisture better than any other form of planting, and the work is easily inspected because the trees are readily seen.

A plow should be used where practicable for laying off contour rows in which to set trees both on gully banks and on slopes bordering them. The contoured rows hold moisture, act as miniature terraces, and make the surface rough, all of which discourages erosion.

Tree Species.—The black or yellow locust is considered the best tree to use on erosion projects for tree planting. It grows rapidly, develops a heavy wide spreading root system quickly, and improves the fertility of the ground on which it grows, thereby encouraging other growths to develop in its midst. It should be set in the gully bottoms, on the bank slopes, and on the tops of the banks as far as is deemed necessary for safety to the project. This distance may vary from a few feet to fifty feet or more, depending largely upon the soil, the gradient of the slope, and the drainage area involved. Good judgment is necessary in deciding how far the planting should extend beyond the banks and above the heads of the gullies to protect the project adequately.

Other species recommended are tulip poplar, white ash, green ash, red oak, cottonwood, willow, hickory, black walnut, white pine, black hill spruce, red pine, shortleaf pine, scotch pine, jack pine, and eastern red cedar. The tulip poplar, ashes, oaks, hickory, and black walnut will be planted chiefly in mixture with locusts, to produce seed trees for replacing the locusts with more valuable species. The white pine, red pine, shortleaf pine, scotch pine, jack pine, black hill spruce, and eastern red cedar will be used mostly as border plantings out on the banks and on other places where erosion is light and locusts are not needed, or where the soil is not suited to locusts. Conifers should not, as a rule, be set in mixture with locust plantings, but in very poor sandy plots they may be set with the locust to become the permanent stand. The only reason for this combination is to secure the locust root system as an aid in checking erosion and improving the soil until the pines can dominate. The locust does not develop well on such areas and should not interfere with the conifers. It should finally be suppressed by them.

Cottonwood and willow should be used in gully bottoms that remain too wet through the year to produce better trees. They may be spaced from 18 inches to 3 feet apart. Cuttings from these should be prepared during the winter and stratified in

Fig. 204.—Black locust seedlings in an Iowa gully one year after planting.

moist sand until time to use them in the spring. They should be made 10 to 12 inches long from limbs one and two years old, from a half to an inch in diameter.

Other species, including fruit-bearing trees such as dogwood, prickly ash, mountain ash, sumac, hackberry, etc., may, as distinct aids in preventing surface wash, find a place on some of the erosion plantings. Areas devoted to tree production will become homes, breeding places, and retreats for wild life. Food is essential for wild life existence. The presence of such food-bearing trees with their attendant wild life offers an additional stimulus to the owner to maintain these areas in good forest condition.

Hickory nuts, red or black oak acorns, and white oak acorns may be planted in selected places anywhere on prepared areas, since they require less fertile soil than the black walnut. They should be spaced 15 to 20 feet apart and covered not more than 1 inch.

Areas planted to trees have little or no chance to fulfil their function if grazing is permitted. Stock will injure or kill the trees by browsing or tramping; they are particularly fond of locusts and the tulip poplar; they also injure or destroy any other vegetation that may be planted, or that may spring out of the ground; they keep the surface packed hard. All of this hastens erosion instead of checking it.

Figure 204 shows black locust seedlings growing in an Iowa gully about one year after planting.

SHRUBS IN GULLY CONTROL

Shrubs may be used for erosion control purposes where their equality or superiority over other means is recognized, or when they are needed to supplement more valuable plants that are scarce or not available. Such instances may occur where shrubs are easily accessible and abundant for use in pasture areas or where, as an under-planting in tree areas, they will materially contribute to erosion control and render the additional service of providing food and cover for wild life.

Coral berry, sumac, and dwarf juniper are mentioned among those that may prove valuable for this purpose.

VINES IN GULLY CONTROL

Vines are used chiefly in gullies within pasture areas and in other places where protection alone is desired and is most easily attained by their use. The kudzu, the wild honeysuckle, and the Himalaya blackberry are considered the most valuable vines for erosion control purposes. Others may be used—perhaps the Virginia creeper, and periwinkle (a form of myrtle).

The same preparation of the ground is necessary for setting vines as for trees.

The Kudzu Vine.—The kudzu vine is an oriental plant imported from China and Japan, but grows as far north in this country as central Ohio and Macon, Mo. It is a legume and a prolific grower. It soon develops a mass of vines and roots that are extremely effective in controlling erosion. Individual vines frequently attain a length of more than 30 feet in one season. It is a climber and should not be planted with trees.

Its vines running on the ground will take root at the leaf joints that come into and maintain contact with moist soil. These leaf joints each become crowns that will produce numerous vines the following year just as the parent vine did. Runners from settings should not be permitted to run in just any direction the first year but should be lifted and placed so as to cover the most ground. Every third or fourth leaf joint should be covered with soil so as to hold moisture sufficiently for it to take root. This precaution should be taken late in June, in July, and early August.

This vine yields an abundance of nourishing food for stock. Its protein content is claimed to be equal to that of alfalfa. It can be propagated for settings either by covering the leaf joints as just described, or by sowing seed in the spring in prepared beds or single rows and cultivating the sprouts during the summer. The seeds should be sown sparingly, so that their vines can run freely and their leaf joints can be rooted to form settings by the above described method.

The kudzu may be planted in the spring from root-crowns one to two years old and spaced anywhere from 4 to 12 feet apart. It should be set in well-made holes that will enable it to develop good thrifty vines the first year.

The Wild Honeysuckle Vine.—The wild honeysuckle vine is known as the wild Japanese honeysuckle. It can be used in southern climates. It develops a dense root system and a tangled mass of vines but is not so rapid a grower as the kudzu. It usually attains a length of less than 6 feet per year.

It provides good winter grazing, and stock will eat it in summer if more palatable food is scarce.

The honeysuckle is easily propagated by setting pieces of it, vines or roots 10 or more inches long, in holes, slits or furrows 6 to 8 inches deep in cultivated ground or in soil caught by dams. It should be set in the spring and spaced 1 to 2 feet apart. It is a climber but far less injurious in tree plantings than is the kudzu vine, and is sometimes planted around temporary dams on tree planting areas.

The Himalaya Blackberry Vine.—The Himalaya blackberry is found growing as far north as Redbud, Ill., and will doubtless grow at a more northern latitude. In its more southern range, its fruit producing value is doubtful. It has one advantage over the kudzu and honeysuckle vines, in that it is uninviting to stock because of its strong, sharp, claw-like thorns.

Where the tips of its vines or runners come in contact with the ground, they take root and start other runners which do likewise. These can be used as settings.

Protection of areas set to vines should be provided against injury or destruction by livestock.

GRASSES IN GULLY CONTROL

Grasses (including the small grains) are considered usually as "helps" in tree planting for erosion control on gullied areas, but there are many situations, notably in pastures, where control by grass alone constitutes the best solution.

Eroded areas will rarely cover themselves with natural grasses and weeds during the first year or two. The help therefore of a quick grass covering is needed the first year to prevent unnecessary surface wash, while the trees together with natural grasses and weeds are becoming established. This can be accomplished by sowing some of the preferred varieties, such as redtop, timothy, and rye in the late summer and early fall on prepared areas, and oats, barley, common lespedeza, and Korean lespedeza in the early spring.

The seeds should be sown when the banks are plowed, if that is the season for sowing the seed, but if the gully banks are plowed out of seed-sowing seasons, and should become packed or baked after a rain, the seeds should not be sown while the banks are in that condition and covered by raking or harrowing, as is sometimes done. Such procedure combs the surface so smooth that erosion is hastened, and many of the seeds are washed away. Instead, the ground should either be scarred by a plow or pitted by striking with a grubbing hoe or mattock and the earth pulled out over the surface with each stroke. The plowed scars should be simple furrows, 3 or 4 feet apart, to make the ground rough and porous. The pits should be spaced about 2 feet apart on the contour and staggered. The seeds should then be sown and the banks perhaps raked to cover them, but not enough to smooth the ground and defeat the purpose of roughening, which is to hinder erosion.

Sometimes pasture fields may contain gullies on which bluegrass or other kinds of grasses are desirable and adequate to control erosion. The Kentucky bluegrass and the Canadian bluegrass are two of the best species for this purpose. Kentucky bluegrass grows best on fertile nonacid soil. Canadian bluegrass can be used on less fertile soil containing more acidity than the Kentucky bluegrass. In establishing stands of these grasses, it is often best to sow the seed in mixtures with redtop, timothy, lespedeza, or one or more of the clovers, depending upon the climate and the soil. Stable manure is a choice fertilizer to use in preparing the banks for a seed bed.

Bermuda grass, sometimes known as wire grass, is one of the most effective grasses to plant in gullies to control erosion. It grows luxuriantly as far north as Washington, Indiana, and will doubtless grow equally well up to the same latitude in other states. It develops rapidly one of the strongest root systems of any of the grasses. It can be propagated by seed or roots, the latter being preferable, if they are readily available in sufficient quantities. If seeds are used, they should be sown in the late spring or early summer and covered by light raking. If roots are used, they should be obtained from sod cut in the spring at the time for planting. This should be chopped at once into small pieces and dropped 12 to 18 inches apart in shallow furrows, or 2 feet apart on plowed gully banks and in silt caught by dams. The pieces of sod when dropped in the furrows should be pressed firm with the foot. Enough soil will roll into the depression to cover the pieces well. The furrows can be made by a plow or by hand with a grubbing hoe or mattock.

Bermuda grass produces an abundance of good grazing stock. Although it spreads rapidly and is sometimes difficult to eradicate in cultivated fields, its good qualities are generally well enough known to place it among the most desirable grasses to use in erosion control, particularly in pastures.

Sodding.—Sod or turf may be used to line terrace outlets, to pave flumes at gully heads, and to patch small breaks in pasture areas of moderate slope. The bottoms and sides of the terrace outlets and flumes should be properly prepared for the sod by smoothing the earth and, if necessary, by placing spreader boards in position.

The sod should be obtained from some convenient place or places where there is reasonable assurance that no erosion will ensue and that the sod will re-establish itself. Usually, the best method is to use a sod cutter drawn by a team. The turf should be cut from 2 to 4 inches thick, in uniform widths of 10 to 12 inches, and then carefully laid and tamped where it is to grow. If the ground is dry, the sod should be well watered after placing, and fertilizer application is desirable on depleted soils.

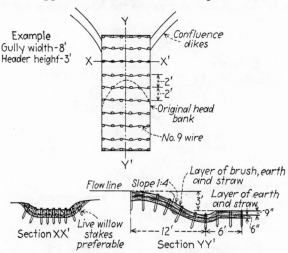

Fig. 205.—Brush flume for gully overfall protection in pastures.

Many eroded areas have medium gullies ranging from 1 to 3 feet deep and with small watersheds that can be controlled by sodding methods. Such gullies are quite often located in pasture areas. Usually the breaks or small gully heads will require sloping of the head and sides before sodding. In some cases it may be desirable to place a small diversion dike above the sodded area to divert the water until the sod has had sufficient time to become established in its new location.

In other gullies with small watersheds it may be advisable to construct a regular sod flume to lower the water into the gully and use board checks to hold the sod and spread the water, similar to the practice followed in establishing vegetation in terrace ditches. Usually a team and slip scraper is used to shape the proposed flume at the head of the gully. The flume must be properly designed with sufficient cross-sectional area to prevent erosive velocities in the flume similar to the method used in vegetative controlled terrace outlets.

About 4 feet of width for each acre of watershed area should be provided. Figures 205 and 206 illustrate two common methods of building brush or sod flumes for gullies of the class being discussed.

The above sodding methods are limited to areas where the sod can be established and where the labor cost is not excessive

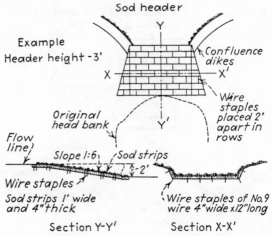

FIG. 206.—Sod flume for gully overfall protection in pastures.

compared with other possible control measures. Within these limitations, however, sodding, either completely or in strips, has valuable possibilities to check erosion, and it should be used wherever its use is at all practical. The success of this work in controlling gullies depends: (1) on having the area properly shaped, root bed well prepared, and sod carefully cut and laid, and (2) upon keeping the sod protected and maintained at all times.

STREAM BANK PROTECTION

All alluvial streams are more or less subject to bank erosion, particularly along the outer curve at bends. This action is the result of a natural process which, if uncorrected, causes the stream to continually change its course and wander back and forth across its flood plain. The points of maximum activity do not necessarily remain at the same location from year to year and banks that have remained stationary for years sometimes become vulnerable to attack for no apparent reason. To conserve fertility of bottom lands and protect the works of man, it is essential that the natural tendency to meander be held in check so far as practicable and that streams be confined to a more or less permanent channel.

The problem of bank protection on the navigable streams of the United States, especially the Mississippi and Missouri rivers, has engaged the attention of Government engineers for many years. By trial and error, definite principles to govern successful practice have gradually been evolved. It has been found that different rivers and different parts of the same river present problems peculiar to their several conditions, and each demands special consideration to determine the most economical and effective control measures. For instance, methods that have proved economical and highly efficacious on the upper Mississippi and Missouri rivers are totally inadequate on the lower Mississippi where the volume and velocity of flood flows are enormously greater. A fluctuation range of 60 vertical feet from extreme low to extreme high water also places the lower Mississippi in a class by itself.

Much less thought, energy, and money have been expended on the small unnavigable streams of the country towards adapting appropriate control measures for their conditions but, in the aggregate, this problem is hardly less important. Innumerable highways, bridges, and railroad properties depend on a stable regimen in the streams they parallel and cross for safe and uninterrupted service, not to mention the hazard to agricultural lands.

Forms of Bank Cutting.—The banks of flowing streams are subjected to two forms of attack: (1) direct rain wash or horizontal scour of the upper bank, and (2) undercutting below the water line with consequent caving along more or less vertical planes of cleavage.

REMEDIES

The following six drawings (Figs. 207 to 212, inclusive) represent recommendations of the Iowa Conservation Commission for small streams under the conditions shown. These designs

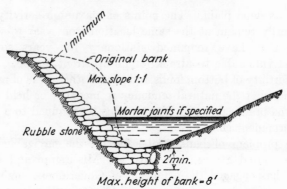

FIG. 207.—Type of stream-bank revetment suitable for small streams and mild erosive condition in localities where rock is available.

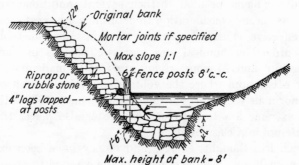

FIG. 208.—Revetment of same type as that shown in Fig. 207 but for moderate erosive conditions.

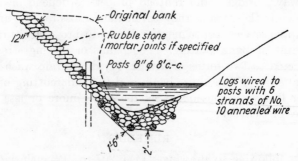

FIG. 209.—Combination stone and log revetment for severe erosive conditions.

are intended to correct both horizontal and vertical erosion. Construction details are apparent from the drawings.

Inclined Tree Planting.—A novel system of tree planting, introduced and patented by O. S. Scheifele of Waterloo, Ontario,

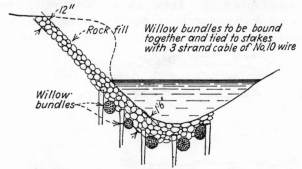

Fig. 210.—Variation of stone and log revetment using willow bundles or fascines instead of logs.

about 10 years ago, has been extensively tried out with considerable success. It is proving quite popular both for erosion protection and landscape beautification of the upper bank between low and high water lines when used in conjunction with

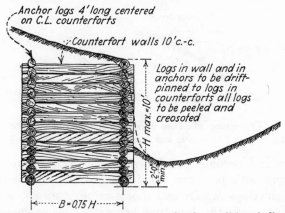

Fig. 211.—Log-crib revetment for use under the conditions indicated.

jetties, retards, riprap, willow mats, or some other means of preventing undercutting below low water.

This system was developed to meet the need for better application of mechanical principles in the use of vegetation to bind and reinforce earth embankments, levees, and river banks. It consists of forming a mattress by means of planting a series of white willow poles (*Salix alba*), 2½ to 6 inches in diameter, laid with butts at or below low water level and extending up the slope to the top of bank. These poles are laid in parallel trenches about 4 feet apart and are bound together with wire and anchored to protect the system from damage until the roots have had time

Plan

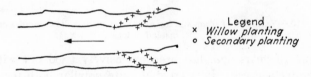

Erosion control in gullies by willow planting

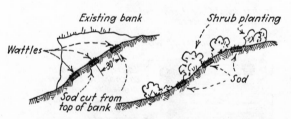

Changing the slope of a bank wattle construction

Fig. 212.—Use of live willows and shrubs in stream-bank and gully control.

to grow and become established. When lightly covered with earth and with butt ends in damp ground an extensive root system develops rapidly and shoots are sent up at every joint. The shoots cover the slope from low water level to the top of the bank and, together with the interwoven roots, form a living mattress which will withstand high velocities when well established. If the lower shoots are removed by ice or killed by prolonged inundation, the top shoots will continue to grow and support the entire root system through the original planted pole.

An investigation of the effectiveness of the Scheifele system was made by a firm of consulting engineers of Omaha, Neb., a few years ago who reported, in part, as follows:

Projects visited were installed for the city of Buffalo, Ontario Hydro-Electric, Canadian Pacific Railway, Ontario Highway Department, and individuals. Specimen poles, 1 to 4 years old, were removed for examination, found alive and in perfect condition. Four days were required for the inspection from Goderich, on Lake Huron, to Port Stanley, on Lake Erie, and from Waterloo to Buffalo. We saw white willow trees 50 to 74 years old growing on milldams near Waterloo. The extensive white willow root system has reinforced these embankments against destructive frost action, seepage, and burrowing animals.

This method was adopted several years ago by the city of Buffalo, N. Y., to protect the banks of a dredged channel along Cazenovia Creek for a distance of about 6000 feet. The plan was advocated by a landscape architect of Buffalo who was interested in providing an attractive vista along boulevards paralleling the stream.

For underwater protection any one of the methods described elsewhere in this chapter may be used, but probably the most appropriate and economical means, where erosive conditions are not severe, is to use a carpet of brushwood tied into fascine bundles and weighted down with riprap, anchored rocks, or concrete slabs.

When used in conjunction with sand traps constructed of planking secured by posts, or of sheet piling* driven below water level and parallel to the shore line, the system of inclined planting is effective and quite well adapted to lake shores subject to erosive wave action. Extensive applications of the system along the shores of Lake Ontario have resulted in complete success.

Retards.—Retards are a series of permeable spurs built out into the stream approximately at right angles to the bank line. Their purpose is to deflect the main thread of the current away from the caving bank and encourage bar formation by slowing up the velocity and causing some of the suspended silt to settle out. A sketch showing the general location and arrangement appears in Fig. 213, and fastening details are shown in Fig. 214.

* Space limitations preclude consideration of heavy masonry seawalls, the design and construction of which involve sufficient material for a book in itself.

The spacing of the retards is usually about the same as the width of the stream, and the length of each is about one-fourth the spacing. As many retards are used as are necessary to fully protect the vulnerable portion of the bank. The particular

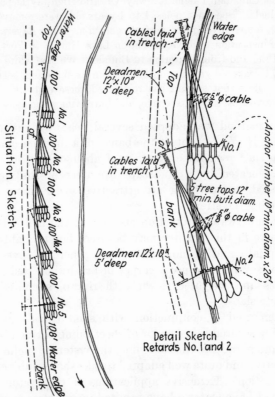

FIG. 213.—Sketch showing general location, arrangement, and construction details of retards.

design shown in Fig. 213 is suited for a stream about 100 feet wide, of moderate depth, and what might be considered mild velocities.

Woods System.—For severe erosive conditions on small streams the Woods Brothers Construction Company of Lincoln, Neb., has developed an inclined steel fence leaning downstream and supported by angle iron props and $\frac{3}{8}$-inch galvanized cables strung every 2 feet of height and anchored to a deadman in the bank. As shown in Fig. 215 each retard is held in position by a

½-inch or ¾-inch cable attached at 12-foot intervals throughout the length of the retard and anchored to other deadmen in the bank. The entire series of retards are then bound together by a cable joining their ends and anchored to the bank. Trees are attached to the top cable running along the fence in the same manner as already indicated in Fig. 214.

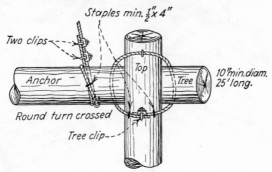

Detail of Fastenings

Table of Quantities per Retard

1 25' Anchor timber
1 12' × 10" Deadman
5 Trees

4 Lines lead cable	470'
1 Line-bank cable	30'
5 Tree connections	60'
Total cable	560'
4 Clips for each lead cable	16
1 Clip for each tree connection	5
2 Clips for each bank anchor	2
Total clips	23
3 Staples for each tree	15
1 Staple for each lead cable	4
1 Staple for each bank cable	1
Total staples	20

Fig. 214.—Detail of fastenings and bill of materials for retards.

All retards are not necessarily the same length nor need the spacing be uniform unless the bank line is quite regular. Each steel unit is 12 feet long and 8, 12, 16, or 20 feet high depending upon the depth of water and height of bank. The retards are built in a series of such lengths, heights, and number as to adequately cover the area to be protected. Note the mass of trees cabled together and serving as a bank head between the inner end of the retard and the bank, which is sloped to an inclination of 1:1 (45 degrees).

A sketch showing a typical layout and the action of a retard series is shown in Fig. 216.

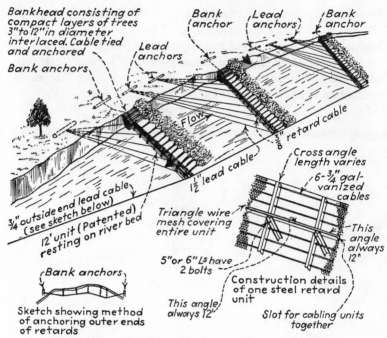

Bankhead consisting of compact layers of trees 3" to 12" in diameter interlaced. Cable tied and anchored

Bank anchors

Lead anchors

Bank anchor

Lead anchors

Bank anchor

Flow

8" retard cable

3/4" outside end lead cable (see sketch below)

12' unit (Patented) resting on river bed

1 1/2" lead cable

Cross angle length varies

6- 3/4" galvanized cables

This angle always 12"

Triangle wire mesh covering entire unit

5" or 6" Ls have 2 bolts

This angle always 12"

Construction details of one steel retard unit

Slot for cabling units together

Bank anchors

Sketch showing method of anchoring outer ends of retards

FIG. 215.—Typical installation of steel current retards.

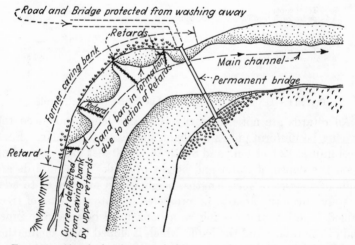

Road and Bridge protected from washing away

Retards

Former caving bank

Retard

Sand bars in formation due to action of Retards

Main channel

Permanent bridge

Retard

Current deflected from caving bank by upper retards

FIG. 216.—Sketch showing a typical layout and action of a retard series.

Photographs of typical small installations are shown in Figs. 217 to 220. These illustrate a wide enough variety of conditions

Fig. 217.—Steel retard installation on a small stream in Oklahoma. (*Courtesy Woods Brothers Construction Company.*)

Fig. 218.—Modified retards as installed in Nebraska.

to indicate that each installation presents a special problem that can best be solved by applying the general principles discussed to the needs of a particular situation. The massiveness of construction and degree of anchorage provided should be propor-

FIG. 219.—View, looking upstream, showing effect of retards.   Note the built-up foreshore.   (*Courtesy Woods Brothers Construction Company.*)

FIG. 220.—View, looking downstream, showing effect of retards in protecting a highway bridge.

tional to the depth and velocity of the stream when at flood stage. The object is not to interpose impervious barriers to the water,

FIG. 221.—Permeable dikes or retards on the Missouri River near St. Joseph, Mo. shortly after construction.

FIG. 222.—Same view one year later. (*Courtesy Woods Brothers Construction Company.*)

which will call into play its full static and dynamic pressure, but merely to retard the flow sufficiently to induce silting. The structures are most vulnerable when first installed, as each subsequent deposit of silt increases their stability.

River Bank Protection.—The kind of installation suitable for rivers like the Missouri and upper Mississippi is typified by the permeable log and brush crib dikes illustrated in Figs. 221 and 222. Structural materials and methods for the jetties or dikes vary widely according to local conditions and the purpose of the training works, but the principles involved remain the same.

Experience on the lower Mississippi, however, has conclusively demonstrated the futility of such structures on that river; so that revetment work is now confined very largely to protective blankets or mats, which lie against the face of the eroding bank or shore. The interests involved justify the expenditure of vast sums for revetment on the lower Mississippi and elaborate plant set-ups and extensive activities are a regular part of the Government's navigation and flood-protection program.

Standard practice in that locality now consists in spreading a flexible mattress against the underwater bank and extending well out into the river bed, supplemented by a monolithic concrete pavement on the upper shore. The materials of which the mattress is composed vary with the funds and equipment available and with other local conditions but most commonly consist of willow saplings woven together and weighted down with rip-rap, sized lumber grillage work; or reinforced concrete slabs precast in units 15 inches by 4 feet, 3 inches thick, and joined together with flexible couplings so that each slab is enabled to move independently of its neighboring slabs and is thus free to "articulate." Articulation permits close conformity with minor bank irregularities and assures protection from undercutting.

The method of anchorage and other details of the articulated concrete mat are shown in the diagram of Fig. 223, and the plant set-up and method of sinking are shown in Fig. 224.

Eroded Material in the Lower Mississippi.—Some years ago the author sought the opinion of a revered member of the Mississippi River Commission who lived beside the river and spent his entire life studying its vagaries. The following excerpts

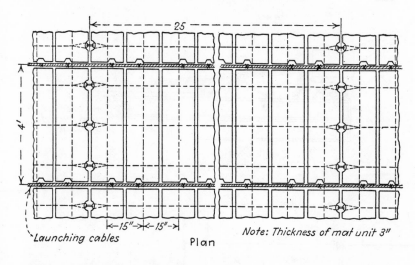

Note: Thickness of mat unit 3″

Plan

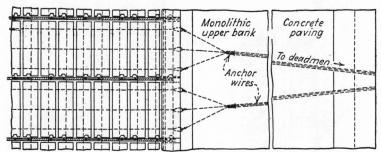

Partial plan showing mat and upper bank pavement

Partial Elevation showing mat and upper bank pavement

FIG. 223.—Diagram showing partial plan and elevation of articulated concrete mat revetment for lower Mississippi River.

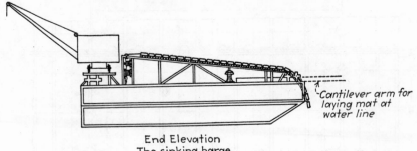

End Elevation
The sinking barge

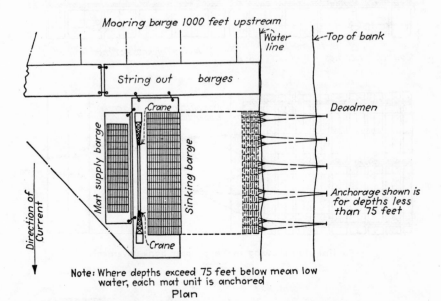

Mooring barge 1000 feet upstream

Water line

←--Top of bank

String out barges

Crane

Deadmen

Mat supply barge

Sinking barge

Crane

Direction of Current

Anchorage shown is for depths less than 75 feet

Note: Where depths exceed 75 feet below mean low water, each mat unit is anchored

Plan

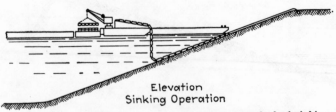

Elevation
Sinking Operation

Fig. 224.—Diagram showing plant set-up and method of sinking articulated concrete mat.

from his letter on the subject are thought to be not only interesting and instructive but quite relevant to the theme of this book:

The amount of silt which is carried in suspension varies very greatly, so also does the amount of larger matter, such as gravel, which is rolled along the bottom of the river. The per cent of turbidity increases with the depth below the surface of the water. While the per cent of silt that can be carried in suspension is dependent on the velocity of the current, it does not necessarily follow that the greatest per cent is transported by the river when its velocity is the greatest; in fact, it has

Fig. 225.—Typical example of bank caving in gullies or small streams. (*Courtesy Caterpillar Tractor Company.*)

been observed at times that a greater per cent of silt was being carried in suspension when the current was, say, 5 feet a second than was the case at other times when the velocity was as much as 8 feet a second. The water can carry so much in suspension, and no more, dependent upon the velocity (and depth); any excess over a certain per cent for a given velocity is, of course, deposited. The per cent and volume of silt transported is greatest during floods and least during protracted low water stages.

The silt carried by the lower Mississippi River, that is the main trunk below Cairo, Ill., comes from two sources: first, that which is supplied by the material which comes from caving in of the banks of the river itself; and second, that which is brought into the river by the tributaries. Of the latter a part comes from caving banks along the tributaries and a part from surface erosion over the watersheds generally.

Careful estimates made of the caving banks along that part of the lower Mississippi from Cairo, Ill., to Donaldsonville, La., a midstream distance of 885 miles and 921 miles following the caving banks, gives the average annual volume per mile that caves into the river along this stretch to be 1,003,579 cubic yards or 27,096,633 cubic feet, or a total volume amounting to 10 square miles 86 feet deep. This is the stretch of river where the greatest caving occurs, but of course some caving takes place all along the stream.

The vast volume of material that caves into the river from its banks is not carried into the Gulf but is deposited a short distance from where it originates, thus going to build up the enormous bars along the river. While caving eats away the bank on one side of the stream, deposits build it out on the other, the result being that the width and depth of the river remain practically the same.

Estimates of the volume of silt deposited annually in the Gulf of Mexico by the Mississippi River vary somewhat, but not greatly. Humphrey and Abbot give for the main river and outlets one mile square and 263 feet deep as the average annual volume carried into the Gulf. This is as reliable an estimate as any that has been recorded and may be taken as representing the true quantity.

While it has not been definitely established, it is estimated that the total volume of silt brought into the main trunk of the Mississippi by the tributary streams is about equal to the volume that is carried into the Gulf of Mexico. That carried into the Gulf is, however, not necessarily the same material that is brought by the tributaries into the main river, for some of this is deposited on the bars along the way and some from the caving banks is carried into the Gulf.

A typical example of bank caving is shown in Fig. 225 which represents a channel that might be classed either as a gully or as an intermittent stream.

CHAPTER XIV

SOIL CONSERVATION AND LAND USE

As the detrimental effect of the promiscuous use of land for intertilled crops becomes more evident and more generally recognized and understood there develops an overwhelming sentiment to do something about it before, indeed, it is too late. Already the political leaders of this country, regardless of partisan affiliation, are all but unanimous in urging an end to the period of exploitation and the initiation of a new era of conservation with the reorganization of our soil resources on a basis of permanent productivity. Such reorganization is an exceedingly complex problem, impinging as it does upon many phases of American life; social, economic, and governmental. A long time will be required to work it out on the basis of the greatest good to the greatest number, and many false starts will doubtless be taken and retraced before a final solution is reached. Meanwhile it is essential that physical data on erosional behavior of different soils under various climatic, topographic, cultural, and cropping conditions be collected as rapidly and on as widespread a scale as possible so that definite recommendations on the best use of land can eventually be based on quantitative facts and not opinions. Certain broad generalizations can of course be made upon the basis of present knowledge, as may be illustrated by the situation depicted in Fig. 226. Obviously the attempt to grow cultivated crops on slopes such as this must inevitably end in complete soil removal and utter exhaustion within a very short time. If maladjusted economic pressure forces continued cultivation of this class of land, bench terraces such as those shown in Fig. 69 provide the only kind of protection possible.

FACT FINDING EXPERIMENTS AND METHODS

Extreme conditions are easily recognized, and the proper remedy may be prescribed almost automatically. Although some confusion arises in the border zones between forest and pasture, and pasture and cropland, quantitative data are most needed in delimiting the upper slope on land suited for intertilled crops and in determining that combination of cultural and cropping practices to yield maximum returns and at the same time insure proper soil and fertility equilibrium.

Federal Experimental Farms.—That progress along this line is being made is indicated in Chap. I with the mention of the 13 experimental farms that have been established to secure

Fig. 226.—Typical scene in many mountainous sections east of the Mississippi River. (*Courtesy U. S. Bureau Agr. Econ.*)

research data for various erosional areas in the United States by the federal government cooperating with the respective states. As a typical example of the variety and scope of the investigations under way on these farms, a list of the experiments being conducted at Bethany, Mo., is quoted, together with a brief description of each and with an accompanying map, Fig. 227.

LIST OF EXPERIMENTS UNDER WAY AT THE BETHANY SOIL EROSION EXPERIMENT STATION

Experiment 1—Field L

Object: To measure the soil loss and surface runoff under different cropping systems and cultural practices on land showing an 8 per cent slope.

Method: Ten plats, nine of which are identical in size and slope, with the tenth one double in length, are so arranged that different cropping systems, fertilizer treatments, and cultural practices can be followed and the resultant water, soil, and plant food losses from each plat accurately determined by catching all the wash-off in large concrete tanks.

Experiment 2—Field L

Object: To determine whether or not it is possible *economically* to make the badly eroded places or bald spots on farms throughout this region productive.

Method: Nine uniform plats, each 80 feet long, 8 per cent slope, have been laid out on exposed subsoil; and by use of divisor flumes the water and soil losses from each plat, on which different cropping systems are used, will be accurately measured and crop yields kept.

Experiment 3—Field L

Object: To determine the effect of incorporating different types of organic matter, either applied direct or through crop residues, on erosion.

Method: Nine uniform plats, each 125 feet long, 8 per cent slope, will receive different types of organic matter, both where the land is cropped to different crops and where the land is left without crop, or kept fallow. Through the use of divisor flumes the amount of soil and water lost from each plat will be determined.

Experiment 4—Field G-1

Object: To compare the different soil treatments and cropping systems for improving badly eroded land recently terraced, using terraces with small cross sections.

Method: A five-acre tract has been divided into three large tracts where different cropping systems and fertilizer practices will be compared. A small tract was also left untreated to serve as check. This is a continuation of Experiment 2, but on a field scale.

Experiment 5—Field E

Object: To compare the effect of reducing the length of slope, either mechanically (terracing) or by having the slope occupied by different crops, on erosion losses and crop yields.

Method: Part of a uniform area was terraced, while the other part was left unterraced. The cropping system for the entire area is so planned that when corn occupies either the upper or lower half of the slope, oats or clover and timothy will occupy the remaining half.

Experiment 6—Fields E-F

Object: To determine to what extent terracing may make it possible to keep land in corn more of the time without serious erosion or decreased crop yields.

Method: Erosion losses and crop yields will be compared on terraced and unterraced land cropped to corn one-fourth, one-half and three-fourths of

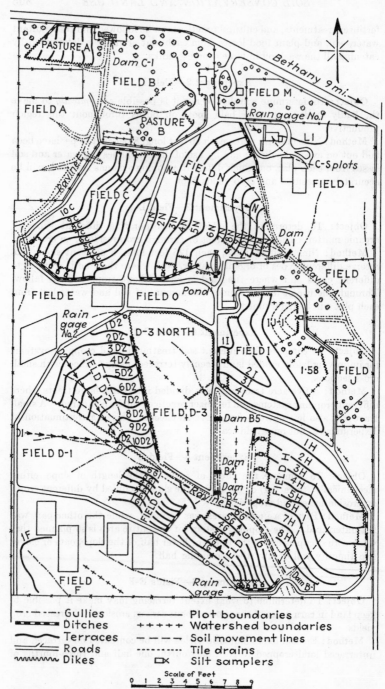

FIG. 227.—Map of Bethany Soil Erosion Farm. (For list of experiments illustrated see opposite page.)

the time, using 3 series of plats so that each crop is to be represented each year.

Experiment 7—Field F

Object: To compare the influence of different crop rotations ·on erosion losses and crop yields.

Method: Twelve one-fifth acre plats have been laid out on an unterraced area, and cropping systems with different proportions of corn or cultivated crops will be used and the resultant crop yields and erosion losses compared.

Experiment 8—Fields C-D-E-F-G-H-I-N

Object: To observe the comparative effect of different cultural practices on erosion losses.

Method: In various places the following farm practices will be compared: (1) Checking corn *vs.* drilling on terraced land; (2) contour farming of terraced and unterraced land *vs.* farming up and down the slope; (3) fall *vs.* spring plowing; (4) deep plowing *vs.* shallow plowing; (5) effect of subsoiling on water penetration and erosion loss.

Experiment 9—Field B

Object: To compare the soil and water losses as well as carrying capacity from bluegrass pasture land when intensely grazed with a similar pasture land moderately grazed.

Method: Two similar areas of one-third acre each have been laid out, divisor flumes installed, and one plat will be intensely grazed with sheep while the other will be moderately grazed, and the erosion losses will be compared.

Experiment 10—Field L

Object: To observe the effectiveness of "contour strip farming" on controlling erosion.

Method: An eight-acre field has been laid out on the contour, using a 6-foot interval between contour lines on the upper strip, and 7-foot vertical

---

Fig. 227.—Experiment: 31. Comparison of cultivated areas; terraced (*D*-2), unterraced (*D*-1 and *D*-3). 32. Comparison of different crops and rotations on terraces 2*H* to 6*H* and 2*G*. 51. Different vertical spacings on 7 per cent slope: 4*N*, 3 ft., 5*N*, 5 ft. and 6*N*, 7 ft. 52. Different vertical spacings on 12 per cent slope: 3*G*-5 ft., 4*G*-7 ft. and 5*G*-9 ft. 53. Different grades: fall in 100 ft. 5*C*-8″; 6*C*-6″; 7*C*-4″; 8*C*-2″; 9*C*-level and 10*C*-0-4″. 54. Level terraces 9*C*, 1*N*, 2*N* and 7*N* to 13 *N*. 55. Different lengths—450 to 2450 ft. terraces 1*I*, 2*I*, 3*I*, and 4*I*. 56. Soil movement—lines *D*-1 *D*-2, *G* and *N*. 57*A*. Terraces— methods and costs of construction—size and cross sections. *B*. Farm machinery design and operation in constructing terraces and farming. 58*A*. Measurement of runoff and erosion from unterraced watersheds—pasture *B*-1-*D*-3, *I*-*J*-1, 1–58. *B*. Stream gaging—Ravines *A*-*B*-*C*. 59*A*. Gully control and reclamation— soil-saving dams. *B*. Terrace-outlet ditches—control of gullying. 60. Terrace breaking—North ends of 5*C*, 6*C* and 7*C*. 61. 62. Runoff and erosion from a terraced pasture—Pasture *A*.

interval on the lower ones. Different crops will be grown between these contour lines, and the crops will be rotated.

Experiment 11—Fields H-L

Object: To observe the effectiveness of black locust and willow trees supplemented by shrubs and various grasses on checking and stabilizing deep and unsightly gullies.

Method: The gullies were first plowed in so that the banks were left with a gentle slope. The small trees were then set and a few woven wire checks installed to help check the washing until the trees were established.

Experiment 12—Fields C-D-E-F-G-H-I-N

Object: To determine the comparative returns from land cropped to different crop rotations and the returns derived from commercial fertilizers.

Method: From the records kept on the many fields on the station, the net returns from each cropping system will be determined after a period of years.

Experiment 13—Fields D-1, L, G-1

Object: To observe the effectiveness of "bluegrass sod bags," supplemented by small woven wire dams in checking small gullies.

Method: Burlap bags half filled with bluegrass sod have been placed in numerous small gullies over the station, and in some places they have been supplemented by woven wire checks.

Experiment 31—Fields D-1, D-2, D-3

Object: To compare erosion losses, crop yields, and net returns on three similar areas where different erosion control practices are used.

Method: (1) Area *D-1, unterraced:* ditch checks, wire dams, sod checks, good crop rotations, and careful farming. (2) Area *D-2 terraced:* terraces, good crop rotations, careful farming. (3) Area *D-3, unterraced:* no ditch control, no terraces, ordinary farm practices, using cropping system common to this region.

Results: Measured by (1) runoff; (2) soil losses; (3) crop yields; (4) net returns over a long period of years.

Experiment 32—Field H

Object: To determine the runoff and soil losses from different crops in different crop rotations on terraced land.

Method: Five terraces of uniform length, (1100 feet), uniform vertical spacing (5 feet): *H-2* two-year rotation (corn, oats, and sweet clover) (sweet clover under as green manure); *H-3,* 4, 5, and 6, four-year rotation (corn, soybeans wheat, clover, and timothy). This will allow a comparison of the erosion from each of the above crops and from the two cropping systems on terraced land.

Experiment 51—Field N

Object: To determine the proper vertical spacing or drop between terraces on moderate slopes. (Slope of Field *N* averages 7 per cent.)

Method: Three terraces, of uniform length (1040 feet) with identical crop rotation, have variable spacings as follows: *N*-4, 3 feet; *N*-5, 5 feet; and *N*-6, 7 feet.

Experiment 52—Field G

Object: To determine the proper vertical spacing on steep slopes (slope of Field *G* averages 12 per cent).

Method: Three terraces of uniform length (700 feet), identical crop rotations, with variable spacings as follows: *G*-3, 5 feet; *G*-4, 7 feet; *G*-5, 9 feet.

Experiment 53—Field C

Object: To determine the proper grade for terraces.

Method: Seven terraces of uniform length (1200 feet), the same vertical spacing (5 feet), and identical crop rotations, with different grades as follows: *C*-4, 10 inches; *C*-5, 8 inches; *C*-6, 6 inches; *C*-7, 4 inches; *C*-8, 2 inches; *C*-9, 0; *C*-10, variable, 4 inches at the outlet reduced to 3, 2 and 1 inch.

Experiment 54—Lower N

Object: (*a*) To observe the effectiveness of level terraces in the control of erosion, and (*b*) to observe the effect of level terraces on crop production.

Method: (*a*) Level terraces with ends closed; (*b*) level terraces varying in length from 250 to 700 feet, each terrace having one end open and the other closed; terraces *N*-7 to 13; (*c*) level terraces 400 to 600 feet long with one end open, terraces *N*-1 and *N*-2.

Experiment 55—Field I

Object: To compare terraces of different lengths to determine the maximum safe or practical length on lands of average slope (7 per cent).

Method: The use of four terraces of uniform vertical spacing (5 feet) and identical crop rotations, varying in length as follows: *I*-1, 420 feet; *I*-2, 1400 feet; *I*-3, 2150 feet; and *I*-4, 2550 feet.

Experiment 56—Fields D-G-N

Object: To determine the comparative rate at which soil moves down the slopes on terraced and unterraced lands.

Method: Each year, with transit and steel tape, take elevations of soil movement lines at one-foot intervals. Plot soil movement profiles.

Location: (1) Unterraced area *D*-1; (2) terraced area *D*-2; (3) terraced area *G*; (4) terraced area *N*.

Experiment 57-A—Fields C-D-G-H-I-N

Object: To determine the best cross-sectional area of terraces and shape of terraces that effectively controls erosion and permits the operation of farm machinery.

Method: (a) Measure cross-sectional area of terrace and water channel; (b) observe machinery operation over terraces; (c) observe crops on terraces and in water channel.

Location: All terraces.

Experiment 57-B

Object: To observe advantages and disadvantages of various types of machinery used in the construction of terraces and in the production and harvesting of crops.

Experiment 58-A—Pasture B, Fields C-H-G-N

Object: To compare the runoff and soil loss from areas (a) terraced and cultivated (fields C-G-H-N); (b) unterraced and cultivated (D-3); (c) unterraced, pasture B.

Method: The runoff of all experimental terraces in fields C-G-H-N is measured with individual flumes and automatic float recorders. The runoff from the six and one-half acre pasture area and the five and one-half acre area in Field D-3 is measured with large flumes and automatic float recorders. Soil losses from all locations are observed by use of wooden silt boxes and sampling devices.

Experiment 58-B—Pastures A and B; Fields G and H

Object: To determine the relation of stream velocity to erosion in the drainage channels of large watersheds.

Method: The velocities of flowing water in Ravines B and C are measured with current meters at times of heavy runoff.

Experiment 59—Fields C-D-G-H-I-N

Object: To determine practical designs of ditch checks for small ditches, and large dams for gullies and ravines.

Method: (a) The combination of small flumes and checks for terrace-outlet ditches. (b) Construction of different types of dams for large gullies.

Location: (1) Earth dams with culvert pipe underneath located in Ravine B, south side of farm; (2) earth dam with galvanized spillway, located in Ravine B, south central part of farm; (3) brush and wire dams in Ravine B, south central part of farm; (4) brush and stone dam in Ravine A, northeast part of farm; (5) ditch checks for terrace-outlet ditch, Field D-2; (6) ditch checks for terrace-outlet ditch, Field I.

MEASURING EQUIPMENT

A view of the measuring apparatus for water and soil lost from Field *D*-3, North, is shown in Fig. 228, and a clearer view of similar equipment at the foot of the slope of terraced Pasture *A* appears in Fig. 229. The chief features of the measuring assembly are, beginning at the inlet end, an automatic water stage recorder, water measuring flume, silt box, and sampling tank for suspended silt. Wherever the silt sampler symbol appears on the map in Fig. 227, it indicates these four units.

Fig. 228.—Measuring apparatus assembly for Field *D*-3, North at Bethany, Mo., erosion experiment station.

Briefly, the water stage recorder consists of a slowly revolving vertical disk that is rotated by clock mechanism and bears against its face a detachable sheet containing graduations to represent hours and minutes. By means of other mechanism, a pencil or ink pointer is held in contact with the detachable sheet and is free to move up or down as the sheet revolves. This up and down or in and out motion of the pointer is actuated by a float that rises and falls with the rise and fall of the water level in the flume. The position of the resulting line or curve charted on the detachable sheet provides a continuous and accurate record of the water level in the flume at any instant.

The measuring device, known as the Parshall or Venturi flume, is so constructed that a definite relation exists between the depth of flow and the discharge, so that the depth in feet as recorded on the chart can easily be converted into discharge in cubic feet per second.*

As the water leaves the flume it falls into a large box with sufficient capacity to catch and hold the heavier silt particles, which are later removed and weighed. The lighter particles remain suspended or mixed with the water and finally pass over a

Fig. 229.—Measuring apparatus assembly on terraced Pasture A, Bethany farm.

weir at the lower end of the box and thence to an outlet channel while still in "solution" with the muddy water. In so doing, however, a definite proportion (aliquot part,[1] say one one-thousandth of the total discharge) passes laterally through an aperture and is caught in the sampling tank shown in the right foreground of Fig. 228 and at the left in Fig. 229. The small white structures in the background each house the clockwork and float mechanism of the water stage recorders. In Fig. 228 duplicate recorders are provided to serve as a check on each other and insure against loss of records in case something goes wrong at a critical time.

* For conversion tables and a complete description of this flume see "Measuring Water in Irrigation Channels," U. S. Dept. Agr. Farmers' Bull. 1683.

[1] Actually, this proportion in apparatus now in use is 1 to 1400.

The four units of equipment just described, together with automatic rain gages placed at strategic points near the hilltop, provide complete records of (1) rainfall intensity and duration, (2) amount and rate of runoff, (3) time of concentration, and (4) quantity of soil and soluble nutrients washed off the watershed.

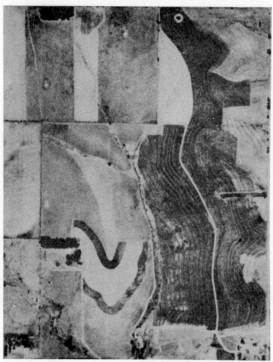

Fig. 230.—Air view of erosion experiment station near Clarinda, Iowa.

When the watershed area is measured, all of the factors in the runoff formula, $Q = CIA$, become known except the coefficient, C, which is easily computed by simply dividing the measured discharge by the product of I and A. The rain gages operate on the same principle as the water stage recorders and all clocks are synchronized to keep the same time.

Data Collected.—Summaries of most of the data so far collected at all of the federal farms have been presented in the preceding chapters, and as time goes on these will continually be augmented and new experiments will be inaugurated with the increase in specialized knowledge.

Clarinda Farm.—An air view of the erosion farm at Clarinda, Ia., is shown in Fig. 230 and is introduced here to indicate the variation existing between layouts on the several federal farms, which are necessary to meet local conditions.

A north and south gully divides the southern one-half to two-thirds of the farm about equally. To the right of the gully a terraced slope averaging 8 to 10 per cent rises to a gently zig-zagging road on top of the ridge, beyond which another terraced

Fig. 231.—Battery of silt samplers and measuring devices installed at the south (outlet) end of the terraces shown on the east slope of Fig. 230. (*Courtesy U. S. Bureau Agr. Eng.*)

slope drops off to the eastern boundary of the farm. A strip-cropping experiment is being conducted in the field west of the gully and near the bottom of the picture, as clearly shown by the two dark bands. An east and west paved highway between Clarinda and Shenandoah, Ia., marks the south boundary of the farm; and the experimental plots are dimly visible in the area just north of the highway and east of the gully. The lysimeters shown in Fig. 15 are also located in this area. Both the plots and the farmstead farther east are south of the two terraced slopes.

One of the interesting features of this layout is a terrace (located just east of the ridge road) more than 4000 feet long and draining in one direction only (to the south).

A view of the measuring apparatus at the outlet of this terrace and its companion terraces on the east slope of the farm is shown in Fig. 231. Note the spreader boards in place in the outlet channel, which was under construction at the time the picture was taken. The view from this angle also shows the small apertures admitting water and suspended silt to the silt sampling tanks.

DEMONSTRATION AREAS

Recently the federal Soil Conservation Service has established demonstration areas on entire watersheds in various parts of the country where the main object is to put into practice the principles of conservation farming on as many farms within the watershed as possible; preferably on all. Experts in the fields of soils, crops, forestry, and engineering are available to consult with individual farmers and assist them in working out the most practicable plan to meet their particular conditions. In return for this service and for other considerations the farmer agrees to cooperate by putting the proposed plan into effect for a minimum period of 5 years, no matter how much adjustment in field layout and in habitual farming practices this may entail.

Results so far are quite encouraging, and already 147 projects have been started in 41 states. A sample list, which is typical of the geographical distribution and size range of these projects, is shown on page 316.

PLAN FOR CONSERVATION FARMING

Data Required.—The first step in formulating any plan is of course the collection of basic data to serve as a foundation. In the case of conservation farming this will require: (1) A topographic map showing the degree, length, and extent of slopes and other usual topographic features; (2) a soil map showing the location of various soil types and present erosive condition; (3) prevailing climatic conditions; and (4) past history of the farm including cropping, cultural practices, and other information pertinent to erosion.

Conventional methods of topographic surveying by the use of a transit, steel tape, and stadia rod, or by the plane table-alidade method, are not generally considered necessary since it is thought that results sufficiently accurate for the purpose intended can be secured by pacing distances and by the use of relatively crude instruments such as clinometers, hand levels, and compasses, or small levels of the wye or dumpy type equipped with graduated horizontal circles for turning off angles. The type

SOIL CONSERVATION PROJECTS

Office location	Name of project	Approximate acres
LaCrosse, Wis..................	Coon Creek	100,000
Bethany, Mo...................	West Tarkio River	175,000
	Big Creek	150,000
Urbana, Ill....................	Sangamon River	140,000
Temple, Tex...................	Elm Creek	200,000
Spartanburg, S. C..............	South Tyger River	125,000
Pullman, Wash.................	South Palouse River	150,000
	Wildhorse Creek	50,000
Santa Paula, Calif..............	Arroyo Las Posas	25,000
	Arroyo Grande	7,000
Stillwater, Okla................	Stillwater Creek	150,000
	Pecan Creek	40,000
Albuquerque, N. M.............	Navajo	16,000,000
Mankato, Kan..................	Limestone Creek	150,000
High Point, N. C...............	Deep River	90,000
	Brown Creek	70,000
Spencer, W. V..................	Reedy Creek	100,000
Zanesville, O...................	Salt Creek	100,000
Minden, La....................	Cooley Creek	100,000
	Cypress Creek	47,000
Albion, Neb....................	Plum Creek	70,000
Conway, Ark...................	East Cadron Creek	125,000
	Crowley's Ridge	25,000
Dadeville, Ala.................	Buck and Sandy Creeks	110,000
Athens, Ga....................	Sandy Creek	100,000
Lindale, Tex...................	Duck Creek	25,000
Meridian, Miss.................	Okatibbee River	150,000
Chatham, Va...................	Banister River	100,000
Safford, Ariz..................	Gila River	8,200,000
LaCrosse, Wis.................	Root River, Minn.	150,000
Dalhart, Tex..................	Dalhart Wind Erosion	15,000
Greensboro, N. C..............	Reedy Fork	44,000
Indiana, Pa...................	Crooked Creek	110,000
Rock Hill, S. C................	Fishing Creek	51,000
Flemington, N. J...............	Raritan River	75,000
Watsonville, Calif..............	Corralitos Creek	67,200
Colorado Springs, Colo...........	Smoky Hill River	120,000
	Black Squirrel Creek	100,000
Huron, S. D...................	Shue Creek	142,000
	Wolsey	38,000
Ithaca, N. Y...................	Cohocton River	150,000

and erosive condition of the soil are determined by field inspection and numerous borings with a soil auger. The prevailing climate is known from the location of the farm, and farming history is determined from field evidence and by questioning the farm operator and his neighbors.

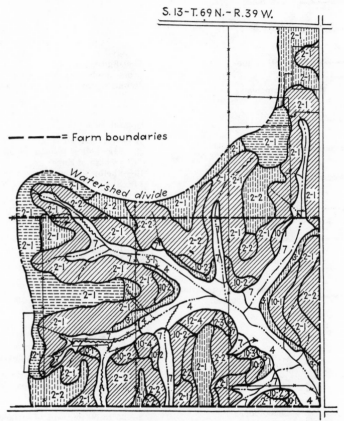

FIG. 232.—Soil map of a typical farm subject to erosion.

An erosion map of a typical farm prepared by the methods just described is shown in Fig. 232. The first numeral in the different areas pertains to soil type, and the second numeral to attained degree of erosion. Slopes are indicated by cross-hatching.

The following conventional symbols have been adopted by the Soil Conservation Service and will be useful in interpreting the map:

KEY FOR INTERPRETING SOIL MAPS

═══════════ Public road

✕———✕— Fence line

●———●— New fence

〜〜 Divide

— — — — Section line

■ Farmstead

+—+—+—+— Railroad

∞∞∞∞∞∞ Hedge fence row

〜〜〜 Continuous stream

〜〜 Intermittent stream

–·—·〜 Inactive grassed waterways

—··— Waterway—can be crossed

—··—· Gullies—small cannot be crossed.

〜〜〜〜〜 Gullies—large—planting and structures.

🌳🌳 Timber

✝ Cemetery

⛪ Church

🏫 Schoolhouse

First figure—soil type
Cross-hatch—degree of slope
Second figure—degree of erosion

Soil Type

Upland soils

  2—Marshall silt loam
  3—Marshall silt loam (deposited at base of slope)
10—Shelby silt loam
11—Shelby loam
12—Shelby silt clay loam
13—Shelby clay (black)

Bench soils

20—Judson silt loam
21—Bremer silt clay loam
22—Bremer silt loam
 8—Ray silt loam

Bottomland

  4—Wabash silt loam
  6—Wabash silt clay loam
  7—Wabash silt loam (colluvial phase)

Degree of Erosion Classification

1—0 to 25 per cent of surface soil eroded (as in Marshall silt loam, dark top soil from 16 to 18 inches in depth).
2—25 to 50 per cent of surface soil eroded
3—50 to 75 per cent of surface soil eroded
4—Over 75 per cent of surface soil eroded

Slope Classification

0 to 3 per cent

3 to 7 per cent

7 to 12 per cent

over 12 per cent

Proposed Cropping Plan.—The data this map affords plus a knowledge of general conditions in the locality will enable an agronomist to select the best cropping system for this particular farm. If necessary to fit the plan recommended, interior fields are rearranged and fences shifted so far as topographic limitations permit. A skeleton map is shown in Fig. 233 which indicates the size and shape of the 16 fields into which the farm is divided.

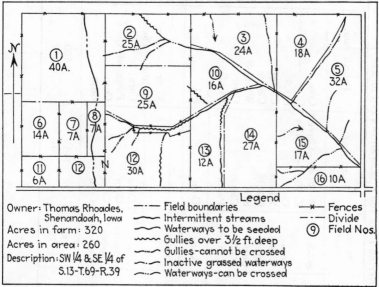

FIG. 233.—Outline map of part of farm in Fig. 232 showing size and shape of fields.

The accompanying crop rotation plan for the first six-year cycle appears in Table 32.

To show the plan for gully control, terracing, and strip cropping, and cultural methods recommended, a similar map and accompanying data sheet would be prepared for clear representation. This phase of the problem is not included here since it already has been fully covered in preceding chapters.

The demonstration work of the Soil Conservation Service is rapidly expanding and probably will soon cover the entire country and have a profound effect on American agricultural practices.

HERBACEOUS COVER AND CONSERVATION

The rôle of trees and shrubs in the conservation of agricultural resources is now recognized as of paramount importance. Steep

TABLE 32.—CROPPING PLAN FOR FIELDS SHOWN IN FIG. 233

Field No.	Part	Acres	First year	Second year	Third year	Fourth year	Fifth year	Sixth year
1	E. 10 A. in area	40	Corn	SG-S	W. 20 A.—Clover / E. 20 A.—Alfalfa	Corn	Corn →	SG-S / Corn
2		25	Pasture	Corn		SG-S	Clover	Corn
3		24	Oats	Wheat	Corn	Clover	Corn	Corn
4		18	Corn	Corn	Wheat-S	Clover	Corn	SG
5		32	Corn	Corn	SG-S	Wheat-S	Clover	SG-S
6	Out of area	14	Corn	SG-S	SG	Corn	Corn	Corn
7	Out of area	7	Rye	Pasture	Clover	Rye-S	Alfalfa	SG-S
8	W. 3 A. Out of area	7	Pasture	Pasture	Pasture →	Corn	SG-S	Alfalfa
9		25	Pasture	Corn	Corn	SG	Wheat-S	Pasture
10		16	C.A.	Alfalfa →			Corn	Clover
11	Out of area	6	Rye	Pasture		S. 20 A.—Corn / N. 10 A.—Pasture	Corn	SG-S →
12		30	Pasture	Alfalfa	Corn	Corn	SG-S	Clover
13		12	Alfalfa	Pasture	Corn	Pastured Rye-S	Pasture	Pasture
14		27	C.A.	Clover	Corn	Corn	SG	Wheat-S
15		17	Wheat	Pasture	Corn	Corn	SG	Wheat-S
16		10	Pasture	Pasture	Corn	Corn	SG	Wheat-S
Total acres in corn			104	100	116	100	112	93
Total acres in legumes				72	70	107	111	78

SG = Small grain.
SG-S = Small grain, seeding.
C.A. = Contracted acres.

slopes covered with trees should not be disturbed; and in older stands, which are deteriorating due to age or other reasons, grazing should be curtailed to permit a new stand to reseed itself naturally. On lands that have been extensively emasculated, tree planting is an important consideration whether or not the original cover consisted of trees. The effect of trees, grass, and shrubs on a badly gullied area in Iowa is well illustrated in Fig.

FIG. 234.—Effect of herbaceous cover on a badly gullied area.

234. Contrast this picture with some of the views shown in Chap. I.

Appropriate Species.—In the light of the discussion in Chap. XIII little need be added concerning tree species. Suffice it to say that the qualities considered more important than ultimate timber value in steep land reclamation are, (1) rate of establishment of forest cover, (2) type of root system, and (3) adaptability to a wide variety of sites. The ideal species is one that grows rapidly, is suited to many site conditions, has an extensive root system, and produces valuable timber for forest products.

Black locust (*Robina pseudo-acacia*), cottonwood (*Populus deltoides*), and the larger varieties of willows (*Salix species*) approach most nearly this ideal. For primary planting cottonwood or willows should be used in moist or wet land and black locust on the drier sites. After erosion has been arrested by primary stands, later plantings may include slower growing but sturdier and more valuable varieties.

A spacing of 4 by 4 feet requires 2740 trees per acre, and the stock used should be seedlings of 18 to 30 inches in height, well rooted. At regular commercial prices the cost per acre of trees in place would be approximately $20, divided about equally between cost of nursery stock and labor for planting.

Other Uses for Trees.—Aside from steep slopes, eroded slopes, and gullied areas, other desirable habitats for trees are, (1) poor soils on any slope, (2) light soils subject to wind erosion, and (3) bottom lands subject to frequent overflow and promiscuous stream cutting.

COORDINATION OF PHYSICAL FACTORS

It is difficult if not impossible, and also inadvisable, to attempt to prescribe a definite conservation program for any area in advance of actual field examination and specific data collection. Yet, for purposes of principle establishment and the dissemination of generalized information, it is desirable to set up some sort of a pattern to serve as a rough guide to standard practice.

From the single viewpoint of erosion damage the ideal land-use policy is that which results in maximum ease of control, and a satisfactory measure of the need for control is susceptibility to damage. Susceptibility to damage has been shown to be dependent upon a number of interrelated factors or variables which in themselves are composed of almost innumerable sub-variables. It will be recalled that there are four such groups of factors, as follows: (1) Climatic conditions which govern the characteristics of rainfall, snowfall, wind and wave action, and frost phenomena; (2) topographic conditions which govern the length and steepness of slopes and the hilltop area contributing extraneous water; (3) soil characteristics including size of particles or texture, cluster arrangement or structure, infiltration and moisture holding capacity, dispersion ratio, depth and fertility of topsoil, and subsoil peculiarities, and (4) biotic life, including native or transplanted vegetation as affected by the activities of man or animals.

The conditions under which agricultural cropping may safely be carried on in the future and suggested uses of land not suitable for agricultural crops are summarized in Table 33. The criteria for this table are steepness of slope and attained degree of erosion which, together, constitute a rough measure of erosivity

TABLE 33.—SUGGESTED USES OF LAND TO CONTROL EROSION
(As affected by slope and degree of erosion)

Group	Erosion‡	Cropping and erosion control practices
A Less than 2 per cent slope	Slight	Agricultural crops with rotation and contour farming.
	Moderate	Agricultural crops 3 to 4 years rotation (1 to 2 years hay) and strip farming.
	Severe	Agricultural crops; terracing supplemented with fertilization; rotation and contour farming.
B Slopes 2 to 12 per cent	Slight	Agricultural crops; terracing supplemented by 3 to 4 years rotation (1 to 2 years hay) and contour farming.
	Moderate	Agricultural crops; terracing supplemented by 5 to 6 years rotation (2 to 3 years hay) and strip farming.
	Severe	Agricultural crops; terracing supplemented by 5 to 6 years rotation (3 to 4 years hay), fertilization and strip farming.
*C** Slopes 12 to 20 per cent	Slight	Close-growing crops for seed, hay or pasture. If necessary, cultivated crops on flatter slopes with 5 to 6 years rotation and strip farming 60 per cent or more in sod farming strips; or reforestation.
	Moderate	Legumes or grasses for hay or pasture; moderate grazing.
	Severe	Permanent legumes or grasses for hay only with fertilization; or reforestation.
D† Slopes 20 to 30 per cent	Slight	Legumes or grasses for hay or pasture; moderate grazing; forestry.
	Moderate	Perennial legumes or grasses for hay only; forestry.
	Severe	Forestry or natural vegetation; no grazing.
E Slopes above 30 per cent	Slight	Perennial, legumes or grasses for hay only, on flatter slopes; forestry.
	Moderate	Forestry or natural cover; no grazing.
	Severe	Forestry or natural cover; no grazing.

These are general recommendations only. Variations to meet individual needs should be worked out with agronomists and soil specialists. Group *E* practices can be used on Group *D* slopes or Group *D* on Group *C*, but generally Group *C* practices should not be used on Group *D* slopes or Group *D* on Group *E*, etc.

* Use of cultivated crops should be discouraged and entire fields with slopes over 12 per cent should not be plowed up at the same time, unless terraced.

† Usually grazing should be discouraged so far as possible. Any plowing should be done only in strips on contour lines, and several years required to plow or reseed entire field.

‡ Erosion: Slight—less than 25 per cent surface soil removed.
Moderate—25 per cent to 75 per cent surface soil removed.
Severe—over 75 per cent surface soil removed.

as affected by past farming practices. The suggested procedure is flexible and subject to any modification that may be necessary to conform to different climatic and soil situations and is offered with all the reservations heretofore expressed or implied. In spite of the necessity for qualifying statements, however, it is believed the table has much value as a general guide.

Wherever the word fertilization appears it is interpreted to mean the kind of treatment suited to the needs of the particular soil to produce good yields and adequate cover whether the treatment be simple manuring, turning under cover crops and crop

Fig. 235.—Illustration of ideal land use, Jackson County, N. C.   (*Photo by U. S. Forest Service.*)

residues, the use of partial or complete commercial fertilizers (nitrogen, phosphorus, and potassium), or indirect fertilization by the addition of lime.

An ideal application of the suggestions in Table 33 to the scene depicted is illustrated in Fig. 235. Note that the steep top slopes are covered with trees and shrubs, the flat land and moderate slopes are in cultivated crops, and the intervening areas are reserved for permanent grasses and forage.

HUMAN AND ECONOMIC HANDICAPS

In a country whose agricultural domain has been settled and utilized on a purely exploitive basis it is inevitable that many nonphysical obstacles will have to be overcome and much maladjustment neutralized before complete conversion to a conservation basis can be expected. Whole populations in sections where productive possibilities are barely at or below a mere subsistence level will either have to be resettled elsewhere or provided with opportunity to earn supplementary income. Single crop farming is not only entangled in the inertia of tradition in the South but also is deeply embedded in the social and economic structure of that region and any appreciable change therefrom is bound to induce upheavals in all phases of communal life. For 25 years or more southern agriculturists have been preaching diversification and their words have been echoed and reechoed in the columns of the daily press and farm journals without producing noticeable effect, yet some adjustment must ultimately come through pressure of sheer self-preservation.

Even in the fertile reaches of the Middle West tenure conditions and prevailing systems of farming are far from conducive to the most sensible use of land. In many instances, size of the farm unit and debt obligations are such as to force the extraction of maximum cash returns with full knowledge of, but without regard to, disastrous effects on the soil. Too often for the individual farmer it is merely a choice between ruthless exploitation or forfeiture of his farm.

To be more specific, it can be stated with complete assurance that the scope of initiative possible for any individual in the adoption of conservation practices is governed by certain influences more or less beyond his control. These may be listed in the following pro and con order. The particular arrangement is prompted by Midwestern conditions, but the principles underlying its preparation apply anywhere.

Adverse Influences	Helpful Influences
Small farm size	Large farm size
Corn-hog type of farming	Dairy and beef cattle type of farming
Lack of supplementary enterprises	Possibility of profitable supplementary enterprises
Tenancy	Owner-operatorship
Short-term leases	Long-term leases
Crop-share leases	Stock-share and cash-rent leases
Tenant unrelated to landlord	Tenant related to landlord
Corporate landlord	Private landlord
Heavy debt burden and high interest rate	Small debt burden and low interest rates
Relatively low farm income level	Relatively high farm income level

In explanation of the effect of these influences the following comment is offered.*

A small farm tends to have the greatest possible acreage of its land in cultivation, and the greatest possible acreage in corn, in order to utilize fully the family labor supply and to obtain the highest possible output per acre; on a large farm, steep hillsides can be kept in pasture, and intertilled crops can be restricted to more level fields.

In the corn-hog type of farming, there is not much use for pasture land and hay crops, because the cattle enterprise is not strongly developed, and the emphasis is placed on hogs fed primarily on corn; the dairy and beef cattle type of farming requires much pasture and hay and usually makes for a smaller percentage of crop land in corn, thereby facilitating the control of erosion. The type of farming is definitely related to the farm size. The beef cattle enterprise is concentrated in the large size groups, while the dairy enterprise, being labor-intensive, is especially adapted to small farms.

Soil conservation, in the final analysis, calls for a shift from corn-hog to dairying in the small size groups, to beef cattle and sheep in the large size groups. To the extent to which this shift towards dairying on smaller farms is economically limited, the only alternative of general significance for permanent erosion control is to increase the farm size and to shift towards beef cattle and sheep.

In some individual instances, supplementary enterprises may be developed which provide for profitable utilization of family labor on the farm without requiring a larger acreage of farm land. Poultry, vegetables, and fruit, for example, may possibly supplement the major enterprises in the farm organization and contribute a significant part of the income, without preying upon the soil resources. In principle, a soil conservation program, particularly on small farms, must not allow the final aggregate output per farm, in terms of income, to decline.

Replacing corn by grasses and legumes sets labor free. Unless some other enterprises are developed to absorb this released labor profitably, the current net income is almost certain to decline and may force the farmer to discontinue his soil conserving rotations. The smaller the farm acreage is per labor unit, the more complete and efficient must be the utilization of labor if a decent standard of living is to be attained. This higher labor utilization on the farm can be brought about by pushing the processing of the soil's products farther into higher-priced commodities, such as dairy products, eggs, vegetables, etc., as compared with hogs, which represent a low degree of processing as far as labor

* "Economic Phases of Erosion Control in Southern Iowa and Northern Missouri," *Iowa Agr. Exp. Sta. Bull.* 333, June, 1935.

requirements are concerned. The problem is to shift labor from erosive crops to other crops and enterprises which yield comparable returns per labor unit. The idea of saving for the future is workable only if there is something left to be saved in the present.

A tenant operator, in general, has no specific interest in keeping up soil fertility, as he is ready to move to another farm any time he sees fit. An owner-operator inherently has a very definite interest in soil conservation, since his future independence and welfare rest upon the perpetuation of his soil's productivity. Tenancy, on the incline since 1920, is very likely stimulating the rate of erosion. Promoting operator-ownership tends to aid erosion control.

Short-term leases accentuate the general tenant attitude toward the soil. The length of farm occupancy affects erosion control particularly because it involves immediate costs, the returns on which are distributed over many years; and involves changes in the crop and livestock system which are definitely of a long-time nature. Long-time leases, therefore facilitate such changes.

The crop-share lease, by far the most common lease type, inherently encourages a large proportion of the farm land to be put in crops, and a large percentage of crop land in corn, the most readily marketable cash crop. Moreover, crop-share leases usually run for only 1 year. Stock-share leases, on the other hand, place the emphasis on livestock, on cattle particularly, and, subsequently, on pasture and hay crops. They commonly are long-term leases. The usual stock-share lease is not well adapted to dairy farms. Promoting an improved stock-share lease for dairy farms would be highly desirable from the viewpoint of erosion control. The cash rent lease allows the tenant complete freedom in adjusting his farming program to soil conditions, provided the rent is adjusted to the price level. If it is not adequate, the tenant may resort to heavy cropping.

A tenant who has family relationship to the landlord is apt to have an attitude toward the soil similar to that of an owner-operator. In many cases, he expects to own the farm later on. Under such circumstances, the length of the lease, and perhaps even the type of lease, may be rather immaterial to the problem of erosion control, because of the genuine community of interest of tenant and landlord with respect to soil fertility maintenance.

Corporations are, by nature, temporary land owners. They are ready to sell the farm as soon as they can get a favorable offer. They have become landowners by accident, not by intention or tradition. A tenant on corporate land has no assurance whatsoever of staying on the farm more than a year. As soil conservation requires a long-time farming program, the corporate landlord, in general, has little interest in it.

Private landlords, on the other hand, usually do not own farms just to dispose of them as soon as possible, but rather as a permanent investment. Hence, they are vitally interested in conserving the producing power of the farm, and are often anxious to keep a good tenant on the farm. A high proportion of corporate land tends to cause instability in land tenure and to foster erosion, unless the majority of corporations can be induced to adopt definite soil conservation programs on their land.

Heavy mortgage indebtedness exerts a specific financial pressure upon the soil by forcing the farmer to squeeze out of his soil whatever he can to meet his financial obligations. It would enhance erosion control work considerably if this pressure could be relieved by arranging for debt adjustments in connection with an erosion control program.

The debt burden has become increasingly intolerable during the depression, which has left many farmers with incomes barely providing for their subsistence. Any policy which raises the general income level of farmers helps to clear the way for soil conservation programs on the farms. The corn-hog program of the AAA doubtless tends to reduce soil losses through erosion, directly by reducing the corn acreage, and indirectly by increasing farm income and relieving farmers from tremendous financial pressure resulting in heavy cropping and subsequent soil losses.

There is another set of economic factors impinging upon the erosion problem which has not been dealt with at all in this study, but which, nevertheless, exerts a potent influence: price relationships between the various products concerned, and the absorptive capacity of local and national markets for these commodities replacing corn and hogs. For instance, high feed grain prices tend to obstruct, low grain prices to facilitate erosion control. High hog prices, relative to dairy products and beef cattle prices, tend to impede, low hog prices to foster erosion control. If erosion control practices became more generally adopted, the resulting reduction in hogs might drive hog prices so high, and the increase in beef and dairy production might force their prices so low that many farmers would be tempted to swing back to the soil exploitive corn-hog enterprise. From the viewpoint of soil conservation, however, it is a fortunate coincidence that the very commodities which prey most heavily upon the soil resources are those which have a weak competitive position in the foreign market, namely hogs, wheat, and cotton. Hence, a reduction in their supply is likely to stimulate their prices less than it would if there were a strong demand for them. Granted that, regardless of what these price relationships are, erosion control is of vital concern to the future of many regions; exploitive commodities will set the pace and determine the methods of erosion control.

Types of farming and farming practices are inherited and rooted in tradition. They may persist much longer than physical and economic conditions warrant. There is conclusive evidence that in the erosive sections of the corn belt soil conditions no longer warrant a highly specialized corn-hog type of farming. The urgent need for soil conservation is more and more realized by society as well as individual farmers.

The foregoing handicaps are cited, not for the purpose of stimulating discouragement, but in the belief that a problem fully recognized is a problem half solved. Profound change in the habits of a nation will not and should not transpire overnight, but those who have faith in the future of America cannot doubt the final outcome.

APPENDIX

SIMPLE METHODS OF CALCULATING LAND AREAS

To compute the area of most fields with straight boundaries, it is necessary only to know the length of the sides. If the field is bounded by four or more sides, no two of which are parallel, the length of the interior diagonal lines must also be known. In the case of a four-sided field, two sides of which are parallel, only the two parallel sides and the perpendicular distance between them need be measured. Fields with curved or irregular boundaries constitute a special problem as shown later.

CASE I. RECTANGLE

The simplest and most common shape is that of a rectangle or square. A rectangle is a figure in which all adjacent sides make angles of 90 degrees with each other. In other words, it is a four-sided figure with opposite sides parallel. A square is a rectangle with all sides equal.

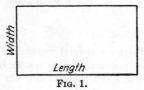

FIG. 1.

To compute the area of a rectangle, multiply the length by the width, as follows:

In Fig. 1 assume a length of 660 feet and a width of 330 feet. Then,

$$\text{Area} = 660 \times 330 = 217,800 \text{ sq. ft.}$$
$$\text{One acre contains 43,560 sq. ft.,}$$

therefore,

$$\text{Area in acres} = \frac{217,800}{43,560} = 5.00 \text{ acres.}$$

CASE II. RIGHT TRIANGLE

The area of a right triangle is one half the product of the base times the altitude, or $\dfrac{\text{Base} \times \text{Altitude}}{2}$

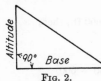

FIG. 2.

Assume in Fig. 2 a base length of 990 feet and an altitude length of 660 feet.

Then,

$$\text{Area} = \frac{990 \times 660}{2} = 326,700 \text{ sq. ft.}$$
$$\text{One acre contains 43,560 sq. ft.,}$$

therefore,

$$\text{Area in acres} = \frac{326,700}{43,560} = 7.50 \text{ acres.}$$

331

Case III. Four-sided Figure; Two Sides Parallel

In this case the area is found by multiplying the average length of the parallel sides by the perpendicular (or shortest) distance between them. Thus, in Fig. 3, if P and P' represent the parallel sides and H the perpendicular distance,

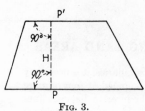

Fig. 3.

$$\text{Area} = \frac{P + P'}{2} \times H$$

For a numerical example, assume that P measures 1320 feet P' 820 feet, and H 450 feet.

Then,

$$\text{Area} = \frac{1320 + 820}{2} \times 450 = 1070 \times 450 = 481{,}500 \text{ sq. ft.}$$

Since one acre contains 43,560 sq. ft.,

$$\text{Area in acres} = \frac{481{,}500}{43{,}560} = 11.05 \text{ acres.}$$

Case IV. Triangle

There are several methods of computing the areas of triangles but the most practical one to use in land mensuration is that which requires only the three sides to be measured. A "base sum" is arrived at by adding the lengths of the sides and dividing by two. From this base sum is subtracted the length of each of the three sides in succession. Then the base sum and the three "remainders" thus obtained are multiplied together. The square root of this product is the desired area.

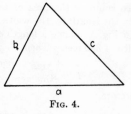

Fig. 4.

If a, b, and c represent the three sides and S the "base sum," the above rule may be expressed as follows:

$$S = \frac{a + b + c}{2}$$
$$\text{Area} = \sqrt{S \times (S - a) \times (S - b) \times (S - c)}$$

In Fig. 4, assume that $a = 640$ ft., $b = 480$ ft., and $c = 600$ ft., then,

$$S = \frac{640 + 480 + 600}{2} = 860 \quad \text{and}$$
$$\text{Area} = \sqrt{860 \times (860 - 640) \times (860 - 480) \times (860 - 600)}$$
$$= \sqrt{860 \times 220 \times 380 \times 260}$$
$$= \sqrt{18{,}692{,}960{,}000}$$
$$= 136{,}722 \text{ sq. ft.}$$
$$\text{Area in acres} = \frac{136{,}722}{43{,}560} = 3.14$$

CASE V. FOUR SIDES; NONE PARALLEL

This kind of a figure is divided into two triangles by measuring a diagonal. Then the area of each triangle is computed by the method of Case IV and the sum taken as the area of the figure.

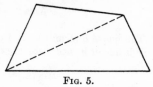

FIG. 5.

CASE VI. ANY NUMBER OF SIDES

In a similar manner any field bounded by more than four sides may be divided into a series of triangles by diagonal lines and the area of each triangle computed as before. The sum of the triangular areas is the area of the figure.

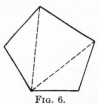

FIG. 6.

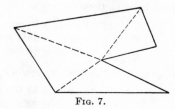

FIG. 7.

CASE VII. CURVED BOUNDARY

If the field contains one or more curved boundaries each such boundary must be treated as follows: First, lay off a straight line (construction line) connecting the extremities of the two sides of the field which intersect the curved side. Measure the length of this line and divide it into that number of *equal* parts which most nearly makes the length of each part 50 feet. Next, measure the perpendicular distance from this line to the curved boundary at the extremity or end of each of its parts. These distances are called "offsets," and the spacing between them must be uniform as noted. The area of the portion of the field between the construction line and the curved boundary is computed by adding together all of the offsets and multiplying this sum by the uniform spacing between them (50 feet as nearly as possible). The area of the balance of the field is then computed

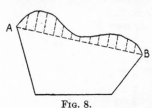

FIG. 8.

as that of any other straight-sided figure as already explained. These areas are then added together to give the total area of the field.

To illustrate how the curved boundary portion of the area is computed, assume that AB, the construction line in Fig. 8, has been laid off and that it measures 700 feet. This permits a uniform distance of 50 feet to be laid off between offsets, thus dividing the line AB into 14 equal parts. Beginning at A the offsets are measured in order and found to be as follows:

0, 80, 110, 115, 90, 70, 40, 15, 20, 25, 60, 75, 60, 35, and 0 feet. The sum
of the offset distances is 795 and

$$\text{Area} = 795 \times 50 = 39{,}750 \text{ sq. ft.}$$

$$\text{Area in acres} = \frac{39{,}750}{43{,}560} = 0.91$$

The line AB should be laid off so that no part of the curved boundary
falls inside of it; otherwise the enclosed area must be subtracted.

HINTS ON MEASURING DISTANCES

For accurate results all distances should be carefully measured with an
error not greater than one foot in 1000 feet. A 100-foot steel tape is most
satisfactory for this purpose and is now in most common use. It may be,
however, that some distances will still be recorded in chains, rods, or yards.
The relation between these units is as follows:

$$
\begin{aligned}
1 \text{ yard} &= 3 \text{ feet} \\
1 \text{ rod} &= 16\tfrac{1}{2} \text{ feet} \\
1 \text{ chain} &= 66 \text{ feet}
\end{aligned}
$$

In square measure the following relations hold true:

$$
\begin{aligned}
1 \text{ acre} &= 43{,}560 \text{ sq. ft.} \\
&= 4{,}840 \text{ sq. yards} \\
&= 160 \text{ sq. rods} \\
&= 10 \text{ sq. chains}
\end{aligned}
$$

CHAINING ON SLOPES

All distances are assumed to have been measured horizontally and are
taken to represent the horizontal projections of all sloping lines. This
means that, when chaining on hillsides, either the tape must be held horizontal (using parts of the tape short enough to enable this to be done) or
else the distance is measured along the slope, the degree or percentage of
slope is estimated, and the slope distance is reduced to its horizontal pro-
jection before being used in computations.

SURFACE OR SLOPE DISTANCES CORRESPONDING TO HORIZONTAL OR TRUE
DISTANCES OF 100 FEET

Grade, per cent	Surface distance, feet	Correction, per cent
5	100.1	0.1
10	100.5	0.5
15	101.1	1.1
20	102.0	2.0
30	104.4	4.2
40	107.7	7.2

Inspection of the table shown at the bottom of page 334 will show that the correction is so small on slopes less than 10 per cent that it may usually be disregarded.

LAYING OFF RIGHT ANGLES

To erect a perpendicular to any line at any point it is only necessary to lay off a triangle whose sides are in the proportion of 3', 4', 5'. Any convenient multiple of 3', 4', 5' may be used to construct a right triangle. This is illustrated in Fig. 9.

Instead of 3', 4', 5' we might have used 6', 8', 10'; 30', 40', 50' or any other convenient multiple.

FIG. 9.

INTERTERRACE AREAS

Areas between terraces can usually be computed with sufficient accuracy by substituting a "give and take" straight line for the curve of the terrace and considering the area as taking the form of some one of the straight boundary figures previously described.

If the adjacent terraces are smooth curves and approximately parallel, the area of any section is the curved length times the average distance between the terraces.

Extreme cases may be treated by the method explained under Case VII and illustrated by Fig. 8. The uniform distance between offsets can be made less than 50 feet and treated in the same manner as that described.

If a planimeter is available, this is, of course, the quickest way of estimating the area of irregularly shaped figures appearing on a map.

PARTIAL LIST OF SOIL CONSERVING, SEMI SOIL CONSERVING, AND SOIL DEPLETING CROPS

I. Soil conserving:
    A. Perennial grasses—established seedings or new seedings under a nurse crop—
        Use—
        1. Pasture.
        2. Hay.
        3. Seed.

NOTE: Any of the following grasses may be considered soil conserving, whether seeded alone or in combination.

Kentucky bluegrass.
Canadian bluegrass.
Timothy.
Redtop.
Smooth brome.
Reed canary.
Orchard.
Meadow fescue.
Tall oat.

Slender wheat.
Crested wheat.
Small-leaved fescues.
Rough-stalked meadow (Poa trivialis).
Perennial rye.
Bermuda.
Any other grasses of known soil conserving value not included in the above list.

(Under some circumstances quack grass may have some value for conserving soil.)

    B. Biennial and perennial legumes—

        Use—

        1. Pasture.   3. Seed.
        2. Hay.   4. Green manure.

          a. Alfalfa (established seedings).
          b. Medium red clover (established seedings).
          c. Mammoth red clover (established seedings).
          d. Alsike clover (established seeding).
          e. Biennial white sweet clover (second year).
          f. Biennial yellow sweet clover (second year).
          g. White clover (established seeding).
          h. Perennial lespedeza (Sericea)—established seeding.

Above crops may be seeded alone or in combination.

NOTE: Any other legumes used strictly as green manures.

        1. Soybeans (close drilled or broadcast).
        2. Dalea—limited adaptation.
        3. Korean lespedeza (*L. stipulacea*).
        4. Common lespedeza (*L. striata.*)
        5. Hubam—annual white sweet clover.
        6. Field peas.
        7. Cow peas.
        8. Vetch (spring seeded).

    C. Orchards, shelter belts or forest plantings (noncropped between planting and seeding down.)

II. Semi soil conserving:

    A. Broadcast or close drilled (Max. row spacing 8″) annuals and winter annuals—

        Use—

        1. Pasture.   3. Green manure.
        2. Hay.   4. Seed or grain.

          a. Oats.   *h.* Sudan grass.
          b. Barley.   *i.* Winter vetch.
          c. Wheats.   *j.* Winter rye.
          d. Flax.   *k.* Field peas or cowpeas (pastured).
          e. Soybeans (pastured). *l.* Rape.
          f. Millet.   *m.* Sorghums.
          g. Buckwheat.   *n.* Hemp.

    B. Exception—Soybeans, field peas, and cow peas used for hay or seed.

NOTE: Any crops falling in Group 2 (semi soil conserving) may be included in Group 1 (soil conserving) when used specifically as nurse crops for seeding of biennial and/or perennial grasses and/or legumes, when used for hay or pasture, or may be clipped and the residues left on the land.

III. Soil depleting:

    A. All clean tilled and other crops not included in Group I (strictly soil conserving) and Group II (semi soil conserving). Such crops may be used for any purpose

SOIL EROSION AND ITS CONTROL

TABLE I.—Two-thirds Powers of Numbers
(For use in Manning's Formula)

Number	.00	.01	.02	.03	.04	.05	.06	.07	.08	.09
.0	.000	.046	.074	.097	.117	.136	.153	.170	.186	.201
.1	.215	.229	.243	.256	.269	.282	.295	.307	.319	.331
.2	.342	.353	.364	.375	.386	.397	.407	.418	.428	.438
.3	.448	.458	.468	.477	.487	.497	.506	.515	.525	.534
.4	.543	.552	.561	.570	.578	.587	.596	.604	.613	.622
.5	.630	.638	.647	.655	.663	.671	.679	.687	.695	.703
.6	.711	.719	.727	.735	.743	.750	.758	.765	.773	.781
.7	.788	.796	.803	.811	.818	.825	.832	.840	.847	.855
.8	.862	.869	.876	.883	.890	.897	.904	.911	.918	.925
.9	.932	.939	.946	.953	.960	.966	.973	.980	.987	.993
1.0	1.000	1.007	1.013	1.020	1.027	1.033	1.040	1.046	1.053	1.059
1.1	1.065	1.072	1.078	1.085	1.091	1.097	1.104	1.110	1.117	1.123
1.2	1.129	1.136	1.142	1.148	1.154	1.160	1.167	1.173	1.179	1.185
1.3	1.191	1.197	1.203	1.209	1.215	1.221	1.227	1.233	1.239	1.245
1.4	1.251	1.257	1.263	1.269	1.275	1.281	1.287	1.293	1.299	1.305
1.5	1.310	1.316	1.322	1.328	1.334	1.339	1.345	1.351	1.357	1.362
1.6	1.368	1.374	1.379	1.385	1.391	1.396	1.402	1.408	1.413	1.419
1.7	1.424	1.430	1.436	1.441	1.447	1.452	1.458	1.463	1.469	1.474
1.8	1.480	1.485	1.491	1.496	1.502	1.507	1.513	1.518	1.523	1.529
1.9	1.534	1.539	1.545	1.550	1.556	1.561	1.566	1.571	1.577	1.582
2.0	1.587	1.593	1.598	1.603	1.608	1.613	1.619	1.624	1.629	1.634
2.1	1.639	1.645	1.650	1.655	1.660	1.665	1.671	1.676	1.681	1.686
2.2	1.691	1.697	1.702	1.707	1.712	1.717	1.722	1.727	1.732	1.737
2.3	1.742	1.747	1.752	1.757	1.762	1.767	1.772	1.777	1.782	1.787
2.4	1.792	1.797	1.802	1.807	1.812	1.817	1.822	1.827	1.832	1.837
2.5	1.842	1.847	1.852	1.857	1.862	1.867	1.871	1.876	1.881	1.886
2.6	1.891	1.896	1.900	1.905	1.910	1.915	1.920	1.925	1.929	1.934
2.7	1.939	1.944	1.949	1.953	1.958	1.963	1.968	1.972	1.977	1.982
2.8	1.987	1.992	1.996	2.001	2.006	2.010	2.015	2.020	2.024	2.029
2.9	2.034	2.038	2.043	2.048	2.052	2.057	2.062	2.066	2.071	2.075
3.0	2.080	2.085	2.089	2.094	2.099	2.103	2.108	2.112	2.117	2.122
3.1	2.126	2.131	2.135	2.140	2.144	2.149	2.153	2.158	2.163	2.167
3.2	2.172	2.176	2.180	2.185	2.190	2.194	2.199	2.203	2.208	2.212
3.3	2.217	2.221	2.226	2.230	2.234	2.239	2.243	2.248	2.252	2.257
3.4	2.261	2.265	2.270	2.274	2.279	2.283	2.288	2.292	2.296	2.301
3.5	2.305	2.310	2.314	2.318	2.323	2.327	2.331	2.336	2.340	2.345
3.6	2.349	2.353	2.358	2.362	2.366	2.371	2.375	2.379	2.384	2.388
3.7	2.392	2.397	2.401	2.405	2.409	2.414	2.418	2.422	2.427	2.431
3.8	2.435	2.439	2.444	2.448	2.452	2.457	2.461	2.465	2.469	2.474
3.9	2.478	2.482	2.486	2.490	2.495	2.499	2.503	2.507	2.511	2.516
4.0	2.520	2.524	2.528	2.532	2.537	2.541	2.545	2.549	2.553	2.558
4.1	2.562	2.566	2.570	2.574	2.579	2.583	2.587	2.591	2.595	2.599
4.2	2.603	2.607	2.611	2.616	2.620	2.624	2.628	2.632	2.636	2.640
4.3	2.644	2.648	2.653	2.657	2.661	2.665	2.669	2.673	2.677	2.681
4.4	2.685	2.689	2.693	2.698	2.702	2.706	2.710	2.714	2.718	2.722
4.5	2.726	2.730	2.734	2.738	2.742	2.746	2.750	2.754	2.758	2.762
4.6	2.766	2.770	2.774	2.778	2.782	2.786	2.790	2.794	2.798	2.802
4.7	2.806	2.810	2.814	2.818	2.822	2.826	2.830	2.834	2.838	2.842
4.8	2.846	2.850	2.854	2.858	2.862	2.865	2.869	2.873	2.877	2.881
4.9	2.885	2.889	2.893	2.897	2.901	2.904	2.908	2.912	2.916	2.920

1. Corn
   Dent
   Sweet
   Pop
   Flint
2. Cotton
3. Tobacco
4. Soybeans (except as specified under I-*B* (Note) and II-*B*
5. Sorghums and Sudan or other clean tilled grasses
6. Potatoes, sugar beets, and any other clean tilled hill or row crops
7. Intertilled and cropped orchard or vineyard.

PARTIAL LIST OF PLANTS OF VALUE IN CONTROLLING EROSION AND IN PROVIDING UPLAND COVER AND FOOD FOR GAME

Mulberry.
High-bush cranberry.
Panicled dogwood.
Red osier dogwood.
Elderberry.
Black raspberry.
Red raspberry.
Blackberry.
Coralberry.
Snowberry.
Bush honeysuckle.
Honeysuckle vine.
Matrimony vine.
Hawthorn.

Wild cherry.
Chokecherry.
Pin cherry.
Black haw.
Wild grape.
Chokeberry.
Sumac.
Hackberry.
Wild plum.
Osage orange.
Red cedar.
Russian olive.
Serviceberry.
Mountain ash.

TABLE II.—SQUARE ROOTS OF DECIMAL NUMBERS
(For use in Manning's Formula)

Number	. − 0	. − 1	. − 2	. − 3	. − 4	. − 5	. − 6	. − 7	. − 8	. − 9
.00001	.003162	.003317	.003464	.003606	.003742	.003873	.004000	.004123	.004243	.004359
.00002	.004472	.004583	.004690	.004796	.004899	.005000	.005099	.005196	.005292	.005385
.00003	.005477	.005568	.005657	.005745	.005831	.005916	.006000	.006083	.006164	.006245
.00004	.006325	.006403	.006481	.006557	.006633	.006708	.006782	.006856	.006928	.007000
.00005	.007071	.007141	.007211	.007280	.007348	.007416	007483	.007550	.007616	.007681
.00006	.007746	.007810	.007874	.007937	.008000	.008062	.008124	.008185	.008246	.008307
.00007	.008367	.008426	.008485	.008544	.008602	.008660	.008718	.008775	.008832	.008888
.00008	.008944	.009000	.009055	.009110	.009165	.009220	.009274	.009327	.009381	.009434
.00009	.009487	.009539	.009592	.009644	.009695	.009747	.009798	.009849	.009899	.009950
.00010	.010000	.010050	.010100	.010149	.010198	.010247	.010296	.010344	.010392	.010440
.0001	.01000	.01049	.01095	.01140	.01183	.01225	.01265	.01304	.01342	.01378
.0002	.01414	.01449	.01483	.01517	.01549	.01581	.01612	.01643	.01673	.01703
.0003	.01732	.01761	.01789	.01817	.01844	.01871	.01897	.01924	.01949	.01975
.0004	.02000	.02025	.02049	.02074	.02098	.02121	.02145	.02168	.02191	.02214
.0005	.02236	.02258	.02280	.02302	.02324	.02345	.02366	.02387	.02408	.02429
.0006	.02449	.02470	.02490	.02510	.02530	.02550	.02569	.02588	.02608	.02627
.0007	.02646	.02665	.02683	.02702	.02720	.02739	.02757	.02775	.02793	.02811
.0008	.02828	.02846	.02864	.02881	.02898	.02915	.02933	.02950	.02966	.02983
.0009	.03000	.03017	.03033	.03050	.03066	.03082	.03098	.03114	.03130	.03146
.0010	.03162	.03178	.03194	.03209	.03225	.03240	.03256	.03271	.03286	.03302
.001	.03162	.03317	.03464	.03606	.03742	.03873	.04000	.04123	.04243	.04359
.002	.04472	.04583	.04690	.04796	.04899	.05000	.05009	.05196	.05292	.05385
.003	.05477	.05568	.05657	.05745	.05831	.05916	.06000	.06083	.06164	.06245
.004	.06325	.06403	.06481	.06557	.06633	.06708	.06782	.06856	.06928	.07000
.005	.07071	.07141	.07211	.07280	.07348	.07416	.07483	.07550	.07616	.07681
.006	.07746	.07810	.07874	.07937	.08000	.08062	.08124	.08185	.08246	.08307
.007	.08367	.08426	.08485	.08544	.08602	.08660	.08718	.08775	.08832	.08888
.008	.08944	.09000	.09055	.09110	.09165	.09220	.09274	.09327	.09381	.09434
.009	.09487	.09539	.09592	.09644	.09695	.09747	.09798	.09849	.09899	.09950
.010	.10000	.10050	.10100	.10149	.10198	.10247	.10296	.10344	.10392	.10440
.01	.1000	.1049	1095	.1140	.1183	.1225	.1265	.1304	.1342	.1378
.02	.1414	.1449	.1483	.1517	.1549	.1581	.1612	.1643	.1673	.1703
.03	.1732	.1761	.1789	.1817	.1844	.1871	.1897	.1924	.1949	.1975
.04	.2000	.2025	.2049	.2074	.2098	.2121	.2145	.2168	.2191	.2214
.05	.2236	.2258	.2280	.2302	.2324	.2345	.2366	.2387	.2408	.2429
.06	.2449	.2470	.2490	.2510	.2530	.2550	.2569	.2588	.2608	.2627
.07	.2646	.2665	.2683	.2702	.2720	.2739	.2757	.2775	.2793	.2811
.08	.2828	.2846	.2864	.2881	.2898	.2915	.2933	.2950	.2966	.2983
.09	.3000	.3017	.3033	.3050	.3066	.3082	.3098	.3114	.3130	.3146
.10	.3162	.3178	.3194	.3209	.3225	.3240	.3256	.3271	.3286	.3302

BIBLIOGRAPHY

BOOKS

1. MEYER, A. F.: "The Elements of Hydrology," John Wiley & Sons, Inc., New York, 1917.
2. AYRES, Q. C., and SCOATES, D.: "Land Drainage and Reclamation," pp. 274–319, McGraw-Hill Book Company, Inc., New York, 1928.
3. BLACK, J. D.: "Agricultural Reform in the United States," McGraw-Hill Book Company, Inc., New York, 1929.
4. KING, H. W.: "Handbook of Hydraulics," 2d ed., McGraw-Hill Book Company, Inc., New York, 1929.
5. HAZEN, A.: "Flood Flows," John Wiley & Sons, Inc., New York, 1930.
6. Technical Staff: "Handbook of Culvert and Drainage Practice," Armco Culvert Manufacturers Assoc., 349 pp., 1930.
7. POWERS, W. L., and TEETER, T. A. H.: "Land Drainage," 2d ed, pp. 284–296, John Wiley & Sons, Inc., New York, 1932.
8. BAKER, O. E.: Utilization of Natural Wealth, "Recent Social Trends in the United States," Part 2, Chap. 2, pp. 93–98, McGraw-Hill Book Company, Inc., New York, 1933.

GOVERNMENT BULLETINS AND REPORTS

(Obtainable from The Superintendent of Documents, Washington, D. C.)

9. FREE, E. E., and WESTGATE, J. M.: The Control of Blowing Soils, U. S. Dept. Agr. Farmers' Bull. 421, 23 pp., Dec., 1910.
10. —— and ——: The Movement of Soil Material by Wind, U. S. Dept. Agr. Bull. 68, 175 pp., 1911.
11. SAMPSON, A. W., and WEYL, L. H.: Range Preservation and Its Relation to Erosion Control on Western Grazing Lands, U. S. Dept. Agr. Bull. 675, 35 pp., 1918.
12. BARTEL, F. O.: First Progress Report on Soil Erosion Experiments, N. C. Bur. Pub. Roads, 1925.
13. RAMSER, C. E.: Runoff from Small Agricultural Areas, Jour. Agr. Research, Vol. 34, No. 9, 1927.
14. ZON, RAPHAEL: Forests and Water in the Light of Scientific Investigation, U. S. Forest Serv., (No number), 106 pp., 1927.
15. BARTEL, F. O.: Second Progress Report on Soil Erosion and Runoff Experiments in Piedmont, N. C., June 1, 1925 to May 31, 1926, Bur. Pub. Roads, 1928.
16. BERMETT, H. H., and CHAPLINE, W. R.: Soil Erosion a National Menace, U. S. Dept. Agr. Circ. 33, 36 pp., 1928.

17. McCRORY, S. H.: Hearing on a Bill for the Conservation of Rainfall in the United States, *U. S. Senate,* 70th *Congress,* 1st *Session, S*-3484, pp. 21–27, May, 1928.

18. SHEPARD, W.: Forests and Floods, *U. S. Dept. Agr. Circ.* 19, 24 pp., 1928.

19. ANON: Relation of Forestry to the Control of Floods in the Mississippi Valley, *House Doc.* 573, 70th *Congress,* 2d *Session,* 740 pp., 1929.

20. BARTEL, F. O.: Third Progress Report on Soil Erosion and Runoff Experiments at the North Carolina Experiment Station Farm, June 1, 1926 to May 31, 1927, *Bur. Pub. Roads,* 1929.

21. MUNNS, E. N.: Relation of Forestry to the Control of Floods in the Mississippi Valley, *House Doc.* 573, 70th *Congress,* 2d *Session,* pp. 57–84, 1929.

22. SHERMAN, E. A.: Relation of Forestry to the Control of Floods in the Mississippi Valley, *House Doc.* 573, 70th *Congress,* 2d *Session,* 1929.

23. ANON: Forest and Range Resources of Utah: Protection and Use, *U. S. Dept. Agr. Misc. Pub.* 90, 101 pp., 1930.

24. FORSLING, C. L.: Study of the Influence of Herbaceous Plant Cover on Surface Runoff and Soil Erosion in Relation to Grazing on the Wasatch Plateau in Utah, *U. S. Dept. Agr. Tech. Bull.* 220, 71 pp., 1930.

25. GRAY, L. C., and BAKER, O. E.: Land Utilization and the Farm Problem, *U. S. Dept. Agr. Misc. Pub.* 97, 54 pp., 1930.

26. MIDDLETON, H. E.: Properties of Soils which Influence Soil Erosion, *U. S. Dept. Agr. Tech. Bull.* 178, 16 pp., 1930.

27. RAMSER, C. E.: Erosion and Silting of Dredged Drainage Ditches, *U. S. Dept. Agr. Tech. Bull.* 184, 54 pp., 1930.

28. CAMERON, D. C.: Great Dust Storm of Washington and Oregon, April, 21–24, 1931, *Monthly Weather Rev.,* Vol. 59, No. 5, pp. 195–197, May, 1931.

29. GEIB, H. V.: Strip Cropping to Prevent Erosion, *U. S. Dept. Agr. Leaflet* 85, 6 pp., 1931.

30. RAMSER, C. E.: Farm Terracing, *U. S. Dept. Agr. Farmers' Bull.* 1669, 22 pp., 1931.

31. SLATER, C. S., and BYERS, H. G.: A Laboratory Study of the Field Percolation Rates of Soils, *U. S. Dept. Agr. Tech. Bull.* 232, 1931.

32. UHLAND, R. E.: Controlling Small Gullies by Bluegrass Sod, *U. S. Dept. Agr. Leaflet* 82, 4 pp., 1931.

33. DULEY, F. L., and HAYS, O. E.: The Effect of the Degree of Slope on Runoff and Soil Erosion, *Jour. Agr. Research,* Vol. 45, No. 6, pp. 349–360, September, 1932.

34. MIDDLETON, H. E., SLATER, C. S., and BYERS, H. G.: Physical and Chemical Characteristics of the Soils from the Erosion Experiment Stations, *U. S. Dept. Agr. Tech. Bull.* 316, 51 pp., 1932.

35. PECK, M., and Others: Economic Utilization of Marginal Lands in Nicholas and Webster Counties, West Virginia, *U. S. Dept. Agr. Tech. Bull.* 303, 64 pp., 1932

36. RAMSER, C. E.: Gullies: How to Control and Reclaim Them, *U. S. Dept. Agr. Farmers' Bull.* 1234, 35 pp., 1932.

37. ANON.: Problems of "Sub-marginal Areas" and Desirable Adjustments with Particular Reference to Public Acquisition of Land, *Nat. Land-use Planning Com. Pub.* 6, 23 pp., 1933.

38. AUTEN, JOHN T.: Porosity and Water Absorption of Forest Soils, *Jour. Agr. Research,* Vol. 46, pp. 997–1014, 1933.

39. MEGINNIS, H. G.: Using Soil-Binding Plants to Reclaim Gullies, *U. S. Dept. Agr. Farmers' Bull.* 1697, 17 pp., 1933.

40. ———: *Report of the Nat. Resources Bd.,* Dec. 1, 1934.

41. ALEXANDER, A. E.: Petrology of the Great Dustfall of Nov. 13, 1933, *Monthly Weather Rev.,* Vol. 62, No. 1, p. 15, January, 1934.

42. BAILEY, R. W., FORSLING, C. L., and BECRAFT, R. J.: Floods and Accelerated Erosion in Northern Utah, *U. S. Dept. Agr. Misc. Pub.* 196, 21 pp., 1934.

43. DULEY, F. L., and ACKERMAN, F. G.: Runoff and Erosion from Plots of Different Lengths, *Jour. Agr. Research,* Vol. 48, No. 6, pp. 505–510, 1934.

44. HAND, IRVING F.: Character and Magnitude of Dense Dust Cloud which Passed over Washington, D. C., May 11, 1934, *Monthly Weather Rev.,* Vol. 62, No. 5, pp. 156–157, May, 1934.

45. ICKES, HAROLD L.: The New Deal in Conservation, *U. S. Dept. Int.,* 15 pp., 1934.

46. RUSSELL, R. J., and RUSSELL, R. D.: Dust Storm of April 12, 1934, Baton Rouge, La., *Monthly Weather Rev.,* Vol. 62, No. 5, pp. 162–163, May, 1934.

47. VINALL, H. N.: Forage Crops for the Sand-hill Section of Nebraska, *U. S. Dept. Agr., Bur. Plant Indus.,* 16 pp., 1934.

48. ANON.: The Resettlement Administration, *Resettlement Admin. Pub.* 1, 27 pp., 1935.

49. YARNELL, DAVID L.: Rainfall Intensity—Frequency Data, *U. S. Dept. Agr. Misc. Pub.* 204, 67 pp., 1935.

50. HOYT, W. G., and Others: Rainfall and Runoff in the United States, *U. S. Geol. Sur. Water Supply Paper* 772, 301 pp., 1936.

51. JARVIS, CLARENCE S., and Others: Floods in the United States, *U. S. Geol. Sur. Water Supply Paper* 771, 497 pp. 1936.

51a. AYRES, QUINCY C.: Hearing on a Bill for the control of flood waters in the Mississippi Valley, *U. S. Senate, 74th Congress, 2d Session, S-3524, Part 1,* pp. 295–330, April, 1936.

STATE PUBLICATIONS

(Obtainable from the various state agricultural colleges, when not out of print)

52. FISHER, M. L.: The Washed Lands of Indiana: A Preliminary Study, *Ind. Agr. Exp. Sta. Circ.* 90, 24 pp., 1919.

53. MILLER, M. F., and DULEY, F. L.: Studies of Water Absorption, Percolation, Evaporation, Capillary Water Movement, and Soil

Erosion Under Field Conditions, *Mo. Agr. Exp. Sta. Bull.* 163, pp. 65–66, 1919.

54. McHARGUE, and PETER, A. M.: The Removal of Mineral Plant-Food by Natural Drainage Waters, *Ky. Agr. Exp. Sta. Bull.* 237, 29 pp., 1921.

55. DULEY, F. L., and MILLER, M. L.: Erosion and Surface Runoff under Different Soil Conditions, *Mo. Agr. Exp. Sta. Research Bull.* 63, 45 pp., 1923.

56. CARTER, DEANE G.: Terracing Farm Land, *Ark. Ext. Circ.* 182, 7 pp., 1924.

57. LEHMANN, E. W., and HANSON, F. P.: Saving the Soils by Use of Mangum Terraces, *Ill. Agr. Sta. Circ.* 290, 19 pp., 1924.

58. COPELAND, J. T.: Terracing in Mississippi, *Miss. Agr. Ext. Bull.* 34, 19 pp., 1926.

59. KARRAKER, P. E.: Soil Washing, *Ky. Agr. Ext. Div. Circ.* 54, pp. 29–31, 1927.

60. HOLMAN, A. T.: Terracing Farm Lands, *N. C. Agr. Ext. Ser. Circ.* 173, 19 pp. 1928.

61. MARTIN, G. E.: Terracing in Oklahoma, *Okla. Ext. Ser. Circ.* 218, 23 pp., 1928.

62. ROBERTS, G., KELLY, J. B., and WELCH, E. F.: Soil Erosion, *Ky. Agr. Ext. Div. Circ.* 129, 38 pp., 1928.

63. BENTLEY, M. R.: Terracing Farm Lands in Texas, *Tex. A. & M. Coll. Ext. Ser. Bull.* 51, 16 pp., 1929.

64. DULEY, F. L., and SHEDD, C. K.: Terracing Farm Lands in Kansas, *Kan. State Agr. Ext. Ser. Bull.* 58, 13 pp., 1929.

65. DULEY, F. L., MILLER, M. L., and SHEDD, C. K.: Terracing Farm Lands in Kansas, *Kan. Agr. Ext. Div. Bull.* 58, 13 pp., 1929.

66. LeBRON, L. C., and NICHOLS, M. L.: Terracing in Alabama, *Ala. Poly. Inst. Ext. Ser. Circ.* 94, 11 pp., 1929.

67. UHLAND, R. E., and WOOLEY, J. C.: Control of Gullies, *Mo. Agr. Exp. Sta. Bull.* 271, 23 pp., 1929.

68. BATES, C. G., and ZEASMAN, O. R.: Soil Erosion—A Local and National Problem, *Wis. Agr. Exp. Sta. Research Bull.* 99, 100 pp., 1930.

69. BODE, I. T.: Tree Planting a Part of Erosion Control, *Iowa Agr. Ext. Ser. Bull.* 166, 4 pp., 1930.

70. CONNER, A. B., and Others: Factors Influencing Runoff and Soil Erosion, *Tex. Agr. Exp. Sta. Bull.* 411, 50 pp., 1930.

71. DICKSON, R. E., and SCOATES, D.: Runoff Water Losses in Relation to Crop Production, *Tex. Agr. Exp. Sta. Report*, pp. 51–52, 1930.

72. MILLER, M. F., and KRUSEKOPF, H. H.: Erosion of Missouri Soils, *Mo. Agr. Exp. Sta. Bull.* 285, pp. 110–112, 1930.

73. SHEDD, C. K.: Terracing Farm Lands: *Mo. Agr. Ext. Ser. Circ.* 248, 10 pp., 1930.

74. TAYLOR, T. V.: Silting of Reservoirs, *Tex. Agr. Exp. Sta. Bull.* 3025, 170 pp., 1930.

75. BENTLEY, M. R.: Gully Control, *Tex. A. & M. Coll. Ext. Ser. Circ.* 49, 12 pp., 1931.

76. CLYDE, A. W.: Terracing to Reduce Erosion, *Iowa Agr. Ext. Bull.* 172, 8 pp., 1931.

77. GEIB, H. V., and HILL, H. O.: Soil Erosion and Moisture Conservation Studies, *Tex. Agr. Exp. Sta. 44th Ann. Report*, pp. 133–134, 1931.

78. SNYDER, J. M.: Research in Soil Erosion at the North Carolina Station, *N. C. Agr. Exp. Sta., 54th Ann. Report*, pp. 47–50, 1931.

79. GLASS, JOHN S.: Terracing to Control Erosion, *Kan. Agr. Ext. Ser. Bull.* 70, 41 pp., 1932.

80. HUGHES, O. E.: Terracing Farm Land in Georgia, *Ga. Agr. Ext. Div. Bull.* 394, Vol. 19, 22 pp., 1932.

81. MILLER, M. F., and KRUSEKOPF, H. H.: The Influence of Systems of Cropping and Methods of Culture on Surface Runoff and Soil Erosion, *Mo. Agr. Exp. Sta. Research Bull.* 177, 32 pp., 1932.

82. SCARSETH, G. D.: Morphological Greenhouse and Chemical Studies of the Black Belt Soils of Alabama, *Ala. Agr. Exp. Sta. Bull.* 237, 48 pp., 1932.

83. THROCKMORTON, R. I., and DULEY, F. L.: Soil Fertility, *Kan. Agr. Exp. Sta. Bull.* 260, 60 pp., 1932.

84. WEIR, WALTER W.: Soil Erosion in California: Its Prevention and Control, *Cal. Agr. Exp. Sta. Bull.* 538, 45 pp., 1932.

85. GRAY, L. C.: Aspects of a State Program of Land Utilization, *Proc. N. J. Land Use Conf., N. J. Agr. Exp. Sta. Bull.* 552, pp. 22–30, 1933.

86. BENNETT, H. H.: Land Use and Soil Erosion, *Proc. N. J. Land Use Conf., N. J. Agr. Exp. Sta. Bull.* 552, pp. 31–47, 1933.

87. WOOD, IVAN D.: Inexpensive Methods of Gully Control, *Neb. Agr. Ext. Ser. Circ.* 741, 16 pp., 1933.

88. CARNES, A., and WILSON, J. B.: Terracing in Alabama, *Ala. Poly. Inst. Ext. Ser. Circ.* 148, 20 pp., 1934.

89. FINNELL, H. H.: Results of Level Terracing on Heavy Silt Loam Soil, *Panhandle Agr. Exp. Sta. Bull.* 53, 12 pp., 1934.

90. KESSLER, L. H.: Erosion Control Structures—Drop Inlets and Spillways, *Wis. Agr. Exp. Sta.* and *Eng. Exp. Sta. Research Bull.* 122, 66 pp., 1934.

91. LUTZ, J. F.: The Physico-chemical Properties of Soils Affecting Soil Erosion, *Mo. Agr. Exp. Sta. Research Bull.* 212, 45 pp., 1934.

92. AYRES, QUINCY C.: Recommendations for the Control and Reclamation of Gullies, *Iowa Eng. Exp. Sta. Bull.* 121, 71 pp., 1935.

93. BAVER, L. D.: Soil Erosion in Missouri, *Mo. Agr. Exp. Sta. Bull.* 349, 66 pp., 1935.

94. JOHNSON, G. I., DANNER, W. N., JR., and PEIKERT, F. N.: Terracing Farm Lands in Georgia, *Univ. Ga. Agr. Ext. Bull.* 394, 24 pp., 1935.

95. MURRAY, W. G., and MELDRUM, H. R.: A Production Method of Valuing Land, *Iowa Agr. Exp. Sta. Bull.* 326, 20 pp., 1935.

96. ROE, H. B., and NEAL, J. H.: Soil Erosion Control in Farm Operation, *Minn. Agr. Exp. Sta. Special Bull.* 170, 20 pp., 1935.

97. ——— and ———: Soil Erosion Control by Engineering Methods, *Minn. Agr. Exp. Sta. Special Bull.* 171, 24 pp., 1935.

98. SCHICKELE, R., HIMMEL, J. P., and HURD, R. M.: Economic Phases of Erosion Control in Southern Iowa and Northern Missouri, *Iowa Agr. Exp. Sta. Bull.* 333, 42 pp., 1935.

PROFESSIONAL AND SCIENTIFIC SOCIETY PUBLICATIONS

Journal of The American Society of Agronomy

99. JARDINE, W. M.: Management of Soils to Prevent Blowing, Vol. 5 No. 4, pp. 213–217, October–December, 1914.
100. CHAPLINE, W. R.: Erosion on Range Land, Vol. 21, No. 4, pp. 423–429, April, 1929.
101. DICKSON, R. E.: Results and Significance of the Spur (Texas) Runoff and Erosion Experiments, Vol. 21, No. 4, pp. 415–422, April, 1929.
102. FINNELL, H. H.: Moisture-saving Efficiency of Level Terraces under Semi-arid Conditions, Vol. 22, No. 6, pp. 522–529, June, 1930.
103. MUSGRAVE, G. W., and DUNLAVY, H.: Some Characteristics of an Eroded Soil, Vol. 23, No. 4, pp. 245–252, April, 1931.
104. BENNETT, H. H.: National Program of Soil and Water Conservation, Vol. 23, No. 5, pp. 357–371, May, 1931.
105. ————: Cultural Changes in Soils from the Standpoint of Erosion, Vol. 23, No. 6, pp. 434–454, June, 1931.
106. STEWART, G., and FORSLING, C. L.: Surface Runoff and Erosion in Relation to Soil and Plant Cover on High Grazing Lands of Central Utah, Vol. 23, No. 10, pp. 815–832, October, 1931.
107. BROWN, P. E.: The Mystery of the Soil, Vol. 24, No. 12, pp. 935–950, December, 1932.
108. GEIB, H. V.: A New Type of Installation for Measuring Soil and Water Losses from Control Plots, Vol. 25, No. 7, pp. 429–440, July, 1933.
109. MUSGRAVE, G. W.: The Infiltration Capacity of Soils in Relation to the Control of Surface Runoff and Erosion, Vol. 27, No. 5, pp. 336–345, May, 1935.

Transactions, The American Geophysical Union

110. McCRORY, S. H.: Runoff Investigations from Small Agricultural Areas, pp. 518–521, April, 1933.
111. BENNETT, H. H.: Dynamic Action of Rains in Relation to Erosion in the Humid Region, pp. 474–488, April, 1934.
112. FULLER, G. L.: Charting the Effects of Erosion in the Old Plantation Belt of the Southern Piedmont, *15th Ann. Meeting*, pp. 495–500, April, 1934.
113. HENDRICKSON, B. H.: The Choking of Pore-space in the Soil and Its Relation to Runoff and Erosion, *15th Ann. Meeting*, pp. 500–505, April, 1934.
114. LOWDERMILK, W. C.: Acceleration of Erosion above Geologic Norms, *15th Ann. Meeting*, pp. 505–509, April, 1934.
115. LOWDERMILK, W. C., and ROWE, P. B.: Studies on Absorption of Rainfall in Its Relation to Surface Runoff and Erosion, *15th Ann. Meeting*, pp. 509–515, April, 1934.

116. MUSGRAVE, G. W.: A Quantitative Study of Certain Factors Affecting Soils and Water Losses as the Logical Basis for Developing Practical Methods of Erosion Control, 15th Ann. Meeting, pp. 515–521, April, 1934.

Agricultural Engineering

(Journal of the American Society of Agricultural Engineers)

117. SHORT, A. K.: The Bank's Interest in Soil Erosion, Vol. 10, No. 9, pp. 289–290, September, 1929.
118. McPHEETERS, W. H.: Soil Conservation as an Aid to Flood Control, Vol. 11, No. 10, pp. 339–341, October, 1930.
119. RAMSER, C. E.: Erosion Control on the Federal Projects, Vol. 11, No. 4, pp. 135–140, April, 1930.
120. HOLMAN, A. T.: Problems Involved in Developing Terracing Machinery, Vol. 12, No. 2, p. 45, February, 1931.
121. RAMSER, C. E.: The Need of Improved Machinery for Terrace Construction and Farming Terraced Land, Vol. 12, No. 2, pp. 39–42, February, 1931.
122. SMITH, H. P.: Types of Terracing Machinery Used in Texas, Vol. 12, No. 2, pp. 43–44, February, 1931.
123. KOTOK, E. I.: Vegetative Cover, The Water Cycle and Erosion, Vol. 12, No. 4, pp. 112–113, April, 1931.
124. LOWDERMILK, W. C.: Studies of the Role of Forest Vegetation in Surficial Runoff and Soil Erosion, Vol. 12, No. 4, pp. 107–111, April, 1931.
125. SAMPSON, ARTHUR W.: Relation of Erosion to Soil Productivity, Vol. 12, No. 4, pp. 114–116, April, 1931.
126. WHITFIELD, A. F.: Soil Building with Terraces, Vol. 12, No. 4, pp. 120–122, April, 1931.
127. McCRORY, S. H.: Land Reclamation Work of the Bureau of Agricultural Engineering, Vol. 12, No. 8, pp. 305–306, August, 1931.
128. KING, JAMES A.: The Place and Function of Land Reclamation in the Agricultural Program, Vol. 12, No. 9, pp. 333–337, September, 1931, and Vol. 12, No. 10, pp. 385–391, October, 1931.
129. NICHOLS, M. L., and SEXTON, H. D.: A Method of Studying Soil Erosion, Vol. 12, No. 4, pp. 101–103, April, 1932.
130. LEHMANN, E. W.: Soil Erosion Control in Illinois, Vol. 13, No. 5, p. 126, May, 1932.
131. WOOLEY, J. C.: Efficiency of Terracing Machines, Vol. 13, No. 7, p. 182, July, 1932.
132. JONES, LEWIS, A.: Engineers and the Control of Erosion, Vol. 13, No. 9, pp. 234–236, September, 1932.
133. RAMSER, C. E.: The Operation of Farm Machinery Over Terraced Land, Vol. 13, No. 9, pp. 231–233, September, 1932.
134. BAIRD, R. W.: The Operation of Power Machinery on Terraced Land, Vol. 13, No. 11, p. 286, November, 1932.

135. BAVER, L. D.: The Physical Properties of Soils of Interest to Agricultural Engineers, Vol. 13, No. 12, pp. 324–327, December, 1932.

136. BAVER, L. D.: Some Soil Factors Affecting Erosion, Vol. 14, No. 2, pp. 51–52, February, 1933.

137. DICKSON, R. E.: Terraces to Conserve Surface Runoff, Vol. 14, No. 2, p. 50, February, 1933.

138. RAMSER, C. E.: Soil Erosion Control by Terracing—History and Accomplishments, Vol. 14, No. 4, p. 103, April, 1933.

139. SEXTON, H. D., and DISEKER, E. G.: A Proposed System of Erosion Control, Vol. 14, No. 6, pp. 150–153, June, 1933.

140. UHLAND, R. E.: Division for Taking Aliquots of Runoff, Vol. 14, No. 7, pp. 186–188, July, 1933.

141. COPELAND, J. T.: Field Observation of Soil Erosion Index Variants, Vol. 14, No. 8, p. 206, August, 1933.

142. GREGORY, W. H.: County Land Terracing Program, Vol. 15, No. 1, p. 22, January, 1934.

143. RAMSER, C. E.: Control of Soil Erosion by Terracing, Vol. 15, No. 5, p. 164, May, 1934.

144. FLEMING, B. P.: A Nationwide View of Essential Soil Erosion Control Measures, Vol. 15, No. 7, pp. 267–272, August, 1934.

145. McCRORY, S. H.: Engineering Phases of Land-use Planning—A Symposium, Vol. 15, No. 8, pp. 315–323, September, 1934.

146. STORIE, R. EARL: Evaluating the Land Factor in Land Classification and Land Appraisal, Vol. 15, No. 9, pp. 330–334, September, 1934.

147. RAMSER, C. E.: Results of Engineering Experiments at the Soil Erosion Stations, Vol. 15, No. 11, pp. 381–386, November, 1934.

148. ROE, H. B.: Soil Erosion Control and Soil Moisture Regulation in Relation to State and National Land-use Planning, Vol. 15, No. 12, pp. 428–430, December, 1934.

149. BAIRD, RALPH W.: Some Requirements of a Terracing Machine, Vol. 16, No. 1, p. 3, January, 1935.

150. COLLINS, E. V., AYRES, Q. C., and JOHNSON, L. W.: A New Type of Terracing Machine, Vol. 16, No. 1, p. 6, January, 1935.

151. DRUMMOND, GARRETT B.: A Nomographic Solution of the Rational Runoff Formula, Vol. 16, No. 1, p. 13, January, 1935.

152. FLETCHER, LEONARD J.: Variable Field Requirements of Terracing Equipment, Vol. 16, No. 1, p. 5, January, 1935.

153. SHEDD, C. K., COLLINS, E. V., and DAVIDSON, J. B.: The Basin Method of Planting Row Crops and a Basin Lister Planter, Vol. 16, No. 1, p. 4, January, 1935.

154. WOOLEY, J. C.: The Development of a Terrace Building Machine, Vol. 16, No. 1, p. 4, January, 1935.

155. BAIRD, RALPH W.: Requirements of Farm Machinery for Terraced Land, Vol. 16, No. 3, p. 97, March, 1935.

156. LIVINGSTON, L. F.: Dams or Ponds to Conserve Water, Vol. 16, No. 3, p. 115, March, 1935.

157. NICHOLS, M. L., and YODER, R. E.: New Power Equipment for Terracing, Vol. 16, No. 3, p. 93, March, 1935.

158. McGREW, P. C.: Engineering Experiments in Soil Erosion Control in the Pacific Northwest, Vol. 16, No. 5, p. 187, May, 1935.

159. SCOATES, D.: Teaching Terracing with Blocks, Vol. 16, No. 5, p. 190, May, 1935.

160. THURMOND, M. F.: Visualizing Soil Erosion Control, Vol. 16, No. 5, p. 191, May, 1935.

161. POWERS, WILBUR L.: Land Classification and Soil and Water Surveys, Vol. 16, No. 6, p. 224, June, 1935.

162. AYRES, QUINCY C.: Cost of Terracing in Iowa, Vol. 16, No. 8, p. 317, August, 1935.

163. BARTEL, F. O.: Results of Recent Engineering Studies in Soil Erosion Control, Vol. 16, No. 8, p. 304, August, 1935.

164. BENNETT, H. H.: Attacking the Soil Erosion Problem on a Nation-wide Front, Vol. 16, No. 8, p. 293, August, 1935.

165. CHAMBERS, T. B.: The SCS Erosion Control Program, Vol. 16, No. 8, p. 301, August, 1935.

166. DRUMMOND, GARRETT B.: The Design of Stilling Basins for Small Dams and Weirs, Vol. 16, No. 8, p. 319, August, 1935.

167. ELLISON, W. D.: Terrace Outlets, Vol. 16, No. 8, p. 298, August, 1935.

168. FARRINGTON, F. N.: Tallapoosa County's (Ala.) Terracing Program, Vol. 16, No. 8, p. 313, August, 1935.

169. MATSON, HOWARD: Design and Construction of Sodded Terrace Outlet Channels, Vol. 16, No. 8, p. 321, August, 1935.

170. RIESBOL, H. S.: Selection of Channel Grade for Terraces, Vol. 16, No. 8, p. 308, August, 1935.

171. HILL, H. O.: Terrace Outlet Control, Vol. 16, No. 10, pp. 403–407, October, 1935.

172. BAIRD, RALPH W., and Others: Terrace Machinery and Terrace Construction Practices—A Symposium, Vol. 17, No. 2, p. 47, February, 1936.

173. FISHER, F. A.: What America's Soil Conservation Program Requires of the Engineer, Vol. 17, No. 2, p. 45, February, 1936.

174. WILSON, N. W., and NICHOLS, M. L.: The Size of Terracing Equipment, Vol. 17, No. 2, p. 55, February, 1936.

175. LOGAN, C. A.: A Pasture Contour Furrowing Machine, Vol. 17, No. 3, pp. 111–113, March, 1936.

175a. HAMILTION, C. L., WOOLEY, J. C., TSCHUDY, L. C., and McPHEETERS, W. H.: Engineering Phases of Soil Erosion Control—A Symposium, Vol. 17, No. 5, pp. 205–214, May, 1936.

Proceedings and Transactions, American Society of Civil Engineers

176. ZON, RAPHAEL, and Others: Comparison of Rainfall and Runoff in the Northeastern United States, *Proceedings*, Vol. 33, No. 8, pp. 924–933, October, 1907.

177. GRUNSKY, C. E.: Rainfall and Runoff Studies, *Transactions*, Vol. 85, pp. 66–136, 1922.

178. JARVIS, C. S.: Flood Flow Characteristics, *Transactions*, Vol. 89, pp. 985–1032, 1926.

179. McCARTHY, E. F.: Forest Cover as a Factor in Flood Control, *Proceedings*, Vol. 53, No. 10, pp. 2511–2518, December, 1927.

180. JARVIS, C. S.: Rainfall Characteristics and Their Relation to Soils and Runoff, *Proceedings*, Vol. 56, No. 1, pp. 3–47, 1930.

181. GREGORY, R. L., and ARNOLD, C. E.: Runoff—Rational Runoff Formulas, *Transactions*, Vol. 96, pp. 1038–1177, 1932.

182. HOYT, W. G., and TROXWELL, H. C.: Forests and Stream Flow, *Proceedings*, Vol. 58, No. 6, pp. 1037–1066, August, 1932.

183. CHAPMAN, H. H.: Influence of Overgrazing on Erosion and Watersheds, *Civil Engineering*, Vol. 3, pp. 74–78, February, 1933.

Journal of Forestry

184. LOWDERMILK, W. C.: Erosion and Floods Along the Yellow River (China) Watershed, Vol. 22, No. 6, pp. 11–18, October, 1924.

185. LENTZ, G. H., and Others: Soil Erosion in the Silt Loam Uplands of Mississippi, Vol. 28, No. 7, pp. 971–977, November, 1930.

186. SINCLAIR, J. D.: Studies of Soil Erosion in Mississippi, Vol. 29, No. 4, April, 1931.

187. WILLIAMS, CARL: Land Use Problems in the South, Vol. 30, pp. 276–283, 1932.

188. BATES, C. G.: Soil Erosion in the Mississippi Valley, Vol. 31, No. 1, pp. 88–96, January, 1933.

189. MEGINNIS, H. G.: Tree Planting to Reclaim Gullied Lands in the South, Vol. 31, No. 6, pp. 649–656, October, 1933.

190. LOWDERMILK, W. C.: The Role of Vegetation in Erosion Control and Water Conservation, Vol. 32, No. 5, pp. 529–536, May, 1934.

Miscellaneous Society Publications

191. MEAD, D. W.: The Cause of Floods and the Factors That Influence Their Intensity, *Jour. Western Soc. Eng.*, Vol. 18, No. 4, pp. 239–289, April, 1913.

192. BAKER, O. E.: Land Utilization in the United States: Geographical Aspects of the Problem, *Geographical Rev.*, Vol. 13, No. 1, January 1923.

193. DULEY, F. L.: Loss of Soluble Salts in Runoff Water, *Soil Science*, Vol. 21, No. 5, pp. 401–409, May, 1926.

194. TUGWELL, R. G.: Farm Relief and a Permanent Agriculture, *Annals Amer. Acad. Pol. and Soc. Science*, Vol. 142, pp. 271–282, March, 1929.

195. POPE, J. D.: Issues Involved in the Readjustment of Farm Organization in the Cotton Belt, *Jour. Farm Economics*, Vol. XI, No. 2, April, 1929.

196. BAKER, O. E.: Outlook for Land Utilization in the United States, *Jour. Farm Economics*, Vol. 13, pp. 203–230, 1931.

197. Cook, C. W.: Why the Mayan Cities of the Peten District, Guatemala, Were Abandoned, *Jour. Wash. Acad. Science*, Vol. 21, No. 13, pp. 283–288, 1931.

198. Stebbing, E. P.: Influence of Forests on Rainfall, Erosion, and Inundation, *Contemporary Rev.*, Vol. 141, pp. 359–366, March, 1932.

199. Knight, H. G.: Land Use and Erosion, *Proc., Amer. Assoc. Advancement Science*, Syracuse Univ., New York, pp. 37–43, June, 1932.

200. Bennett, H. H.: Quantitative Study of Erosion Technique and Some Preliminary Results, *Geog. Rev.*, Vol. 23, No. 3, pp. 423–432, July, 1933.

201. Bayer, A. W.: The Relationship of Vegetation to Soil Erosion in the Natal Thornveld, South Africa, *Jour. Science*, Vol. 30, pp. 280–287, October, 1933.

202. Leighly, John: Turbulence and the Transportation of Rock Debris by Streams, *Geog. Rev.*, Vol. 24, No. 3, pp. 453–464, July, 1934.

203. Musgrave, G. W.: A Device for Measuring Precipitation Waters Lost from the Soil as Surface Runoff, Percolation, Evaporation, and Transpiration, *Soil Science*, Vol. 40, No. 5, pp. 391–401, November, 1935.

Proceedings, Soil Conservation Conferences

204. Trent, D. P.: Formulating a Land Policy for Oklahoma, *Proc., State Soil Conserv. Conf.*, Oklahoma City, Okla., p. 38, November, 1, 1929.

205. Lentz, G. H.: Soil Erosion in Western Mississippi, *Proc.*, 2d *Southwest Soil & Water Conserv. Conference*, pp. 23–31, June, 1930.

206. Hazen, L. E.: Handling Runoff from Terraced Fields, *Proc.*, 2d *Southwest Soil & Water Conserv. Conf.*, pp. 55–57, June, 1930.

207. Zon, Raphael: National Economic and Social Objectives in Forest Policy, *Proc. Nat. Conf. Land Utilization*, Chicago, Ill., pp. 77–83, November, 19–21, 1931.

208. Duley, F. L.: The Formation of a Soil and Water Conservation Program for the Southwest, *Proc., 4th Southwest Soil and Water Conserv. Conf.*, pp. 34–49, July, 1933.

209. Glass, John S.: The Effect of Contour Farming on Soil and Water Control, *Proc., 4th Southwest Soil and Water Conserv. Conf.*, pp. 26–31, July, 1933.

210. Bennett, H. H.: Relation of Soil Erosion to Flood Control, *Nat. Rivers & Harbors Congress*, April, 1934.

211. Allison, R. V.: Essential Character of Water Conservation and Erosion Control, *Proc., 5th Southwest Soil and Water Conserv. Conf.*, pp. 3–10, July, 1934.

212. Harper, H. J.: Effect of Organic Matter in the Control of Soil Erosion, *Proc., 5th Southwest Soil and Water Conserv. Conf.*, pp. 20–23, July, 1934.

213. Henrickson, B. H.: Recent Developments in Strip-cropping and Water-furrowing for Erosion Control, *Proc., 5th Southwest Soil and Water Conserv. Conf.*, pp. 24–26, July, 1934.

214. GLASS, JOHN S.: New Type Terraces and New Terracing Machines, *Proc., 5th Southwest Soil and Water Conserv. Conf.*, pp. 26–31, July, 1934.

215. UHLAND, R. E.: Soil Erosion and Land Utilization for Missouri and Iowa, *Proc. 5th Southwest Soil and Water Conserv. Conf.*, pp. 38–41, July, 1934.

216. MEYER, A. H.: Soil Erosion and Land Utilization for Louisiana, *Proc., 5th Southwest Soil and Water Conf.*, pp. 41–44, July, 1934.

217. PERSON, H. S.: Little Waters. Booklet published jointly by Soil Conservation Service, Resettlement Administration and Rural Electrification Administration. Obtainable from Superintendent of documents. 82 pp., April, 1936.

INDEX

A

A-frame level, 124
Adjustment of levels, farm-dumpy type, 128, 129
  farm-turret type, 127
  peg test for, 128
Adverse economic influences, 325
Agricultural cropping, requisites for safe continuation of, 322, 323
  (*See also* Contour farming; Conservation farming; Land use)
Agricultural crops, list of conserving and depleting, 335–337
Agricultural experiment stations, Alabama, 50
  Missouri, 17
    comparison of continuous corn and corn in rotation, 49
    effect of cultural and cropping systems at, 43
    results of fourteen years' measurements at, 36
  North Carolina, 24
  Texas, 17, 24, 50
  (*See also* Federal erosion farms)
American terracer, 149
American tragedy, An, 15
Apparatus, measuring, for erosion experiments, 311–313
  for infiltration capacity of soils, 41
Appendix, 331–365
Appraisal, means for weighing value of various control methods, 40
Areas, land, methods of calculating, 331–335
  of pipe culverts, 259
Articulated concrete mat, 298–300
Automatic rain gages, 95, 313

B

Bank caving, illustration of, 301
  (*See also* Stream-bank erosion)
Bartel, F. O., 36
Basin-forming machine, 71
Basin lister-planter, 51
Bench terraces, 101
Bennett, H. H., 33, 44–47, 50
Bermuda grass, 284
Bethany erosion farm, experiments in progress at, 303–310
  map of, 306
Bibliography, 341–352
  Agricultural Engineering, 347–349
  books, 341
  Federal bulletins and reports, 341–343
  Journal of the American Society of Agronomy, 346
  Journal of Forestry, 350
  Miscellaneous society publications, 350, 351
  Proceedings and Transactions, American Society of Civil Engineers, 349
  Proceedings, Soil Conservation Conferences, 351, 352
  State publications, 343–346
  Transactions, The American Geophysical Union, 346, 347
Black locusts (*see* Trees)
Blade graders (*see* Graders)
Blasting (*see* Explosives)
Box culverts, capacity of, 266
  use in earth dams, 261–268
Broad crested weirs, 272
  discharge capacity of, 238
Brush, use of, for overfall protection, 212, 285
  for stream retards, 292–296

Brush dams, 217–222
  (*See also* Check dams)
Buffalo, N. Y., use of inclined tree
  planting at, 291
Bull dozer, 139

C

C, values of, 87
Calculating areas, methods of, 331–
  335
Canadian bluegrass, 284
Capacity computations, example of,
  113, 114
Capacity formula, 111
Carrying capacity (*see* Discharge
  capacity)
Channels, shape of, 191
Charts, for solution of Manning's
  formula, 115
  rainfall intensity-frequency, 89–96
Check dams, as aid in gully planting,
  275
  brush, 217
    cost of, 221
    double-post row type, 213, 219
    performance of, 220
    pole type, 222
    single-post row type, 217
  cost comparison of, 229
  definition of, 217
  height of, 210
  log, 232
    loose rock, 229
    plank, 234
  notch capacity of, 206
  principles governing use of, 205
  requirements for stability in, 211
  spacing of, 210
  for terrace outlets, 197–201
  wire, cost of, 228
    fixed-basket type, 226
    suspended-net type, 224
    V-type, 223
Chemical properties of soils, 30
Chisel cultivator, 52, 53
Civilian Conservation Corps, 18

Clarinda erosion farm, air view of,
  313
  description of, 314
Coefficients, roughness, *n*, 112, 113
  runoff, *C*, 87
Collins, E. V., 70, 157
Collins terracer (*see* Whirlwind
  terracer)
Colloidal soils, frost phenomena in,
  37
Colloid-moisture equivalent ratio, 29
Colloids, definition of, 25
  measurement of, 29
Combating agencies, experimental,
  303–310
  historical, 16, 17
Commercial fertilizers, 324
Concrete dams, 239–251
  design of, 240–251
  types of, 240
Concrete pipe, for drop-inlet culverts, 255
Conservation associations, local, 18
Conservation farming, data required
  for planning, 315, 317
  outline map for, 319
  suggested guide for (table), 323
  (*See also* Contour farming)
Conservation projects, 316
Conserving and depleting crops, list
  of, 335–337
Conventional symbols for erosion
  maps, 318
Contour farming, 49
  benefits of, 50
  on permanent pastures, 73
  on terraced land, 67, 183
  (*See also* Conservation farming;
    Cultural practices)
Contour plowing, of gully banks, 279
  (*See also* Contour farming)
Contour ridging, 73
  (*See also* Cultural practices)
Control, erosion (*see* Erosion control)
Corrugated metal, for drop-inlet
  culverts, 257
  for flumes, 214

Corrugated metal, for highway ditches, 204
Corrugated pipe, for drop-inlet culverts, 257
estimated life of, 257
Corsicana terracer, 148, 150
Cost, of check dams, 221, 228, 229
of equipment for terracing, 135, 146, 149, 157, 160
of planting trees, 322
of sloping gully banks, 277
of terrace construction, 165–177
form for cost data, 178
of terrace maintenance, 180
Critical rate of runoff, definition of, 83
quantitative determination of, 86
Crop rotations (*see* Cropping systems)
Crop stripping (*see* Strip cropping)
Cropping plan, for typical farm subject to erosion, 320
Cropping systems, for conservation farming of typical farm, 320
effect of, on denudation of soil, 34
on runoff and erosion, 36, 43, 44–49
experiments in progress on effect of, 303–310
on fields terraced and strip cropped, 56–59, 64–67
on strip-cropped fields (unterraced), 55, 60, 62, 69
Crops, list of conserving and depleting, 335–337
Cultivation, effect of, on erosion, 34
number of days soil is denuded by, 35
Cultural practices, comparison of effect of, on four soil types, 50
contour ridging, 73, 74
effect of, on runoff and erosion, 36, 43–47
on terraced land, 180–186
(*See also* Strip cropping)
Culverts, drop inlet on highway, 271

D

Dams, masonry, 200
for terrace outlets, 197–201
(*See also* Check dams; Soil-saving dams; Storage dams)
Data, on cost of terracing, 165–177
standard form for, 178
required to plan conservation farming, 315, 317
Demonstration areas of Soil Conservation Service, 315, 316
Denudation, effect on runoff and erosion, 34
Depleting crops, list of, 335–337
Diagram for solution of Manning's formula, 115
Discharge capacity, of box culverts, 266
of broad-crested weirs, 238
of pipe culverts, 258
of weir notches, 207
Discharge formula, 112
Dispersion ratio, effect on erosion, 25
measurement of, 29
Distances, relation of slope to horizontal measurement of, 334
Diversion ditches, for overfall protection, 216
for sod flumes, 285
for terrace outlets, 194
Dodge, A. F., 31
Double-post row brush dam (*see* Check dams, brush)
Drainage area (*see* Watersheds)
Drop-inlet culverts, pipe capacity for, 258
Drop-inlet dams, 254–271
Drop inlets, on existing culverts, 271
Duckfoot machine, results from use of, 50
Dumpy level, 128
Duration of rainfall rates, 88–96
Dynamite (*see* Explosives)

E

Earth dams, 252–271
drop-inlet type, 254–271

Earth dams, high-head type, 261–268
side-spillway type, 252–254
storage with bleeder outlet, 269
Economic factors, effect on erosion, 38, 325
Economics of land use, 305, 324–329
Elevating graders (*see* Graders)
Equipment, measuring, for erosion experiments, 311–313
for infiltration capacity of soils, 41
(*See also* Terrace construction)
Eroded material in lower Mississippi river, 301
Erosion, causes of, 1, 8, 20, 325
diagrammatic representation of, 8
effect of frost action on, 36, 37
of vegetation on, 71–77, 273–291, 321–324
of miscellaneous factors, 38
essential elements for, 20
extent in U. S., 2, 3
factors affecting rate of, 20, 322, 325
forces responsible for, 7
formula for, 38
illustration of, Cal., Ga., 6
inventory in the U. S., 4
losses, categories of, 7
man's responsibility for, 1, 20
natural rate of, 1
as related to land use, 39, 322
significance of, 1
suggested uses of land for control of, 323
types of, 7
by water, 8
by waves, 16
by wind, 15
Erosion control, annual expenditure for, 7
benefits of, 7
correlation of methods of, 81, 323
on cultivated slopes, 38
fact-finding experiments and methods, 303–310
in highway ditches, 200, 204, 234
on intermediate slopes, 38

Erosion control, list of desirable trees and shrubs for, 337
order of priority, 202
in relation to land use, 1, 39, 70, 72, 323
role of vegetation in, 30, 31, 273–291, 319–322
on steep slopes, 38
of stream banks, 286–302
use of sod bags in, 202
of vegetation for, 75, 76, 273–291, 321–324
yardstick for comparison of, by various methods, 40
Erosion experiment stations (*see* Federal erosion farms; Agricultural experiment stations)
Erosion maps, conventional symbols for, 318
typical, 306, 317, 319
Erosion ratio, 26
definition of, 29
Experiments in progress at federal erosion stations, 303–310
measuring apparatus for, 311–313
Explosives, use of, for sloping gully banks, cost, 277
for sub-soiling, 53

F

Farm levels, dumpy type, 128
turret type, 126
adjustment of, 127
use of, 130
utility of, 129
Farming to conserve soil and moisture (*see* Conservation farming; Contour farming; Cultural practices)
Federal erosion farms, Clarinda, Iowa, 314
experiments in progress at, 303–310
location of, 17
results from, 36, 44–48, 50, 79
typical map of (Bethany), 306

Field layout of typical farm subject to erosion, 188, 319
Field stripping (*see* Strip cropping)
Fills, soil-saving dams, 269
Fixed-basket wire dam, 226
Flumes, discharge capacity of, 238
  for terrace outlets, 199, 201
  use of, in overfall protection, 214
    for high drops, 215
  width required for each acre of watershed, 286
Forests, care and improvement of, 75
  economic returns from, 75, 322
  effect of, on runoff and erosion, 31, 33, 34, 74–77
  (*See also* Trees; Vegetation)
  new plantings in, 76
  role of, in land use, 31
  use of, for gully control, 75, 76, 321–324
Formulas, capacity, 111
  discharge, 112
  erosion, 38
  Manning, 112
  runoff, 86
  velocity, 112
Forsling, C. F., 71–73
Frequency of rainfall rates, 88–96
Fresno scraper, 162
Frost action, 37

G

Graders, blade, four-wheel, 150
  light terracing, 148, 149
  two-wheel special, 151–153
  use of, in terrace construction, 143–145, 155
  elevating, heavy type, 154
    light type, 156
Gradients, maximum for gully stabilization, 210, 275
  of terrace channels, 108, 109
Grass lands or grazing lands (*see* Permanent pastures)
Grasses, directions for seeding in gully banks, 283
  effect on runoff and erosion as compared with forests, 33

Grasses, seed mixtures of, 193, 284
  use of, in gully control, 283–286
  (*See also* Cropping systems, Vegetation)
Grazing, effect on tree planting; 281
  (*See also* Permanent pastures)
Gullies, control of, by corrugated metal checks, 204
  by dams, 275
  by mechanical means, 202–271
  by shrubs, 281
  by sod bags, 202
  by trees, 273–281
  by vegetation, 273–286
  by vines, 281–284
  by wire prongs, 203
  crossing with terraces, 136
  filling in preparation for terracing, 138
  "Hordes of Gullies" (poem), 19
  small, treatment of, 202
  terminology for, 203
Gully banks, directions, for seeding, 283
  for sloping, 275
Gully erosion, control of, by vegetation alone, 55, 74–77
  description of, 8, 10
  illustrations of, 6, 11–15
Gully gradients maximum for stability, 210, 275
Gully head banks (*see* Overfall protection)

H

Handicaps, economic, affecting land use, 324–329
Helpful economic influences, 325
Herbaceous cover (*see* Shrubs; Trees; Vegetation)
High head dams, 261–268
  bill of materials for, 265
  California type, 268
  construction of, 266–268
  design of, 263

High head dams, runoff requirements
    for, 262
Himalaya blackberry vine, 282
Hole digger, results from use of, 50
"Hordes of Gullies," 19
Hydraulic capacity (*see* Discharge
    capacity)
Hydraulic radius, 112, 191
Hydraulics, of head spillways, 272
    laws of, affecting runoff and
    erosion, 21, 22

I

Inclined tree planting, 289–291
Infiltration rates, difference for
    Marshall and Shelby silt
    loams, 41
    (*See also* Soils)
Intensity of rainfall rates, 88–96
Iowa Conservation Commission,
    recommended remedies for
    stream-bank erosion, 288–290
Iowa Emergency Relief Administra-
    tion, 18
Irregular fields, calculating areas
    of, 332–335

K

Kelly terracing plow, 146
Kentucky bluegrass, 284
Kudzu vine, 281

L

Lake Ontario, shore protection of,
    291
Land areas, methods of calculating,
    331–335
Land mensuration, 334
Land slopes, effect on terrace layout,
    120–124, 131–134
    on terrace spacing, 103
    experiments on effects of, 22, 304–
    310
    method of measuring, 132
    in relation to soil conservation,
    317, 323

Land use, 1
    coordination of physical factors
    affecting, 322
    effect of, on erosion, 38
    illustration, of improper, 304
    of proper, 321, 324
    place of herbaceous cover in, 321
    plan for, to conserve soil and
    moisture, 323
    in relation to soil conservation,
    303–329
Land use economics, 305, 324–329
Layout of terraces (*see* Terrace
    location)
Legend for erosion maps, 318
Length of terraces (*see* Terraces)
Level terraces, 105
Leveling, application to terrace
    layout, 132–134
    procedure for, 130
    sketches of, 132–134
    sample form of notes for, 131
Leveling instruments (*see* Farm
    levels)
Lineal measurement, units of, 334
Log-crib revetment, 289
Log dams, 232
Logs, use of, for stream retards, 297
Loose-rock dams, 229

M

Maintenance of terraces, 143, 177–
    186
Mangum, P. H., 100
Manning's formula, 112, 191
    diagram for solution of, 115
    tables to aid in solution of, 338,
    339
Maps, annual precipitation in U. S.,
    84
    Bethany erosion farm, 306
    extent of erosion in U. S., 3
    rainfall intensity, frequency, dura-
    tion, 89–96
    rainfall-intensity zones, 208
    soil, 317
    key for interpreting, 318

Maps, topographic, 315
typical field outline, 319
Marshall silt loam, infiltration rate of, 42
Meandering streams, control of, 286–302
Measuring distances, 334
Measuring equipment, for erosion experiments, 311–313
for infiltration capacity of soils, 41
Middleton, H. E., 25
Mississippi river, 298–302
range from low to high water, 287
Moisture equivalent, definition of, 29
Musgrave, G. W., 40

N

n, 112, 113
National Resources Board, 7
Navigable streams, 287–302
Nichols, M. L., 50, 141
Notch capacities, computation of, 209
Notches for check dams, capacity of, 206
shape of, 210

O

Object lessons, Old World, U. S., 2
Outlet structures, 161, 197–201
Outlets, for terraces, 187–201
Outline map for conservation farming, 319
Overfall protection, 199, 201, 212
by brush, 212, 285
by diversion ditches, 216
by flumes, 213
by paved channels, 214
by sod, 286
by tree planting, 290
by watertight structures, 215
Overgrazing, extent and seriousness of, in U. S., 4
(*See also* Permanent pastures)

P

Parshall flume, 311
Pastures, apparatus for measuring runoff and erosion from, 312
experiments in progress on runoff from, 310
seed mixtures for, 193, 284
(*See also* Contour ridging; Cropping systems; Cultural methods; Permanent pastures; Vegetation)
Patented devices, 203
Peg test for level adjustment, 128
Permanent pastures, consequences of abuse of, 4, 16, 70, 72
land suited for, 39, 70, 323
machine for making water pockets in, 71
treatment of, for conservation, 70–74
Physical factors affecting land use, coordination of, 322
Physical properties of soils, 26
Pipe culverts, capacity of, 258
cross-sectional areas of, 259
use in earth dams, 255–261
Plank check dams, 234
Plant setup, for articulated concrete mat, 300
for high head earth dams, 266
Plants (*see* Cropping systems; Forests; Vegetation)
Plot data, 36, 43–50
limitations on interpretation of, 47
Plowing terraced land, 67, 180, 181
Alabama practice of, 143, 182
Plows, multiple disk, 157
single disk, 156
for sloping gully banks, 276
terracing or wing, 146
Pole-type brush dam, 222
Pondage fill, 269
profile of, 270
Precipitation (*see* Rainfall)

R

Rainfall, annual amounts and distribution, map of, 83, 84
characteristics of, 83
damaging, 21
duration of intense rates, 88–96
effect on runoff, 21
frequency of recurrence, 21
intensity-frequency of, 88–96
meteorological laws governing, 83
relation to runoff, 85, 86
Rain gages, automatic recording, 95, 313
Rainfall intensities, zone map of, 208
Ramser, C. E., 86, 107
Range lands (*see* Permanent pastures)
Rational formula (*see* Runoff)
Recommended cropping plan for typical farm subject to erosion, 320
Recommended use of land to conserve soil and moisture, 323
Recording rain gages, 95, 313
Reforestation (*see* Forests; Trees)
Results of erosion experiments (*see* Agricultural experiment stations; Federal erosion farms)
Retards, definition of, 291
spacing of, 292, 293
for stream bank protection, 291–297
Revetment, on lower Mississippi river, 298
of stream banks, 288, 289, 298–300
River banks (*see* Stream bank erosion)
Road ditches, for terrace outlets, 190
protection of, 200
Roe, H. B., 162
Rotary terracer (*see* Whirlwind terracer)
Rotation of crops (*see* Cropping systems)
Roughness coefficient, *n*, 112
table of values of, 113

Row crops on terraced land, 67, 182–186
Rubble masonry dams, 236
use of, in overfall protection, 216
Runoff, coefficient for, 86, 87, 97
critical rate of, 83
quantitative determination of, 86
effect of, on erosion, 9, 20
of frost action on, 36, 37
of land slope on, 21
of rainfall on, 21
of size and shape of watershed area on, 20, 22
of soil variables on, 23
of vegetation on, 30, 31, 71–77
(*See also* Vegetation)
formula for, 86, 89, 102
applications of, 97, 117, 192, 313
relation to rainfall, 85, 86
time of concentration of, 85–88
watershed characteristics governing, 85
Runoff coefficient, 86, 87
from terraced watersheds, 97
Runoff computations, examples of, 96
in terrace channels, 97
Runoff curves, 208, 236, 262
Runoff formula, 86, 89, 102
applications of, 97, 117, 192, 313

S

Scheifele, O. S., 289
Seeding mixtures, for pastures, 284
for terrace outlets, 193, 197
Seismic disturbances, 20
Setting trees, 278
Shape of channels, effect of, on velocity, 191
Sheet erosion, description of, 8, 9
illustrations of, 9, 10
Shelby silt loam, infiltration rate of, 42
Shrubs, list of desirable species, 337
use of, in erosion control, 31, 281
(*See also* Forests; Vegetation)

Side spillway dams, 252–254
  discharge capacity of, 238
Silica-sesquioxide ratio, 30
Silt content of lower Mississippi river, 301–302
Silt sampling tanks, 311–313
Single-post row brush dams (*see* Check dams)
Slope measurements reduced to horizontal, 334
Sod, directions for placing, 285, 286
  as outlet for terraces, 190
  use of, for overfall protection, 286
    in cultivated fields, 55
    in pasture restoration, 284–286
    in stream bank protection, 290
    for terrace outlets, 195
Sod bags, use of, in gully control, 202
Sod strips, use of, in gully control, 204
Soil conservation, in relation to herbaceous cover, 321
  to land use, 303–329
Soil Conservation Service, 18
  demonstration projects of, 315, 316
Soil-conserving and -depleting crops, list of, 335–337
Soil erosion (*see* Erosion)
Soil map, 317
  key for interpreting, 318
Soil profiles, description of, effect on infiltration, 24
Soil-saving dams, 235–271
  concrete, 239–251
    design of, 240–251
    types of, 240
  definition of, 217, 235
  earth, 252–271
    drop-inlet type, 254–271
    high-head type, 261–268
    side-spillway type, 252–254
    rapidity of fill, 270
  rubble masonry, 236
Soil tests, description of, 25, 26
  determination of infiltration rates, 41
  results of, 27, 28

Soil variables, dispersion ratio, 25
  effect on runoff and erosion, 23
  structure, 23
  texture, 23
Soils, absorption range of, 40
  chemical analysis of, 29
    correlation of, with erosional behavior, 30
  chemical characteristics of, 20
  colloid content of, 29
  comparison of effect of cultural practices on four types of, 50
  criteria for determining erodibility of, 30
  dispersion ratio of, 29
  erosion ratio of, 29
  infiltration rates of, 40–42
    improvement of, by mechanical means, 51, 52, 71
    by use of explosives, 53
  moisture equivalent of, 29
  pH value of, 30
  physical characteristics of, 20
  physical tests of, 27, 28
    correlation with erodibility, 30
  resisting power of, 20
  silica-sesquioxide ratio of, 30
Spacing, of dams (*see* Check dams)
  of terraces (*see* Terraces)
Spreader boards, 195, 285, 314
Square roots of decimal numbers, table, 339
Storage dams, 269
Stream-bank erosion, combating by tree planting, 322
  forms of, 287
  inclined tree planting, 289–291
  remedies for, 287–300
Stream banks, protection of, 286–302
Stream erosion, 14, 301
Stream meandering, control of, 286–302
Strip cropping, 53–70
  advantages and disadvantages of, 68
  combined with terraces, 56–59, 64–67

Strip cropping, experiments in progress on effect of, 303–310
limitations of, 56, 63
methods of laying out fields for,
54, 62
as practiced in Texas, 54–59
in Missouri and Wisconsin, 60–
70
photographs of, 60, 67, 313
on terraced land, 64–69, 184
without terracing, 54, 55, 63, 69
use of, as prelude to terracing, 59,
67
width of strips for, 54, 61
Strip farming (see Strip cropping)
Structures, for terrace outlets, 197–
201
Surveying, for contour ridging, 73
hints on, 334
procedure for leveling, 130, 131
for strip cropping, 54, 61
for terrace layout, 131–134
for topographic and soil maps, 315
Suspended-net wire dam, 224
Symbols for erosion maps, 318

T

Taber, Stephen, 37
Tables to accompany Manning's
formula, 338, 339
Terminology for gullies, 203
Terrace channels (see Terraces)
Terrace construction, best time to
operate, 135
with blade graders, 143–145
Nichols method, 143
ten-foot blade, from both sides,
144
from upper side, 145
checking grades in, 163
example of, 164
completion of, 160–162, 166
correct method of crossing gullies,
136
cost of, at Clarinda, Ia., 175
cost factors in, 165, 176
details of procedure, 140

Terrace construction, direction earth
should be moved, 137, 138
with elevating graders, 154–157
cost of, 170–172, 176
equipment for, 135
cost of, 135, 146, 147, 149, 152,
157, 160
experiments in progress on, 310
test comparison of, 170
extra work on, 166
filling low spots in bank in, 161,
162
first step in, 136
form for cost data on, 178
with four-wheel graders, 150
cost of, 175
with light terracing graders, 149
cost of, 168, 169, 175, 176
making pilot cut in, 136
with multiple-disk plow, 157
with plow and slip-scraper, 161
cost of, 168, 176
with plow and V-drag, 142
cost of, 168, 175, 176
preliminary preparation for, 59,
67, 138
surveying procedure for, 131–134
with two-wheel graders (special),
151–153
cost of, 170–174
use of bull dozer in, 139
of Fresno scraper in, 162
of tile in, 161
V-drag, dimensions for, 141
homemade for, 140
with whirlwind terracer, 145, 159
cost of, 169, 170
work on outlets, 167, 174
Terrace cross-sections, specifications
for, 118
(See also Terraces)
Terrace farming (see Conservation
farming; Contour farming)
Terrace location, planning the layout, 120
typical examples of, 122–125
Terrace outlets, constructed, channel design for, 191

Terrace outlets, constructed, control by vegetation alone, 191
  depth of, 193
  establishing vegetation in, 195–198
  seeding of, 193
  use of sod, 195
  use of spreader boards, 195, 196
  use of structures, 197–201
  widths of, 192
location of, 122, 123, 187
natural, 189
need for, 187
temporary, 194
use of road ditches for, 190
  pastures for, 190
  woodland for, 189
  (*See also* Terraces)
Terraced land, acres of, in U. S., 17, 81
  agronomic practices on, 64–69, 177, 180
  cultivation of, 180, 182
  experiments on use of cultivating and harvesting machinery on, 310
  plowing of, 143, 180–182
  row crops on, 182–186
Terraces, acreage protected by in U. S., 17, 81
  advantages and disadvantages of, 81
  computing areas between, 335
  construction of, 135–164
    (*See also* Terrace construction)
  cross sections of, 111, 118, 143, 145, 151, 155, 162, 164
  cultivation of, 180, 182
  description of, 77
  design principles for, 77, 101
  drainage of low spots in, 161
  economics of, 98, 120
  effect of shape of channel, 112
    of depth of flow in, 116, 117
  example of, 113, 114
  experimental results from use of, 78–80, 106

Terraces, experiments in progress on effect of, 305–310
  grades (or gradients) for, level, 105
    loss comparisons of, 106
    special tables of, 109, 110
    uniform vs. variable, 107, 117
    variable, 108
  historical, 2, 100
  illustrations of, 77, 78, 111, 125, 158, 177, 160
  intervals for (*see* Terraces, spacing of)
  length of, 110
  level, 105, 124
    outlet for, 161
    results from use of, 50
  limitations of, 120
  lineal feet per acre, 103
  location of, 120–134
    (*See also* Terrace location)
  losses from variable graded, 106
  maintenance of, 177
    cost of, 180
  order of construction of, 121
  outlets for, 187–201
    (*See also* Terrace outlets)
  place of, in control program, 78, 323
  relation to interpretation of plot data, 47–49
  row crops on, 67, 182–186
    contour method, 183
    crop-stripping method, 184
    key-terrace method, 184
    straight-row method, 185
  spacing of, 102, 103
    Alabama and Georgia practice, 104
    level, 105
    recommended in various bulletins, table, 104
    rule for, 102
    special table for, 119
  supporting agronomic practices for, 177, 180
  types of, 100
    bench, 101
    broad-base ridge, 101

Terraces, types of, narrow-base ridge, 101
  use of, for erosion control, 77–81
  in gully restoration, 205, 216
  for overfall protection, 216
  with strip cropping, 56–59, 64–67
  value of cooperation between neighbors in using, 121, 146
Terracing (*see* Terraces; Terrace construction; Terrace outlets)
Texas terracer, 148, 150
Tile drains, for reclamation of small gullies, 205
  for storage dams, 269
  use of, in terracing, 161
Tillage, number of days soil is denuded by, 34
  (*See also* Cultural practices)
Time of concentration, 85–88
Topography (*see* Land slopes; Watersheds)
Trees, advantages of, for gully control, 273
  list of desirable species, 337
  miscellaneous uses for, 322
  relation to shrubs, vines and grasses, 274
  role of, in relation to conservation and land use, 31, 321
  use of, for retards, 292–296
  in gullied areas, 273–281
  for wild-life preservation, 280
Tree planting, advisability of, 274
  cost of, 322
  crew organization for, 278
  directions for, 277
  setting white willow poles, 290
  effect of grazing on, 281
  estimated spacing and number per acre, 322
  for gully control, 290
  by inclined propagation, 289–291
  need for, 274
  preparation of cuttings for, 280
  for stream bank protection, 290
  tools for, 277
Tree species, 276, 279–281, 321, 337

Turf (*see* Sod)
Turret level, 126
Two-thirds powers of numbers, 338

V

V-drag, homemade, 140
  use of, 142
  steel, 147
  use of, 142
V-type wire dam, 223
Vegetation, effect of, on runoff and erosion, 30, 31, 43, 71–77
  experimental results from use of, 71–73
  holding power of various kinds of, 32
  list of conserving and depleting, 335–337
  role of, in erosion control, 30, 31, 322
  in relation to conservation, 321
  special uses of, 273–291
  use of, to control small depressions in cultivated fields, 55
  for control of terrace outlets, 191–194
  for gully control, 75, 76, 204, 273–291
Velocity, effect of land slope on, 22
  tables for computation of, 338, 339
  (*See also* Manning's formula)
Venturi flume, 311
Vines, use of, in gully control, 281–284
Vitrified sewer pipe, for drop-inlet culverts, 255

W

Watersheds, characteristics governing runoff from, 85
  methods of computing size of, 331–335
  time of concentration of, 85–88
Water-stage recorders, 311–313

Wetted perimeter, 112
Whirlwind terracer, 143, 145, 159, 167
Wild honeysuckle vine, 282
Wild-life preservation, list of desirable trees and shrubs for, 337
Willows (*see* Trees)
Wind erosion, description of, 15
  illustration of, 16
  use of trees for prevention of, 322
  wave action caused by, 16

Wire check dams, 223–228
Wood lots (*see* Forests)
Woods Brothers Construction Co., 292
Wooley, J. C., 156
Wooley terracer (*see* Graders; Light elevating)

Y

Yarnell, David L., 89, 98, 99

Use and Abuse

of

America's Natural Resources

An Arno Press Collection

Ayres, Quincy Claude. **Soil Erosion and Its Control.** 1936

Barger, Harold and Sam H. Schurr. **The Mining Industries, 1899–1939.** 1944

Carman, Harry J., editor. **Jesse Buel:** Agricultural Reformer. 1947

Circular from the General Land Office Showing the Manner of Proceeding to Obtain Title to Public Lands. 1899

Fernow, Bernhard E. **Economics of Forestry.** 1902

Gannett, Henry, editor. **Report of the National Conservation Commission, February 1909.** Three volumes. 1909

Giddens, Paul H. **The Birth of the Oil Industry.** 1938

Greeley, William B. **Forests and Men.** 1951

Hornaday, William T. **Wild Life Conservation in Theory and Practice.** 1914

Ise, John. **The United States Forest Policy.** 1920

Ise, John. **The United States Oil Policy.** 1928

James, Harlean. **Romance of the National Parks.** 1939

Kemper, J. P. **Rebellious River.** 1949

Kinney, J. P **The Development of Forest Law in America.** *Including,* Forest Legislation in America Prior to March 4, 1789. 1917

Larson, Agnes M. **History of the White Pine Industry in Minnesota.** 1949

Liebig, Justus, von. **The Natural Lawss of Husbandry.** 1863

Lindley, Curtis H. **A Treatise on the American Law Relating to Mines and Mineral Lands.** Two volumes. 2nd edition. 1903

Lokken, Roscoe L. **Iowa—Public Land Disposal.** 1942

McGee, W. J., editor. **Proceedings of a Conference of Governors in the White House, May 13–15, 1908.** 1909

Mead, Elwood. **Irrigation Institutions.** 1903

Moreell, Ben. **Our Nation's Water Resources—Policies and Politics.** 1956

Murphy, Blakely M., editor. **Conservation of Oil & Gas: A Legal History, 1948.** 1949

Newell, Frederick Haynes. **Water Resources:** Present and Future Uses. 1920.

Nimmo, Joseph, Jr. **Report in Regard to the Range and Ranch Cattle Business of the United States.** 1885

Nixon, Edgar B., editor. **Franklin D. Roosevelt & Conservation, 1911–1945.** Two volumes. 1957

Peffer, E. Louise. **The Closing of the Public Domain.** 1951

Preliminary Report of the Inland Waterways Commission. 60th Congress, 1st Session, Senate Document No. 325. 1908

Puter, S. A. D. & Horace Stevens. **Looters of the Public Domain.** 1908

Record, Samuel J. & Robert W. Hess. **Timbers of the New World.** 1943

Report of the Public Lands Commission, with Appendix. 58th Congress, 3d Session, Senate Document No. 189. 1905

Report of the Public Lands Commission, Created by the Act of March 3, 1879. 46th Congress, 2d Session, House of Representatives Ex. Doc. No. 46. 1880

Resources for Freedom: A Report to the President by The President's Materials Policy Commission, Volumes I and IV. 1952. Two volumes in one.

Schoolcraft, Henry R. **A View of the Lead Mines of Missouri.** 1819

Supplementary Report of the Land Planning Committee to the National Resources Board, 1935–1942

Thompson, John Giffin. **The Rise and Decline of the Wheat Growing Industry in Wisconsin** (Reprinted from *Bulletin of the University of Wisconsin,* No. 292). 1909

Timmons, John F. & William G. Murray, editors. **Land Problems and Policies.** 1950

U.S. Department of Agriculture—Forest Service. **Timber Resources for America's Future:** Forest Resource Report No. 14. 1958

U.S. Department of Agriculture—Soil Conservation Service and Forest Service. **Headwaters Control and Use.** 1937

U.S. Department of Commerce and Labor—Bureau of Corporations. **The Lumber Industry,** Parts I, II, & III. 1913/1914

U.S. Department of the Interior. **Hearings before the Secretary of the Interior on Leasing of Oil Lands.** 1906

Whitaker, J. Russell & Edward A. Ackerman. **American Resources:** Their Management and Conservation. 1951